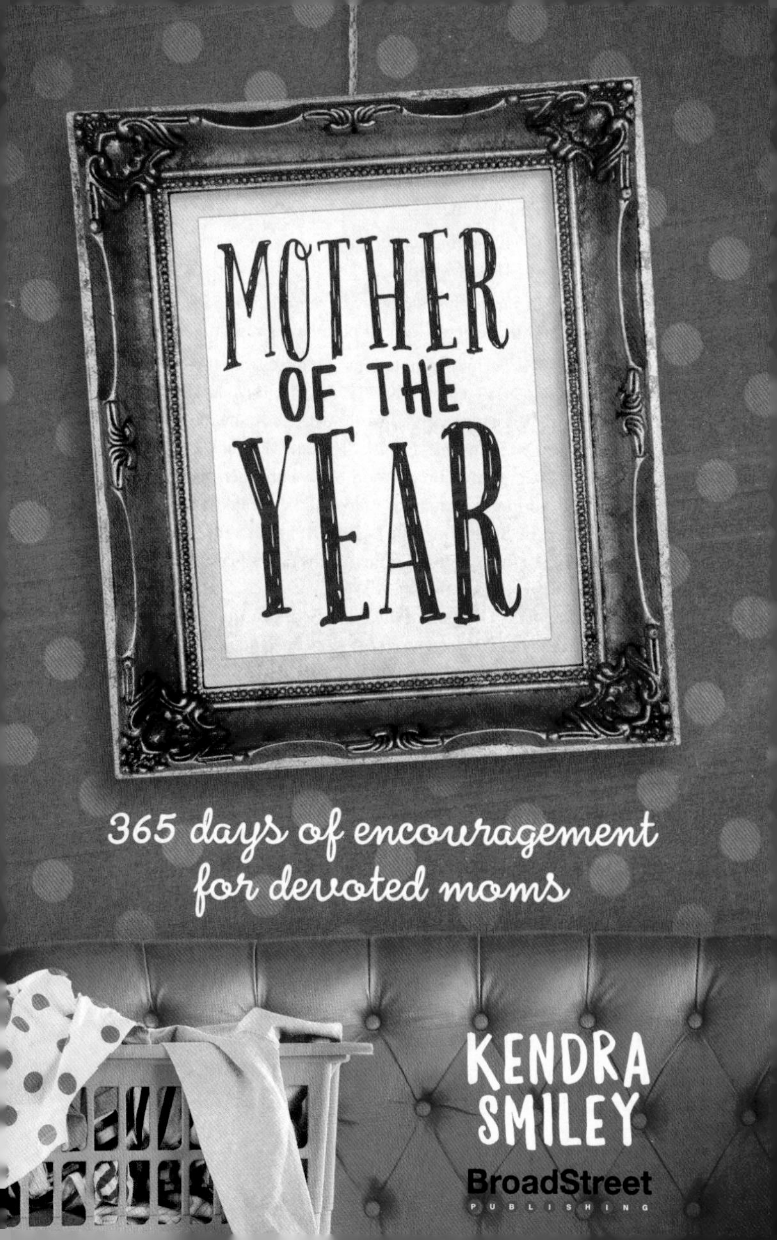

MOTHER OF THE YEAR

365 days of encouragement for devoted moms

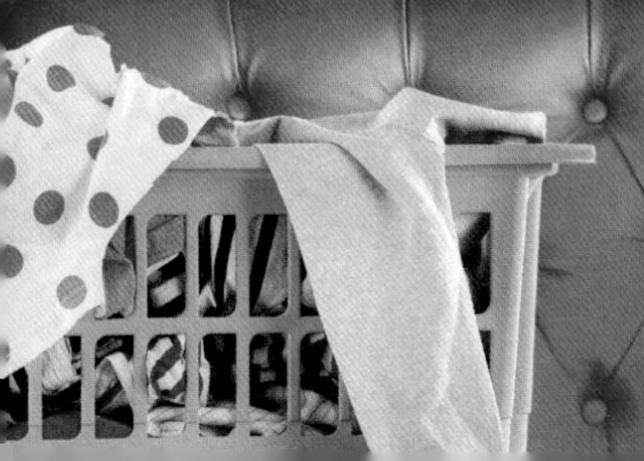

KENDRA SMILEY

BroadStreet
PUBLISHING

BroadStreet Publishing Group, LLC
Racine, Wisconsin, USA
BroadStreetPublishing.com

MOTHER OF THE YEAR: *365 Days of Encouragement for Devoted Moms*

ISBN-13: 978-1-4245-5409-6 (hardcover)
ISBN-13: 978-1-4245-5410-2 (e-book)

Stock or custom editions of BroadStreet Publishing titles may be purchased in bulk for educational, business, ministry, fundraising, or sales promotional use. For information, please e-mail info@broadstreetpublishing.com.

Cover design by Chris Garborg, garborgdesign.com
Interior design and typeset by Katherine Lloyd, thedeskonline.com

Printed in China
17 18 19 20 21 5 4 3 2 1

INTRODUCTION

A Mother Understands the Heart of a Mother

Rejoice with those who rejoice,
weep with those who weep.
—Romans 12:15 ESV

Motherhood is an *adventure*, and as with any adventure, there are peaks and valleys. One day you feel like an enormous success; the next like a total failure.

Motherhood is a *roller coaster ride* that can bring you overwhelming joy and sorrow you never imagined.

Motherhood is an incredibly *important responsibility*, with the goal being to work your way out of a job. When it begins, you have a starring role—but as the years pass by, you become a supporting actress. Finally, your children reach adulthood, and you have a bit part. And with that, dear mother, you are deemed a success.

Motherhood is a *gift from God*, the One who created both you and your child.

Let me join you on this adventure, this roller coaster ride of responsibility. Let me hold your hand as you work your way out of the most precious and important job you will ever have—the one given to you by God.

IT'S A ROLLER COASTER RIDE

"A woman giving birth to a child has pain because her time has come; but when her baby is born she forgets the anguish because of her joy that a child is born into the world."

—John 16:21

JANUARY 1

Happy New Year!

You became imitators of us and of the Lord,
for you welcomed the message in the midst of severe
suffering with the joy given by the Holy Spirit.
—1 THESSALONIANS 1:6

Happy New Year! That exclamation was shouted many times as the clock struck midnight, and it will be spoken many more times throughout the coming week. But having a happy New Year, a happy day, or even a happy few hours can be difficult when you're busy raising a family.

Why? Because happiness is based on happenings, and the happenings in our lives aren't always pleasant. Perhaps we should consider a different encouragement for the New Year. How about wishing others a "Joy-filled New Year"?

As I ponder the possible change, I realize it might not be much better as a greeting. All too often the happenings in my life not only make me unhappy, but also they rob me of my joy. To be more accurate, I allow them to steal my joy.

When that happens, I need to remember I can have "the joy given by the Holy Spirit"—regardless of my circumstances.

LET'S PRAY

Lord, I admit that at times I allow circumstances to steal my joy. As this New Year begins, help me find my joy in the knowledge of your love.

JANUARY 2

Learning Contentment

I have learned to be content
whatever the circumstances.

—PHILIPPIANS 4:11

Have you ever noticed how content your children are when they're sleeping? (And so well-behaved too!) There are some days when those hours of rest are the only hours of contentment. Let's face it; it's not just kids who struggle with feelings of discontent. Thankfully, God's Word gives us a clue to finding contentment.

The apostle Paul *learned* to be content. It wasn't automatic for him, and it isn't for you. The very word *learning* implies a change of behavior. We have no idea what Paul specifically did to change his behavior, but he found contentment.

For each one of us, learning to be content involves more than reading a well-written book or hearing a gripping sermon on contentment. Those two sources can give you helpful instructions for achieving your goal, but ultimately you are the one to initiate a change. Just like Paul, you can learn to be content "whatever the circumstances." You can choose a change in behavior.

FOR YOU TO CONSIDER

Are you feeling discontented in a particular area of your life? Ask God to help you learn to be content as you develop a healthy change in behavior.

JANUARY 3

Never, Never, Never

Jesus was telling the disciples a parable to make the point that at all times they ought to pray and not give up and lose heart.

—Luke 18:1 AMP

I am not a history buff, but there are some quotes from noted historical events that have found their way into my memory. One of those is from Winston Churchill. He addressed the people of England during the Second World War with these words: "Never give in, never, never, never, never!"* His urgency and passion made it a quote to remember.

A verse from the book of Luke made me think of Churchill's words because both sources remind us to never give up. In addition, Jesus' words go beyond those of the prime minister of the United Kingdom. Jesus' instruction is twofold. He tells believers what *not* to do (give up and lose heart) and also what they should do—pray!

As a mom, there are moments when you might feel like giving up. That's the time to remember what you should and should not do. Pray and never, never, never give up!

NOW IS THE TIME

Close your eyes and take a deep breath. Exhale and do the same thing again. Let God's Spirit give you a new resolve to pray when you feel like giving up.

---

* Winston Churchill, "Never Give In," address given at Harrow School, London, England, on October 29, 1941.

JANUARY 4

Actions and Decisions

Even a child is known by his doings,
whether his work be pure, and whether it be right.
—PROVERBS 20:11 KJV

When my boys were little, they learned that the words *I'm sorry* were almost magical. They would utter that sentence, and it instantly would disarm me. I'd accept the apology at face value and praise them for their good decision.

It didn't take long, however, for me to discover that many times those words were spoken simply to absolve them of responsibility or to avoid retribution. Fortunately, while my boys were still young, I wised up. I realized that unless the "I'm sorry" was followed by actions reflecting those words, they were meaningless. If a person, young or old, is truly sorry, their actions will give them away.

When I finally saw the light, I would follow their hollow apologies by saying, "If you were truly sorry, you wouldn't have repeated that behavior. Your actions gave you away."

HOW ABOUT YOU?

Are you telling God you're sorry and then repeating your poor choice? Remember, your actions are giving you away. Ask him to help you make a change.

JANUARY 5

Under Her Wings

"Jerusalem, Jerusalem, you who kill the prophets
and stone those sent to you, how often I have longed
to gather your children together,
as a hen gathers her chicks under her wings,
and you were not willing."
—MATTHEW 23:37

Even though I live on a farm, I have no experience whatsoever with hens and chicks. I do, however, have an idea of how a hen might feel (if indeed a hen can feel) when it comes to protecting her chicks. The hen has a nurturing nature, and she wants to keep her little ones safe. I think there's actually a "motherhood thing" going on—not just a "chicken thing." Perhaps what's really going on is a Jesus thing.

The Lord has a nurturing nature when it comes to his children. He wants to guide you and keep you safe, to draw you close to him just as that hen does when she gathers her chicks under her wings. As a mom, you exhibit that same nature when you draw your children to your side—to the shelter of your presence.

THINK ABOUT IT

As a mother you know how heartbreaking it would be for your children to stay at arm's length and resist the safety and love you provide. Are you keeping the Lord at a distance by rejecting his love and protection?

JANUARY 6

Not What I Expected

"People look at the outward appearance,
but the LORD looks at the heart."
—1 SAMUEL 16:7

My husband, a US Air Force Reserve pilot, had been gone more than usual, and I was feeling a little lonely. A temporary answer to my loneliness popped up one afternoon when our fourteen-year-old son invited me to go to the high school girls' volleyball game with him. I was pleased and immediately answered yes.

When we entered the school, he headed for the student cheering section, and I located a friend among the adults. After the match was over, my son asked if he could stay at school for a while to work on their class float for the homecoming parade. Our neighbor was helping with the project and was willing to drive him home, so permission was granted.

As I drove home alone, I realized the volleyball game wasn't exactly the mother-son bonding experience I'd expected. Had I been conned into providing transportation? Or had he, sensing I was missing his dad, included me to exhibit compassion? (Fourteen-year-old boy compassion, that is.) Until further notice, I'm going with the compassion explanation.

FOOD FOR THOUGHT

You always have a choice when it comes to your perspective. Remember, God looks at the heart.

JANUARY 7

Never and Always

Then Jesus declared, "I am the bread of life.
Whoever comes to me will never go hungry,
and whoever believes in me will never be thirsty."
—John 6:35

It's interesting to listen to kids, especially teenagers, trying to manipulate their parents. I'm not saying I condone manipulation; I'm just fascinated with their techniques. Kids, through trial and error, develop a method that is most effective in their home.

My boys, for example, discovered that I respond best to humor or hyperspiritualism. "Mom, I just witnessed a miracle! The truck ran off the icy road, hit a telephone pole, and I walked away unscathed!" (Yes, I did actually hear those words.)

One technique that didn't work in our home was the popular "always and never" argument. "I *always* have to babysit!" or "You *never* let me go to the movies!"

Very few things fall into the *always* or *never* categories—with one obvious exception. When words come from the Lord, you can count on them. He is *always* true to his word.

LET'S PRAY

Lord, you are trustworthy and your word is true. Help me walk in that knowledge and know you are always with me.

JANUARY 8

This Is the Day

This is the day which the LORD hath made;
we will rejoice and be glad in it.
—PSALM 118:24 KJV

"I can't wait until the baby is born. It's getting harder and harder to get comfortable."

"Surely the baby will sleep through the night before too long. Won't he?"

"I wish we were done with this potty training thing. How long does this usually take?"

"Pretty soon he'll be in school. Then I'll get a lot more done around here."

And on and on, we wish away stage after stage of parenting, hoping "the tough one I'm in now" won't last long.

Years ago I framed a cartoon. A mom is standing with her hands on her hips, looking with disgust at her son's messy room. "You need to grow up," she scolds. Then she instantly imagines what life will be like with him grown-up and gone. She quickly adds, "But not too soon."

HOW ABOUT YOU?

Are you rushing through your days as a mom, looking forward to tomorrow and missing today? If so, remember to enjoy today. This is the day the Lord has made. Rejoice and be glad in it.

JANUARY 9

God's Love

God shows his love for us in that
while we were yet sinners Christ died for us.
—Romans 5:8 rsv

My husband taught a high school Bible study in our home every other Wednesday evening for almost eight years. More often than not, he began the study by writing several basic concepts on a whiteboard. One of those basics was this: *God loves you.*

You might think that statement would get repetitious after so many sessions, or you might wonder why he bothered to write it almost every time. It's because the reminder of God's love is so basic, so supernatural, and so incredible, it deserves to be said again and again.

God doesn't wait for you or your children to deserve his love. In fact, he doesn't even demand that you appreciate his love. He simply blesses you with it. Helping your children remember that truth is fundamental. God loves you!

JUST FOR YOU

God loves you. Jesus died for you. It's not based on your performance. It is because of his very nature. His desire is for you to love him back.

JANUARY 10

All-Purpose Answer

At the name of Jesus every knee should bow,
in heaven and on earth and under the earth.

—PHILIPPIANS 2:10

I have fond memories of countless children's sermons I heard in our little church. The kids loved those messages, and so did the adults. There were times, in fact, when the nugget of truth offered in those few minutes stayed with me for days.

Regardless of the message presented, the adult in charge tried to engage the kids by asking questions. That was typically when the humor—planned or unplanned—began. Family secrets tended to pop out when children answered the innocent questions that were posed, occasionally resulting in an embarrassed mom or dad.

But beyond those amusing moments, my favorite memory is how kids answered questions by shouting out the name of Jesus—whether or not it applied. When in doubt, they simply went to the all-purpose answer to any question: *Jesus.*

IT'S TRUE

No matter what is happening in your life or in your home today, Jesus is the answer.

JANUARY 11

In Our Family

Do not love the world or anything in the world.
If anyone loves the world, love for the Father is not in them.

—1 John 2:15

"We don't do that in *our* family," I'd say whenever one of my children had done something disgusting or disrespectful. Then one day it dawned on my eldest that the statement wasn't entirely true.

After I uttered that frequently heard phrase, he looked at me and said innocently, "Well, we just did." And he was correct. Whatever disagreeable action I was attempting to squelch had just occurred.

Perhaps it would have been more accurate to say, "Let's not do that anymore. We don't *want* to do that in our family." But that might not have been exactly right either.

You understand what I was trying to say, don't you? "Do not do that!" That's more to the point.

God gets right to the point with his family. Loving the world? We don't do that in God's family!

A QUESTION FOR YOU

As a child of God, are you paying attention to the family rules?

JANUARY 12

Prayer Changes Things

"You have heard that it was said,
'Love your neighbor and hate your enemy.'
But I tell you, love your enemies
and pray for those who persecute you.'"

—MATTHEW 5:43–44

There are many catchphrases when it comes to prayer. One I've heard and said more than once is: "Prayer changes things."

One day, I started to wonder: Does prayer change things, or does prayer change me? When I pray about a situation or concern, does praying alter the way I view the circumstances? That was something I hadn't considered before.

At that point, I admitted that when I truly seek the Lord—when I don't just go through the motions and run through my list of concerns—my perspective changes. Sometimes I have a change of attitude. Other times I realize something I've overlooked in the past. On occasion, I gain compassion or wisdom.

LET'S PRAY

Lord, help me remember that prayer is not a monologue; it's communication with you. I want to hear your voice and be changed.

JANUARY 13

Countercultural

"But to you who are listening I say:
Love your enemies, do good to those who hate you."
—LUKE 6:27

It can be easy to overload your children with stuff. There are many reasons to purchase more and more "things" for your kids. There is peer pressure, for one. Keeping up with the Joneses can take quite an investment. Add to that your children's demands and the things you buy to compensate for time spent away from them, and you've got a pretty hefty list of reasons to spend money on stuff.

But if your goal is to raise creative problem-solvers who can think outside the box, the abundance of things can hamper that goal. There are positive aspects to having less, but that idea is countercultural.

More importantly, many of the teachings of Christ are not mainstream. Consider his instructions: "Love your enemies" and "Do good to those who hate you." As a believer, following the example of Jesus may mean being countercultural.

LET'S PRAY

Lord, give me the courage to follow your instruction even when the world sees it as foolish.

JANUARY 14

Working Together

Though one may be overpowered,
two can defend themselves.
A cord of three strands is not quickly broken.
—ECCLESIASTES 4:12

The four-year-old handed her mother the papers she had gotten in Sunday school and heard a question many children hear each week. "What did you learn this morning?"

The little girl thought for just a minute, then answered with confidence. "Two are better than one! That means if you're strong, you and your friend together are even stronger. And if you are smart and have good ideas, you and your friend are even smarter together."

Sounds like she got the picture. The truth is that working together with a friend can lighten the load. It can bring a fresh perspective to the circumstances in your life.

In our home we like to say, "The two of you together are much smarter than either of you alone." The smartest and strongest friend is Jesus—who knows you, loves you, and wants to make you even stronger and smarter too.

WHAT ABOUT TODAY?

If you find yourself needing a friend's help, call on Jesus. He wants to be that friend, and he is available now and waiting for your call.

JANUARY 15

A Gift for You

Encourage one another daily,
as long as it is called "Today."
—HEBREWS 3:13

"I wish it was Friday already!" said my friend. It was only Monday, but between home duties and work, she had a stressful week in front of her. I also knew how she felt. As a mom, I had those times when I looked at my day or my week and thought the demands were just too many and too difficult. I imagined that somehow flashing forward would be the best thing to do.

Then I'd remember a quote I heard (probably from an anonymous source). "Every day is a gift. That's why they call it the present."

That isn't really why they call it the "present," but I appreciate the thought. Every day is a gift—a gift from God. There are no guarantees of quantity or quality of life on this earth, so be encouraged and unwrap the gift of Today!

HERE'S AN IDEA

Maybe there's another mom you could encourage today. Pray and ask God to lead you to that special woman who needs to recognize the gift of Today.

JANUARY 16

Please Listen

To answer before listening—
that is folly and shame.
—PROVERBS 18:13

Occasionally I'll remember some amusing thing one of my parents used to say, and the recollection will flood me with memories. My dad had a line he repeated more than once, and—come to think of it—he was the only one who found it amusing.

As a teenager, I'd be in the middle of a compelling argument about why I should be allowed to go somewhere or do something, and my dad would hold up his hand, smile, and say, "Don't confuse me with the facts. My mind is made up."

That was code for: *No. That's not a good idea. Permission denied.* He wasn't answering before listening; he'd just heard enough to give an educated answer.

That memory helped me as a mom. I wanted to listen before answering, but I learned that I didn't have to listen to endless pleas when I already knew the correct answer.

HOW ABOUT YOU?

Does your child go on and on and on and wear you down? Listen attentively until you're certain of the correct answer, and then feel free to gently stop the one-sided conversation.

JANUARY 17

Daddy's Tricky

The appeal we make does not spring
from error or impure motives,
nor are we trying to trick you.

—1 THESSALONIANS 2:3

I sat in my oldest son's family room on the evening of the last day of school. His two older daughters would be entering the third and first grades in the fall, and his third daughter, Ava, would be in preschool once again.

"Okay, girls," he said. "It's time to go to bed. You have school in the morning."

All three kids stayed right where they were, looked at him, and giggled. Then Ava turned to me. Thinking I might not understand the obvious humor in her father's request, she whispered loudly, "There's no school tomorrow. Daddy's tricky!"

Indeed he was tricky, but not in a mean or deceitful way. His motive was not impure; his words were meant to entertain. And from the continued laughter I heard coming from his children, it was clear he had succeeded.

WHAT IF?

Make certain your words are not misunderstood. Make certain your motivation for speaking comes from a pure and honest heart.

JANUARY 18

Tears of Joy

When the LORD restored the fortunes of Zion,
we were like those who dreamed.
Our mouths were filled with laughter,
our tongues with songs of joy.
Then it was said among the nations,
"The Lord has done great things for them."
The LORD has done great things for us,
and we are filled with joy.

—PSALM 126:1–3

I sat in a chair at the back of the sanctuary. The worship began, and before the first song was finished, I was aware of God's presence. The knowledge of God's love became more real as everyone sang another song together.

As I thought of the words we were singing, I started to cry. The tears of joy gently rolled down my cheeks as the truth of God's amazing grace pierced my heart.

Then I felt the touch of a small hand on my arm. I opened my eyes to see a sweet little girl with whom I worship each week. This two-year-old was gently patting my arm as she looked at my tears. She'd mistaken my tears of joy and thanksgiving for tears of sadness. She was comforting me.

LET'S PRAY

Lord, your grace is amazing. Let me never overlook that truth. May I never refrain from crying tears of joy and thanksgiving as I live in that grace.

JANUARY 19

No One to Chat with

"God does speak—sometimes one way and sometimes another—even though people may not understand it."

—JOB 33:14 NCV

When Megan's dad got home from work, he asked her about her day. "How was preschool today? Was it thumbs-up, thumbs-down, or in the middle?"

Megan responded by pointing her thumb to the side. It was neither a very good nor very bad day.

"Why was your day just in the middle?"

Without missing a beat, she answered, "No one would chat with me. Not even Nathan, and he's my good friend."

Maybe you're like me and you can understand Megan's frustration. She wanted to "chat" and couldn't find anyone who was interested. That's when it's good to know the One who is always available for a good chat—the One who speaks and listens.

JUST FOR YOU

Have you ever felt lonely, even with someone nearby? When that happens, remember who is as close as the air you breathe. He is longing to chat with you.

JANUARY 20

Seven Pounds of Baby, Fourteen Pounds of Guilt

For I have kept the ways of the Lord;
I am not guilty of turning from my God.
—Psalm 18:21

My oldest son likes to say I practiced on him to get ready for the next two. There is some degree of truth in that statement, but he's giving me more credit than I deserve. When he arrived I didn't even have enough mothering skills to call what I was doing practice. I needed "Parenting 101."

Here's my explanation: I'm the baby in my family, and I only had one babysitting job in my life. When I came home from that particular evening, I announced that there "had to be an easier way to make money." I mowed lawns.

Then my first baby arrived. I was certain I was doing everything wrong, and occasionally an experienced mother (purposely or accidentally) confirmed my feelings of inadequacy. I imagined God had given me seven pounds of baby and fourteen pounds of guilt.

In all truth, God had given me a great blessing, and little by little he gave me confidence that extinguished the guilt.

THINK ABOUT IT

Is someone or something giving you an undeserved guilt trip? If you've done nothing irresponsible or purposefully wrong, you can throw that guilt away. You've been declared not guilty!

JANUARY 21

Good Medicine

A cheerful heart is good medicine,
but a crushed spirit dries up the bones.

—Proverbs 17:22

Not all medicine is easy to take. I've seen capsules so big that they should have been prescribed to a horse or some other large animal. Then there is the medicine that smells and tastes so bad your child won't get within ten feet of the serving spoon.

On the other hand, there is one medicine that is not unpleasant at all. In fact, God's Word calls it "good medicine." It's a cheerful heart that can laugh in spite of circumstances.

Maybe it's been a long time since you laughed with your child. Not a polite little tee-hee, but a robust belly laugh. When was the last time you laughed so hard you had tears in your eyes or found yourself doubled over, trying to catch your breath? When did you see your child doing the same thing? If it's been a while, now is the time to take some "good medicine" and enjoy a cheerful heart.

HERE'S AN IDEA

Watch a funny movie together. If you or your kids like slapstick comedy, try a movie with the Three Stooges. Those are hard to resist for their sheer silliness.

JANUARY 22

Hardest Job You'll Ever Love

Whatever you do, work at it with all your heart,
as working for the Lord, not for human masters.

—Colossians 3:23

In my lifetime I've had various jobs. When I was a teenager, I worked at the local swimming pool as a lifeguard and later managed the pool. As a newlywed I taught gymnastics at the area YMCA, and after I finished my college degree, I taught elementary school and coached high school girls' athletics.

The jobs I had before motherhood had challenges, but none compared to the ones I encountered as a mom. I was a mediator, disciplinarian, tutor, chauffeur, cook, investor, and first responder all at once. Being a mom was the toughest assignment I'd ever had.

My teenage jobs also had rewards, but by the same token, none of those rewards compared to the ones I encountered in motherhood. Being a mom is the toughest job you'll ever love!

LET'S PRAY

Lord, you know it can be difficult to be a mom. You also know the joy my kids can bring me. Help me to stick with it and continue to love my job, even in the rough times.

JANUARY 23

A Disinterested Cook

Therefore, as God's chosen people, holy and dearly loved,
clothe yourselves with compassion,
kindness, humility, gentleness and patience.
—COLOSSIANS 3:12

I'll be the first to admit I'm not fond of cooking. But as the mother of three sons, it was irrelevant whether or not I enjoyed spending time in the kitchen. It was my responsibility to be certain those boys had three square meals a day. I wasn't concerned about presentation; it was all about quantity—especially when they reached their teen years.

After they were out of the house and well on their way to adulthood, my middle son heard me refer to myself as a bad cook. Perhaps out of gentleness and compassion he corrected me. "Mom, you're not a bad cook. You're a disinterested cook."

I considered that title an upgrade and appreciated his kindness.

THINK ABOUT IT

Have you been a little too rough on yourself? It might be time for an upgrade. How about your kids? Is there a label someone has attached to them that should be changed? Take action today.

JANUARY 24

It's Contagious

Do not make friends with a hot-tempered person,
do not associate with one easily angered,
or you may learn their ways
and get yourself ensnared.

—Proverbs 22:24–25

When you have more than one child, the odds are very slim anything contagious will attack just one of them. I can still remember the fall when the chicken pox managed to haunt our home for weeks and weeks!

After the first child who'd contracted the disease seemed to be on the verge of total health, one of his brothers began to develop all the sadly familiar symptoms. Then when child number two was on the mend, the third one started to develop the telltale rash.

We experienced a chicken pox epidemic in our own home. The only way I could have possibly stopped the cycle of contagion would have been to quarantine the sick one or send the healthy ones to Grandma's house.

The childhood disease of chicken pox is not the only thing that is contagious. Kids can also catch your attitude, so make sure it's the kind of attitude you want them to catch.

IT'S TRUE

Attitudes are contagious. Is yours worth catching?

JANUARY 25

God Isn't Finished

He who began a good work in you
will carry it on to completion until the day of Christ Jesus.
—PHILIPPIANS 1:6

Years ago my brother gave me a T-shirt imprinted with the words "Under Construction." That exceptionally loud, orange-colored shirt became one of my favorites, not because of the atrocious color but because of the message on the front. I was "under construction" then, and I will continue to be until God finishes his work in me.

Ever since God began the good work in you and in your children, you've been under construction too. You might clamor for the construction of your home to be finished or wonder if the carpenters will ever finish the job. But you can relax and be assured that God's work will someday be complete. He never begins a good work without the intention of finishing the job.

It's a process, and a process takes time. The key is to celebrate each step closer to the finished product and to have confidence in the fact that God will complete the good work he began in you.

THIS IS GOOD NEWS

God loves you with an everlasting love and will continue the good work he began in you until it is complete. Put your confidence in him to do what he has promised.

JANUARY 26

Sweater Obedience

Walk in obedience to all that the LORD your God has commanded you, so that you may live and prosper and prolong your days in the land that you will possess.

—DEUTERONOMY 5:33

Do you know the definition of the word *sweater*? You might be thinking, *What? Of course I know the definition.* My guess is you know the traditional definition, but in the *Kids' Dictionary of Actual Life*, I found one that is a little different. According to that seldom-used reference book, a sweater is "something you put on when your mother is cold."

To a child, putting on a sweater just because Mom told you to do it may or may not seem logical. It may, in fact, appear to be rather arbitrary, but out of sheer obedience, children will dutifully comply.

The instructions of the Lord do not always seem logical either, but the big difference is they are never arbitrary. Unlike Mom, God sees the big picture perfectly and always knows what's best.

FOR YOU AND YOUR KIDS

It's easy to question the instructions in God's Word. Always remember, they are never uninformed. He knows what's best for you.

JANUARY 27

The Blues

Because of the LORD's great love we are not consumed,
for his compassions never fail.
They are new every morning;
great is your faithfulness.
—LAMENTATIONS 3:22–23

Things can become rather overwhelming when you're raising kids. I call those overpowering feelings of exhaustion sprinkled with temporary inadequacy, the Blues.

Different moms handle the Blues in different ways. I have a friend who gets out her journal and records her thoughts and feelings. Another friend of mine puts on her running shoes and goes for a jog.

Me? I tend to hit the sack. A quick nap is my antidote for a rough morning. When I shared my remedy of choice with another friend, she was able to make it sound rather spiritual.

"Good idea," she said. "After all, God's mercies are new every morning, so in a sense you get to experience a new morning when you wake up from your nap!"

I know that was stretching it, but I did appreciate her positive spin.

A QUESTION FOR YOU

How do you handle those days when everything seems to go wrong—days when you have the Blues? The key is to handle them wisely.

JANUARY 28

Give Up

A time to search and a time to give up,
a time to keep and a time to throw away.
—ECCLESIASTES 3:6

There was a sweet little boy in Sunday school who was having a difficult time adjusting to being away from his mom and older sisters. He whined and cried until one day, in frustration, his mother asked me if I would help and I agreed.

The next Sunday rolled around, and I was in charge of helping Jason adjust to his class. At first he cried and protested, but I calmly and lovingly explained that he had no option. That wasn't what he wanted to hear, so he sat on my lap with a disgusted look on his face.

Before long, my oldest son, a teenager at the time, came into the room and saw the drama unfolding. "Jason," he said, looking at the forlorn child on my lap, "I know my mom, and she's going to win—so you might as well give up now."

Jason believed him, relaxed, and returned to his chair in Sunday school within minutes—only to discover his class really was fun!

LET'S PRAY

Lord, there are times I don't want to give up my will and trust you. Help me always remember that surrendering to your will is best.

JANUARY 29

Children of God

Yet to all who did receive him,
to those who believed in his name,
he gave the right to become children of God.

—JOHN 1:12

Years ago, the idea of wearing a garment with the manufacturer's label prominently displayed on it would have been considered ridiculous. It would have been akin to wearing something with the tag showing.

That was years and years ago. Now, in many cases, pieces of clothing are chosen simply *because* of the manufacturer's label. Labels have become significant and influential.

When it comes to people, the labels placed on them have always been meaningful. Consider the child who is labeled as a member of the "terrible twos." Or the older child who is tagged a "turbulent teen." Those labels are significant, and they're not as flattering as the label on your tennis shoes.

How about some positive labels—the ones God uses to describe his kids? You are a joint heir with Jesus. You are a child of the living God. You are saved by grace!

HOW ABOUT YOU?

It's very easy to tag a child with an unflattering label. It can also be very detrimental. Stop and think about the names you call your kids and make an adjustment if necessary.

JANUARY 30

Good News, Bad News

Every good and perfect gift is from above,
coming down from the Father of the heavenly lights,
who does not change like shifting shadows.

—JAMES 1:17

When you think of a "good and perfect gift," you may think of the gift your children are to you. Maybe you think of your parents or your spouse or your job. Any or all of those things could fall into the "good and perfect" category of gifts from God.

Something in your life at first may appear to be very far from either good or perfect—much less a good and perfect gift. If you wait long enough, though, you might discover that what you considered bad and imperfect just might be one of the most perfect things to ever happen.

It may be an unwanted gift that draws you closer to the Lord and encourages you to spend more time in his Word. Bad news can sometimes be good news in disguise. Don't be too quick to label the unsettling events in your life in a completely negative way.

THE ALTERNATIVE

Rather than categorizing something seemingly unpleasant as bad news, be quick to use every circumstance in your life as a reason to draw closer to God.

JANUARY 31

Discernment

The mocker seeks wisdom and finds none,
but knowledge comes easily to the discerning.
—PROVERBS 14:6

My dad gave me a great tip years ago. I was in driver's education class, and he let me drive to my older sister's home about ninety miles away. As I cautiously drove through one small town, I reached a four-way stop exactly when another car did. That car had its left-hand blinker going strong, so I started to make my move across the intersection.

That was when Dad shared these words of wisdom. "When someone has their turn signal on, all you really know is that the car's signal works." In other words, even though the car's signal says one thing, it might not indicate what the driver intends to do.

You must be wise not only about turn signals—which may or may not display accurate information—but also about more important things. Teaching your children to be discerning when it comes to spiritual matters is critical. For example, when someone wears a necklace with a cross, all you really know is that the person is wearing a necklace with a cross.

THIS IS IMPORTANT

It can be easy for both young and old to be deceived. As a mom, teaching your children to be discerning is an important lesson. It will lead them to the path of knowledge.

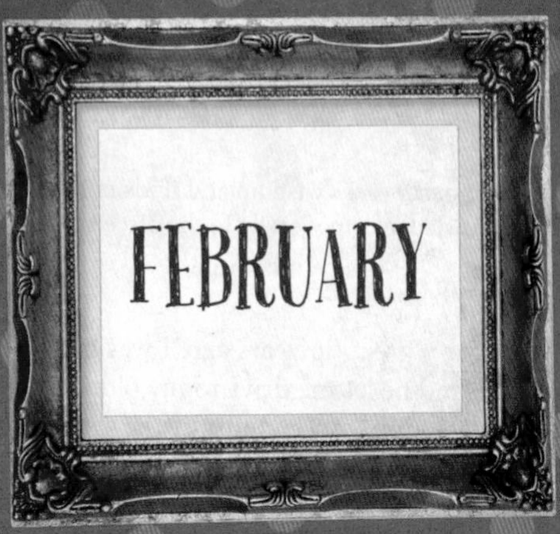

DO THESE THINGS

For you know that we dealt with each of you
as a father deals with his own children,
encouraging, comforting and
urging you to live lives worthy of God,
who calls you into his kingdom and glory.

—1 Thessalonians 2:11–12

FEBRUARY 1

Encouraging an Encourager

Therefore encourage one another and build each other up, just as in fact you are doing.

—1 THESSALONIANS 5:11

You cannot have too many encouragers in your life, and neither can your children. The world—whether it's the office, the classroom, or sometimes even the church—can be a discouraging place. People don't tend to encourage one another even though that's what the Word of God instructs believers to do.

I wonder how long Paul had to wait before he could utter the sentence in the Scripture above. Look again at the last phrase: "just as in fact you are doing." He saw the Thessalonians encouraging one another, and he cheered them on: "Way to go. Keep up the good work!"

What a great idea for your home! It's time to start encouraging the encouragers. The chances are great that when your children are applauded for applauding others for a job well done, the encouragement will grow.

FOR YOUR TO-DO LIST

Make an effort to encourage your kids when you hear or see them encouraging one another. I have a feeling it will make a noticeable difference.

FEBRUARY 2

Expectations

When those came who were hired first,
they expected to receive more.
But each one of them also received a denarius.
—MATTHEW 20:10

Expectations are powerful. I used to teach elementary school, and one of the things I believed was that my students would live up or down to my expectations. In an effort to encourage them to behave appropriately, I referred to them as ladies and gentlemen instead of as girls and boys.

I didn't have a control group to determine the success or failure of my plan, but my feeling was that the results were positive. It's tough to pull the hair of the girl sitting in front of you when your teacher has just called you a gentleman. It's difficult to call the boy across the aisle a mean name if your teacher has just called you a lady.

My students lived up to my expectations. Your kids will too—or they might live down to them. Calling your son a "troublemaker" or your daughter a "whiner" might encourage them to live out the full meanings of those names.

IT'S TRUE

A negative nickname can bring out negative behavior. Think before you call your child anything but his or her name.

FEBRUARY 3

Courage and Encouragement

"Be strong and courageous.
Do not be afraid or terrified because of them,
for the LORD your God goes with you;
he will never leave you nor forsake you."
—DEUTERONOMY 31:6

I was writing a note to a dear friend to thank her for, among other things, giving me courage and encouragement. As I reread the note, I wondered about the connection between those two words.

The definition of *encourage* is to inspire with hope, courage, or confidence. The word *courage* was the very root of the word *encourage*.

Today you may need courage to persevere in a difficult circumstance with your children or simply to start your day. Perhaps you need courage to share the good news of Jesus with a friend or neighbor. Whatever the case, I am here today to encourage you just as my friend encouraged me. You can have courage, for God will not forsake you.

PRAY WITH ME

Lord, please give me courage today. I only have an idea of the situations I might face. You know exactly what the day will bring. I am encouraged to know you are walking before me.

FEBRUARY 4

Powerful Words

Encourage and cheer me with your words.

—PSALM 119:28 TLB

"Hi, kids," the youth pastor said to the children gathered around him on the platform. "It's great to see you today. You'll have to excuse me for just a minute. I brought my toothbrush and toothpaste with me because I didn't have time to brush at home. It won't take me long."

At that point, he squeezed some toothpaste onto his brush. Needless to say, the kids started to laugh. I know what they were thinking: *How is he going to brush his teeth at church? Where is he going to spit?*

The young pastor paused as the kids laughed even harder. "This is silly, isn't it? I guess I'll just push the toothpaste back into the tube and we'll get started. Excuse me for just a second."

When he couldn't return the toothpaste to the tube, he paused and delivered the punch line of his lesson. "This toothpaste is like our words. Once they come out of our mouths, we can't stuff them back in."

A LESSON FOR YOUNG AND OLD

This is a lesson you can share with your children. The toothpaste you waste as you illustrate the point might produce a life-changing result.

FEBRUARY 5

Do Love

Love is patient, love is kind.
It does not envy, it does not boast, it is not proud.
It does not dishonor others, it is not self-seeking,
it is not easily angered,
it keeps no record of wrongs.
Love does not delight in evil but rejoices with the truth.
—1 CORINTHIANS 13:4–6

Love is an action word; it's more than a feeling. If you spend an entire day telling your kids you love them but don't "do love," it will be hard for them to believe you.

So how can you "do love"? The key is in 1 Corinthians 13, where you can learn what love is. You "do love" by being patient and kind and rejoicing in the truth.

In the same passage, Paul explains what love does not do—and that list is even longer. It doesn't envy or boast. It isn't proud or rude or self-seeking or easily angered. If you are doing those things, you aren't doing love.

Doing love is a choice you make each day. Doing love means choosing actions that reflect the nature of God, for God is love.

SO

Love in action is a call to live and love like Jesus. Make it your goal today to extend an extra dose of patience and kindness to everyone who crosses your path—and you can begin with the people at home.

FEBRUARY 6

Be Good to Your Kids

Parents, don't be hard on your children.
Raise them properly.
Teach them and instruct them about the Lord.

—EPHESIANS 6:4 CEV

I saw a bumper sticker that read: "Be good to your kids. They will choose your nursing home." I got a chuckle out of the thought, and then I began to imagine the ways a mom can "be good to her kids."

On the most basic level, a good mom makes certain her children have the bare necessities for survival—like food and shelter. Beyond that, children need the security of their mother's love. A good mom makes certain her children receive that love.

Perhaps the most important thing moms do is to teach their children about the Lord and his love. That lesson is fundamental, and the time to start teaching it is long before your kids are searching for your new place to live . . . long before they choose your nursing home.

LET'S PRAY

Lord, I want to be good to my kids. I want to teach them about you—about your love, your grace, and your goodness—urging them to live lives worthy of you.

FEBRUARY 7

Do It

If anyone, then, knows the good they ought to do
and doesn't do it, it is sin for them.

—JAMES 4:17

A teenager I know gave horseback riding lessons during the summer. His students ranged in age from three years old to the age of his grandmother. Occasionally I'd go to the riding stables and watch him work with those eager riders.

As I watched one day, a ten-year-old student was helping the instructor brush down the horse, getting ready to put the saddle on her back. The young man walked a little too close to the backside of the horse and his teacher spoke up.

"You need to walk farther away from the back of the horse."

"I know," was the reply.

When it happened again, the teacher was firmer—repeating the same instruction once again.

The boy's reply was also the same: "I know."

His teacher simply said, "Well, if you *know* it, then *do* it!"

HOW ABOUT YOU?

As a mom you might find yourself repeating an instruction over and over, only to hear your child claiming he "knows" what he should do. Next time, try the words of the horseman: "If you know it, then do it." And expect nothing less.

FEBRUARY 8

Good Gifts

Each of you should give what you have
decided in your heart to give,
not reluctantly or under compulsion,
for God loves a cheerful giver.

—2 CORINTHIANS 9:7

When my boys were young, they were well-dressed thanks to the many hand-me-downs we received. At the change of every season, they'd get a bag or box of clothes from friends who had outgrown an assortment of shirts and slacks and shorts. It was like getting Christmas presents throughout the entire year.

After my children were the thankful recipients of "recycled clothing," they became the donors. Many jeans and shirts were outgrown and handed down. And each time they filled the sack, they followed a simple rule: Give away treasures not trash, good things not garbage, jewels not junk.

The rule for the hand-me-downs reflects God's very nature. He gives good gifts to those who ask him.

THINK ABOUT IT

The hand-me-down rule can also apply in a spiritual sense. Encourage your kids to give away prayer, support, and the gospel message—giving away treasures not trash, good things not garbage, jewels not junk.

FEBRUARY 9

He Carries You

"There you saw how the LORD your God carried you,
as a father carries his son,
all the way you went until you reached this place."
—DEUTERONOMY 1:31

These words in Deuteronomy paint a wonderful picture. When I read them, I remember carrying each of my children when they were little. They would cuddle and bury their faces close to my neck. There they felt warm and protected and could feel the beat of my heart. Those memories remind me of the trust and comfort they found in my arms and in the arms of others who loved them.

God offers you and your children comfort and love. He is able to carry you and to carry your kids from today into adulthood and beyond. He will carry those he loves when they cannot walk on their own.

A mother's privilege and joy is not only to carry and comfort her children, but also to help them understand that God is always available and willing to carry and comfort them. He will be there when you cannot.

LET'S PRAY

Lord, I want my kids to know that you're always near to comfort them. Help me communicate that truth to them.

FEBRUARY 10

Tunnel Vision

Give thanks in all circumstances;
for this is God's will for you in Christ Jesus.
—1 THESSALONIANS 5:18

God's Word is very clear about having a thankful heart. Admittedly, that isn't an easy thing to do. Being thankful is most difficult for me when I find myself in an uncomfortable situation and cannot escape. If something is unpleasant, it's difficult to respond with a thankful heart. Always giving thanks is hard for me.

Why is that the case? Maybe it's because I have tunnel vision and can't see the big picture. All I see is my disappointment over the immediate circumstances. I don't see how the current situation fits into God's plan.

God, however, can see the big picture. He's not limited by time or space or imagination, and he's given me the instruction to give thanks in everything. I don't have to understand it or see the big picture. My responsibility and yours is to choose to obey.

FOOD FOR THOUGHT

You might find it difficult to give thanks in your current situation. Maybe the key can be found in one little word: God says to give thanks in everything—not for everything. Consider that as you walk through today.

FEBRUARY 11

Put on Your Shoes

Stand firm then . . . with your feet fitted
with the readiness that comes from the gospel of peace.

—EPHESIANS 6:14–15

Where I live in Central Illinois, we have our share of tornadoes. Twisters happen so frequently they're almost routine. When the kids were young, the first thing I did when I heard of a tornado watch or warning was to tell them to put on their shoes. That's because heading to the basement for cover is easier if you're wearing shoes, and if things get serious, there might be debris to avoid.

My kids knew the routine and also knew it was in their best interest to get their shoes on as soon as they heard the order.

God tells his kids to put on their shoes too. In Ephesians 6, we're told to put on the full armor of God, which includes arming our feet. Knowing the gospel of Jesus Christ assures that we're ready for action.

TO DO

Help your kids "get their shoes on." Teach them the truth of the gospel of peace. Doing so will prepare them for the storms of life.

FEBRUARY 12

A Gentle Whisper

The Lord said, "Go out and stand on
the mountain in the presence of the Lord,
for the Lord is about to pass by."
Then a great and powerful wind tore the mountains
apart and shattered the rocks before the Lord,
but the Lord was not in the wind.
After the wind there was an earthquake,
but the Lord was not in the earthquake.
After the earthquake came a fire,
but the Lord was not in the fire.
And after the fire came a gentle whisper.

—1 Kings 19:11–12

The Lord is powerful and capable of amazing, extraordinary things. He is a mighty God who is all-powerful, yet in the Scripture above we learn he chose to speak through a gentle whisper.

As a mom, it is too easy to think that increasing the volume of your voice will increase your children's ability to actually listen to what is being said. Perhaps a gentle whisper would be a better choice. After all, hearing a whisper takes more effort and demands more attention.

AHA!

Perhaps getting the attention of your child might be as simple as turning down the volume and speaking in a gentle whisper.

FEBRUARY 13

Thank You

Praise the LORD.
Praise God in his sanctuary;
praise him in his mighty heavens.
—PSALM 150:1

Writing a thank-you note is almost a lost art. An e-mail, as wonderful as it is, doesn't have the same impact as a handwritten note of thanks to someone who has shown you kindness or given you or your child a gift.

There has never been a greater gift than the gift of God's Son: "For God so loved the world that he gave his one and only Son, that whoever believes in him shall not perish but have eternal life" (John 3:16).

Maybe it's time to write a thank-you note to God. Although no letter can actually be delivered, you can write your note of thanks in a journal. When you have recorded your words of thanksgiving and praise, you can read them and be reminded again and again of God's goodness.

START TODAY

You don't need a journal to begin the process. Find a piece of paper and a pen and write down your note of thanks to God. "God, today I praise you for . . ."

FEBRUARY 14

Keeping It Simple

"Everyone who calls
on the name of the Lord will be saved."

—Acts 2:21

I like keeping things simple. The fewer ingredients in a recipe, the better. The simpler the driving directions, the better chance I'll make it to my destination without stress. I like wash-and-wear clothes and wash-and-wear hair. I like e-mail addresses, short sermons, and simple earrings that go with almost everything in my closet.

I also like the message of the gospel, and in many respects that message is simple. It's straightforward and so alarmingly uncomplicated that some find it difficult to believe.

It may be too simple for some, but even a young child can accept the message of truth. Everyone who calls on the name of the Lord will be saved.

THE TRUTH

God wants your child to "come to a knowledge of the truth" (1 Timothy 2:4). Keep it simple as you share the gospel message with your children.

FEBRUARY 15

No Fear

The LORD is my light and my salvation—
whom shall I fear?
The LORD is the stronghold of my life—
of whom shall I be afraid?

—PSALM 27:1

Fear is a powerful thing. It can push its way into many areas of your life and the lives of your children. Fear comes in various forms. Some people fear accidents, illness, or death; or they fear those things might happen to someone they love. It's possible to fear defeat or even to fear trying something new. The list of possible fears is long and can include irrational fears, such as fearing the darkness or make-believe monsters.

Fear has the potential to be desperately discouraging. It can undermine your faith, paralyze your progress, and blur the vision you've received from God. Fear can rob you of joy and peace. It can do the same destructive things to your children.

The psalmist chose to replace his fear with confidence in the Lord. You and your children can choose to do the same.

SOMETHING TO NOTE

There are things children should be taught to respect, such as fire, traffic, and strange animals. Respecting those things is important for your child's safety, but respect is different from fear.

FEBRUARY 16

Not in Vain

Therefore, my dear brothers and sisters, stand firm.
Let nothing move you.
Always give yourselves fully to the work of the Lord,
because you know that your labor in the Lord is not in vain.

—1 CORINTHIANS 15:58

Many of the jobs that go hand in hand with motherhood are so very *daily*. I used to laughingly lament that after feeding the kids a great meal they would just want to eat again in five hours. Yes, many of the motherly "labors of love" are everyday labors, and they are oftentimes unappreciated.

This can make the tasks seem burdensome. When you feel that way, the key may be to see those labors from a different perspective. To quote Paul, "Your labor in the Lord is not in vain."

The meals you cook, the clothes you wash, the carpool trips you make, the classroom excursions you chaperone—they are all labors of love. They demonstrate your love for your child, who is a gift from the Lord. These acts of labor are not in vain.

IT'S TRUE

Being a mom can be exhausting. It is a daily commitment to do the things, the everyday things, that are necessary for raising responsible children capable of loving and serving the Lord.

FEBRUARY 17

Woe

Woe to those who call evil good and good evil,
who put darkness for light and light for darkness,
who put bitter for sweet and sweet for bitter.

—Isaiah 5:20

As a mom, it's important to help your children identify what's good and what's evil. When my kids were little I had more than one opportunity to do just that while we watched TV together.

Without warning an inappropriate scene would suddenly appear. "Wow, that's not good," I'd say. "Maybe we should change the channel."

The boys would immediately do their best to reassure me. "Mom, it really isn't *that* bad."

They couldn't have said anything worse. I'd literally jump out of my chair and rush toward the remote, saying something like, "If you think that sort of thing is okay, I've *got* to change the channel. Maybe we should just turn the TV off!"

Their sheepish replies? "Oh no, Mom. You're right. It is bad. How about just changing the channel?" They got the idea. I wanted them to identify good and evil.

IT'S TRUE

You will have many opportunities to help your children distinguish good from evil. Take advantage of those teachable moments and encourage them to follow God's standards for behavior.

FEBRUARY 18

Music Trivia

"The LORD himself goes before you and will be with you;
he will never leave you nor forsake you.
Do not be afraid; do not be discouraged."

—DEUTERONOMY 31:8

Are you ready for a little music trivia? Here are a few lines from a song written in the 1800s. It is considered to be one of the top Western songs of all time, so hopefully you'll be able to imagine the tune when you read the words.

"Home, home on the range. Where the deer and the antelope play. Where seldom is heard, a . . ." Your turn; finish the refrain.

I'm guessing you knew the right answer, but just in case, here it is: "Where seldom is heard a *discouraging word*."

The range sounds like it might be a good place to live. Somehow the folks who inhabit that location have managed to limit the number of discouraging words. That's not a bad idea. Regardless of your location—the range, the city, the suburbs, or the farm—cutting back your discouraging words is a very good idea.

WHY NOT?

How about teaching your children the song "Home on the Range"? Then rather than scolding them when you hear a "discouraging word," you can hum the tune—a fun reminder in code.

FEBRUARY 19

Missed Opportunity

A word fitly spoken is like apples of gold
in pictures of silver.
—PROVERBS 25:11 KJV

There are many ways you can be an encourager to your children. Perhaps the most powerful way is through the words you speak, the words they hear. Chances are, you can remember specific words of encouragement that made an impression on you. It may have been something said by a teacher, or a friend, or one of the most important people in your life—your mom.

But moms aren't always speaking those encouraging words. There are some days when they find themselves constantly correcting their kids. On days like that, it can be difficult to notice those little darlings doing anything right.

There are other times when the kids are doing a great job and Mom notices, but she doesn't say a word. Why? It's because she expects them to do what's right. Regardless of what's expected, don't miss any opportunity to speak an encouraging word.

THE SIMPLE CHALLENGE

Remember the power of an encouraging word. Then catch your kids in the act of doing something right and encourage them.

FEBRUARY 20

Wise Counsel

The way of fools seems right to them,
but the wise listen to advice.

—PROVERBS 12:15

There is a difference between asking someone for *wise* counsel and finding someone who will give you *agreeing* counsel. It's important that as you make decisions in your life you seek wise counsel. It's also important to teach your children to do the same.

Too often kids simply find someone who will agree with them. "Do you think I should skip class?" Wise counsel would say no, but agreeing counsel would affirm that poor choice and maybe even decide to skip class too.

A wise mom seeks wise counsel. She doesn't merely look for agreeing counsel or choose to avoid all counsel or advice. A wise mom teaches her child to do the same—to look for help from others who have wisdom and experience that can make him or her wiser still.

IT'S TRUE

You can benefit from advice, and so can your children. The key is to get that counsel from a wise source. Be an example to your kids. Be a mom who looks for wise counsel.

FEBRUARY 21

A Heavy Load

Anxiety weighs down the heart,
but a kind word cheers it up.
—PROVERBS 12:25

It's tough to carry a heavy load. When you come home after shopping for a week's worth of groceries, it's always good when someone volunteers to carry them into the house even if you're the one who puts them all away.

It was very helpful when my kids used to volunteer to carry the cooler I'd packed for our picnic lunches or the luggage we were toting for a family vacation. Those things can weigh a great deal even when they're empty.

An anxious heart is a more burdensome load than groceries, sandwiches, or luggage, and no one else can lift and tote it for you. There is a way, however, that someone can help. The Word explains that a kind word is the solution; it does wonders for a heavy heart, whether it is your heart or the heart of your child.

REMEMBER

Even a child can have a heavy heart. Perhaps that is because we live in a fallen world where hurts and disappointments abound. The next time you notice your child feeling anxious, offer a kind, encouraging word.

FEBRUARY 22

Pray the Word

This is my prayer: that your love may abound more
and more in knowledge and depth of insight,
so that you may be able to discern what is best and
may be pure and blameless for the day of Christ.

—PHILIPPIANS 1:9–10

I've often felt compelled to "pray the Scriptures" for folks I love. By that I mean inserting the name of someone directly into the Word. The verses above from the book of Philippians are a wonderful prayer to personalize, praying it specifically for someone in your life: "that your love, (insert name), may abound more and more in knowledge and depth of insight . . ."

It is also encouraging to make the Word more personal by inserting your own name into the love letter from God. The Word is not a collection of generalizations; it is written communication from the Lord who loves you and your children with an everlasting love. With confidence, you and your children can personalize John 3:16: "For God so loved *me*, that he gave his only begotten Son . . ."

A CHALLENGE

Take time right now to pray the Word for your children. Insert their names into the words of John 3:16.

FEBRUARY 23

Your Home

Our citizenship is in heaven. And we eagerly await
a Savior from there, the Lord Jesus Christ.
—Philippians 3:20

When I was a child, the road trips our family took were usually to visit my grandmother, who lived in a suburb of Chicago. Somewhere between our home and hers was a community whose welcome sign announced the name of the town, followed by: "If you lived here, you'd be home now." We thought that was so amusing that we often adapted the message to fit other small towns on our way to Grandma's.

After I came to a saving knowledge of Christ, it dawned on me that setting up residence in a certain town or country didn't necessarily mean that your "home" was located there—at least, not your permanent home.

Currently I am a citizen of the United States of America, and I have a home in the state of Illinois, but I'm not home yet. If you've received the gift of eternal life, you're not home either.

SOMETHING TO CONSIDER

You share your earthly home with people you love. Helping your children understand the love of Christ and encouraging them to receive that love may mean you'll also share a heavenly home in the future.

FEBRUARY 24

Saved

If you declare with your mouth, "Jesus is Lord," and believe in your heart that God raised him from the dead, you will be saved.

—Romans 10:9

I was raised in a home where Scripture was not taught or valued. That meant that I did not even have a basic knowledge of the Bible.

The first time I ever heard the word *saved* in reference to Christianity, I was a teenager visiting a kindly older woman. Her words to me were something like, "It doesn't matter where you go to church. What matters is that you've been saved."

At that point I nodded my head knowingly, having absolutely no idea what she was talking about. I didn't begin to learn the Christian language until a few years later when I heard the gospel message presented clearly in words I could understand.

That puzzling interchange from years ago comes to my mind each time I try to communicate with someone about the love of God and his sacrifice. Whether your audience is young or old, the gospel message can only be heard when the words you use can be understood.

SO

Make certain your children understand what you are saying when you tell them about the love and sacrifice of Jesus. That's the most important message anyone can bring.

FEBRUARY 25

The Word

Consequently, faith comes from hearing the message,
and the message is heard through the word about Christ.
—Romans 10:17

God's Word encourages his children to "live lives worthy of God" (1 Thessalonians 2:12). In other words, we are to live a life filled with faith in the Lord. The question becomes: How can you encourage your child's faith in God and ensure their faith—their life-changing choice—becomes a reality? Let's begin by establishing the truth about the origin of faith.

Faith is not a factor of heredity. It is not something that automatically comes through the bloodline.

Faith is not obtained through osmosis. In other words, it isn't transferred unconsciously.

Faith is not caught like a communicable disease.

According to Scripture, faith comes through hearing the message in the Word of God. To build children of faith, you must see to it they hear that all-important message.

A KEY

Since you want your children to hear the message, take time to read the Word to them every day. Enrolling them in a children's or teen program where the Bible is taught is also an excellent idea.

FEBRUARY 26

Think About It

Finally, brothers and sisters, whatever is true, whatever is noble, whatever is right, whatever is pure, whatever is lovely, whatever is admirable—if anything is excellent or praiseworthy—think about such things.

—PHILIPPIANS 4:8

As a mom it can be tough to get a full night's sleep. That's true when there's a newborn in the house, and it doesn't end when all the children sleep through the night. When my boys reached elementary school, I imagined I saw the "light at the end of the tunnel" in terms of uninterrupted sleep.

However, before long they became teenagers; and I realized the "light" was the reflection of the car headlights as they pulled into the driveway. By the time your kids are teenagers, you'll miss sleep again, waiting for them to get home.

It's not just kids that interrupt your sleep. Sometimes I wake up in the middle of the night for no reason at all. When that happens I start thinking . . . thinking about what's on my calendar for the next day . . . thinking about a project I need to finish . . . thinking about how much fun our upcoming trip will be. I'm thinking and losing valuable sleep.

FOR YOU TO DO

If you happen to find yourself awake for no reason at all, forget the calendar, the project, and the upcoming vacation. Instead use Philippians 4:8 as your guide and "think about such things."

FEBRUARY 27

Growing Up

Jesus grew in wisdom and stature,
and in favor with God and man.

—LUKE 2:52

When a baby is born we want to know the gender (if it hasn't already been revealed), the height, and the weight. More importantly, we want to hear that baby and mother are both doing well.

It doesn't take long for the height and weight of the newborn to change dramatically. Babies usually double their birth weight before they're six months old. Growing in stature typically goes hand in hand with the proper nourishment.

Growing in wisdom and in favor with God and man will take more effort, but that kind of growth is also a matter of proper nourishment. As a mom you have the privilege and the responsibility of introducing your child to the nourishment of God's Word from a very early age.

THE DIRECTIONS

Follow these instructions for growing in wisdom and in favor with God and man: "Let the message of Christ dwell among you richly as you teach and admonish one another with all wisdom through psalms, hymns, and songs from the Spirit, singing to God with gratitude in your hearts" (Colossians 3:16).

FEBRUARY 28

Encourage Her Children

Therefore encourage one another
with these words.

—1 THESSALONIANS 4:17

I was on a long, boring drive and decided to turn off the radio and amuse myself another way. My thoughts turned to the blessing God had given me through the women I worshiped with each Sunday. So many of them had become good friends and encouragers.

A question popped into my mind: How could I be a blessing to them? My first thought was that I could make each one a pan of lasagna, my go-to entrée that is both easy and delicious. I'd do one a week until each friend had received my gift of love.

Within minutes a new idea trumped that one. Rather than cooking something or baking something, what if I gave each friend the gift of encouraging her children? I knew each one of their kids personally and frequently interacted with them. Yes! That was how I could bless each friend. That was how I could encourage these moms.

FOR YOU

Who can you bless with the gift of encouragement? Waste no time; begin today.

FEBRUARY 29

The Bonus Day

In the beginning God created the heavens and the earth.
Now the earth was formless and empty,
darkness was over the surface of the deep,
and the Spirit of God was hovering over the waters.
And God said, "Let there be light," and there was light.
God saw that the light was good, and he separated
the light from the darkness. God called the light "day,"
and the darkness he called "night." And there was evening,
and there was morning—the first day.

—GENESIS 1:1–5

Today we take notice of a day that only occurs every four years. It's the bonus day that may or may not be on the calendar this year. Nevertheless, we're celebrating this unique and special day.

Some might view February 29 as simply a placeholder, guaranteeing that the calendar year will be synchronized with the solar year. But truly, it can be seen as so much more.

What if you chose to see February 29 as a reflection of the creative power of God? It was God who created the sun and the path of the earth's rotation.

TODAY

Take time to talk with your kids about creation. You might honor God's mighty power by celebrating leap year in a special way.

YOU ARE A ROLE MODEL

Dear children,
let us not love with words or speech
but with actions and in truth.

—1 JOHN 3:18

MARCH 1

You Are a Role Model

Be shepherds of God's flock that is under your care, watching over them—not because you must, but because you are willing, as God wants you to be; not pursuing dishonest gain, but eager to serve; not lording it over those entrusted to you, but being examples to the flock.

—1 PETER 5:2–3

NBA Hall of Fame player Charles Barkley made headlines years ago. In the instance I'm referring to, he made news not for his talent on the court, but for his appearance in a commercial where he declared, "I'm not a role model."

When I first heard those words, I remember thinking how wrong he was. He *was* and *is* a role model. I am a role model and you are a role model too, whether we like it or not.

Someone is always watching you, and that "someone" includes your children. They're watching you and taking note of your behavior and your responses. God knew that would be the case when he gave you guidelines in 1 Peter 5.

THERE'S NO DENYING IT

You are a role model. It's inevitable. Your children are watching you, so take responsibility and do your best to be a good role model for them.

MARCH 2

Instant Oatmeal

Wait for the LORD;
be strong and take heart
and wait for the LORD.
—PSALM 27:14

We live in a society that values the instantaneous. I, for one, am usually a big fan of speed and efficiency. I enjoy instant oatmeal, texting (my favorite form of instant messaging), and instant pudding. It's nice to have all of those things available with very little waiting, but the Word specifically tells us to wait on the Lord.

The Old Testament prophets had to do their fair share of waiting. In Jeremiah 42, all the army officers and all the people approached Jeremiah the prophet, saying, "Please hear our petition and pray to the LORD" (v. 2).

Jeremiah did as the people requested, and then he waited for the Lord's answer. It was not instant: "Ten days later the word of the LORD came to Jeremiah" (Jeremiah 42:7).

KNOW THIS

God's reply is not always as rapid as you wish it would be. You may pray and wait ten minutes, ten days, ten weeks, or longer. Don't grow weary. Instead, know that the wait is for your good. Model patience for your children.

MARCH 3

Complaints Department

Moses also said, "You will know that it was the LORD
when he gives you meat to eat in the evening
and all the bread you want in the morning,
because he has heard your grumbling against him.
Who are we? You are not grumbling against us,
but against the LORD."

—EXODUS 16:8

I wonder what it would be like to work in a complaints department—hour after hour, day after day, listening to someone complain.

As you read in Exodus, it seems as though Moses found himself at the head of the complaints department. The Israelites grumbled to him and about him, complaining about every aspect of their journey.

How did Moses handle all that complaining? He challenged the people to look at the truth: "You are not grumbling against us, but against the LORD."

PARTIAL JOB DESCRIPTION

Kids can be complainers, and you're probably the head of the complaints department. When you hear a complaint that constitutes grumbling against the Lord (i.e., "I want to be taller. It's not fair."), nip it in the bud. And remember, attempting to eliminate complaints applies to you too.

MARCH 4

The Explanation Is No Excuse

"They all alike began to make excuses.
The first said, 'I have just bought a field,
and I must go and see it.
Please excuse me.'"

—LUKE 14:18

"Of course I was late. I don't really bother to tell time. That's just the way God made me. It's not my fault."

Is that true? Is that the way God made your teenage daughter? To some degree, the answer is probably yes. There are different personalities, and some are better at paying attention to detail.

So does that mean the explanation of a God-given personality equals an excuse? Not a chance! What it does mean is that your son or daughter—and even you—will need to identify weaknesses and work to overcome them. If you happen to be a person who doesn't "really bother to tell time," now is the *time* to learn!

Mom, you don't want to make excuses because you don't want to hear your kids doing the same thing. The explanation is no excuse.

LET'S PRAY

Lord, you created me with strengths and weaknesses. Help me refrain from using those weaknesses as excuses. That's not the behavior I want to model for my kids.

MARCH 5

"I Know Everything"

If anyone thinks he knows all the answers,
he is just showing his ignorance.
—1 CORINTHIANS 8:2 TLB

Years ago I heard a young man declare that he knew "everything" about women. My recollection is that after he made that outlandish statement, a burst of uproarious laughter came from the listeners who were a little older and wiser. I wonder how long it took this man to discover the error of his words. I can only imagine his shock when ultimately he realized the truth.

The truth is that God is the only One who knows everything about women. He also knows everything about men and children. The Lord knows everything about everything. Any young man, mom, or child who says or believes they know *everything* about *anything* is mistaken.

The Word goes further. Not only is a know-it-all attitude mistaken; it is also a show of ignorance. The knowledgeable person is teachable.

YOUR CHOICE

Mom, you can choose to model a teachable attitude for your kids. A man, woman, or child who is teachable can be used by the Lord in a mighty way.

MARCH 6

Fight-or-Flight

You, man of God, flee from all this,
and pursue righteousness, godliness, faith,
love, endurance and gentleness.

—1 TIMOTHY 6:11

I remember learning about adrenaline in my college physiology class. That's the chemical produced in your body that is responsible for the fight-or-flight response. When you're under stress, adrenaline is secreted in order to boost your energy and enable you to handle the situation. With this energy you can rescue yourself with might (the fight) or escape from the conflict or harm (the flight).

Adrenaline prepares you to do one of those two things, and the Word has given you guidelines in 1 Timothy 6 to help you know when to use your extra energy for flight.

Among other things, you are to flee from envy, strife, malicious talk, and evil suspicions (v. 4); and you are to pursue "righteousness, godliness, faith, love, endurance and gentleness" (v. 11).

Modeling the flight from evil to good will encourage your children to do the same.

LET'S PRAY

Father, I want to be wise when it comes to escaping evil. I want to be an example to my children—choosing to flee from evil and to run toward what is good.

MARCH 7

Walk This Way

When Jesus spoke again to the people, he said, "I am the light of the world. Whoever follows me will never walk in darkness, but will have the light of life."
—John 8:12

The young mother had a serious accident and tore her Achilles tendon. Fortunately the surgeon was able to repair her leg, but even after weeks of therapy, she still walked with a limp that was exaggerated when she'd had a long day.

She had a young daughter, only two years old, whose legs were completely healthy. Nevertheless, when the little girl walked with her mother, she walked with a limp too—an exact replica of her mom's gait. She wanted to be just like Mom.

Your children want to be just like you. They want to talk the way you talk and even walk the way you walk. That might seem like a scary proposition, but God can help you be the kind of example your children need. That is especially important when it comes to following Christ. When your children follow him, they will never walk in darkness.

A QUESTION FOR YOU

Do you want your kids to walk the way you walk? If your answer is no, now is the time to make some changes in your life. Ask God for help and start the change today.

MARCH 8

Rotten Potatoes

Walk with the wise and become wise,
for a companion of fools suffers harm.
—PROVERBS 13:20

I walked into my pantry and knew something was wrong. There was a distinctive smell I immediately identified as a rotten potato. Yuck! I knew I now had the task of digging through the potato sack to find the rotten, stinky potato.

It didn't take long to find the culprit. No, wait—I should say *culprits*. There was one potato that had obviously started the whole thing, and several others, its companions, were leaning against it and working their way toward complete and utter uselessness.

One potato was spoiling the others. That can happen with people too. One companion who is a fool can influence others to behave foolishly. If you choose to keep company with a fool, the Word says you will suffer harm. And you'll be modeling that behavior for your children.

FOOD FOR THOUGHT

Peer pressure is a real thing for kids and for adults, so it is important to personally model choosing good peers. Take time to let your kids know why you have chosen your friends. What characteristics do they have that you admire?

MARCH 9

The Leader

Then I said to you, "Do not be terrified;
do not be afraid of them. The LORD your God, who
is going before you, will fight for you,
as he did for you in Egypt, before your very eyes."
—DEUTERONOMY 1:29–30

"Line leader!" the four-year-old shouted, then raced to the front of the pack. She was very confident and enthused about determining the route that would be taken, and the rest of her friends dutifully lined up behind her. They sensed she was more than capable in her leadership role.

A leader's confidence or lack of confidence seems to be infectious. As a mom, your confidence or lack of confidence is transferred to your children. When you have courage in a situation, when you are not afraid, that same courage empowers your kids.

THINK ABOUT IT

Was there a time when your courage gave your kids the courage to try something new and ultimately to succeed? Yay, Mom! Conversely, have you ever transferred an irrational fear to your children? That can happen too. When you confront any possible fear again, know that God is going before you—then you can lead with boldness.

MARCH 10

PPS

"Therefore I tell you, do not worry about your life,
what you will eat or drink; or about your body,
what you will wear. Is not life more than food,
and the body more than clothes?"

—MATTHEW 6:25

I've discovered—or perhaps I should say I have named—a disease. A syndrome, actually. You might be wondering how I, a person who has absolutely no education or training in the field of medicine, can find myself in the potentially prestigious position of naming a previously unnamed syndrome.

No one really cares about the label I've created, so my lack of medical credentials is unimportant. Nevertheless, let me familiarize you with my discovery. The syndrome? PPS: Premature Panic Syndrome.

PPS is the panicky feeling you have when you can't find your car keys even though you took them out of the ignition and threw them into your purse only moments before. Have you ever experienced PPS?

YIKES!

In case you now have a name for something you've experienced more than once, let me give you the cure. It's found in the words of Matthew 6:25. Do not worry!

MARCH 11

Actions Give You Away

The LORD appeared to us in the past, saying:
"I have loved you with an everlasting love;
I have drawn you with unfailing kindness."

—JEREMIAH 31:3

"It really doesn't matter what you say. Your actions and decisions give you away." Those sentences caused me to think.

Consider those who tell their spouse "I love you" and then they're unfaithful? Those actions and decisions give them away. How about the mom who tells her child, "Keep control. Don't act out your anger," and then verbally lashes out as a car cuts in front of her? Her actions and decisions give her away. The child who claims he'll stay on the sidewalk with his bike and then pedals down the street? His actions and decisions give him away. When there is an obvious discrepancy between words and actions, the actions tell the truth.

Everything the Lord said and did was in perfect harmony. He declared his "everlasting love" for his children, and he demonstrated that love by the sacrifice of Jesus.

LET'S PRAY

Lord, I want my words and my actions to bring the same message to my children. Give me the help I need to make that happen. Let my words perfectly illustrate my actions and decisions.

MARCH 12

An Easy Outline

Don't let anyone look down on you because you are young,
but set an example for the believers in speech,
in conduct, in love, in faith and in purity.

—1 TIMOTHY 4:12

I love it when God's Word gives you an easy outline for living, such as the one in the verse above. As a believer you are to be a role model in the areas listed in 1 Timothy 4—in speech, in conduct, in love, in faith, and in purity.

In speech: The Lord is always listening to the words you speak. It doesn't matter where you are or how softly you speak; he hears you.

In conduct: You are called to demonstrate a life of discipleship as a follower of Christ.

In love: The love of Christ is available to permeate all you do.

In faith: Faith the size of a mustard seed pleases God.

In purity: God will create a clean and pure heart in you.

SOME QUESTIONS FOR YOU TO PONDER

Are you modeling speech that is pleasing to God? Is your life an example to others? Are you allowing the love of God to shine in all you do? Is your faith big enough to serve God? Are you allowing God to give you a pure heart?

MARCH 13

Show-and-Tell

"Why do you call me, 'Lord, Lord,'
and do not do what I say?"
—LUKE 6:46

Parenting is a lot like show-and-tell. Do you remember that elementary school activity? You would bring something special to show to your classmates, and then you'd tell them about it.

As a mom, you tell your children how you want them to behave or respond in certain circumstances, but that's not all: You also show them. And a problem can arise when your show-and-tell doesn't match.

"Don't lie. It's bad to lie," Mom says to her daughter amid a teachable moment. Then the phone rings and Mom picks it up. Dad is in his easy chair in the family room, and the words out of Mom's mouth are confusing.

"I'm sorry, my husband isn't home right now."

The daughter thinks, *What? He's in the other room. Mom just lied, didn't she? I guess it's okay to lie sometimes.* Her words and actions didn't match.

That problem isn't new, which is why Jesus spoke to his disciples about the discrepancy between their words and deeds—the problem with their show-and-tell.

THINK ABOUT IT

When your show and your tell don't match, your children will be confused. Remember that what you do shouts much louder than what you say.

MARCH 14

God's Glory

So whether you eat or drink or whatever you do,
do it all for the glory of God.

—1 CORINTHIANS 10:31

The chances are great you've already had breakfast this morning. Maybe you had a cup of coffee or tea or a glass of orange juice. The verse above instructs you to eat or drink to the glory of God. And that's not all.

"Whatever you do," you're to do for God's glory. As I thought about this verse, I started making a list of things moms do besides eating and drinking.

In no particular order, there's: shopping for groceries, changing the baby's diaper, washing your daughter's uniform before the next game, driving the carpool to school, putting those groceries away, changing another diaper, washing your son's uniform, and hopping into the car to pick up the kids from school.

God knew what your days would be like, and his desire is for you to do it all for his glory.

THE NEXT STEP

Think about what you planned to do after you put this book down. Whatever you do, do it with purpose. Do it for God's glory.

MARCH 15

Stretching the Truth

"Then you will know the truth,
and the truth will set you free."
—John 8:32

As adults, we have developed a vocabulary of easy excuses—excuses that downplay personal responsibility. We use terms like "stretching the truth," "fibbing," or "little white lie" instead of the more blunt and accurate word, *lie*. The substitutes we choose make lying more palatable.

The truth of the matter is, it's the truth that matters! Knowing the truth and living in it are two of the most freeing things we can do. Not only does the truth set you free, but Jesus defines himself as the truth, saying, "I am the way and the truth and the life. No one comes to the Father except through me" (John 14:6).

If that's not enough, there's the bonus of John 8:36: "If the Son sets you free, you will be free indeed."

LET'S PRAY

Father, you know that oftentimes I'm tempted to stretch the truth—to lie to others and to myself. Give me the courage to live in the truth. I want to live in the freedom that only you can bring to my life.

MARCH 16

Forgiveness

"In accordance with your great love, forgive the sin of these people, just as you have pardoned them from the time they left Egypt until now."

—NUMBERS 14:19

God's Word has a great deal to say about forgiveness. According to my concordance, in the New International Version, the words *forgive*, *forgiveness*, *forgiving*, and *forgiven* are used 126 times in Scripture. The numbers indicate that forgiveness in its many forms is an important topic.

It only makes sense. Forgiveness is something every person deals with in two ways; at some point, everyone needs to *ask* for forgiveness and to *extend* forgiveness to someone else.

As your children watch you, they will learn how to accept forgiveness and also how to give it to others. Both actions are essentially a choice. When you model either accepting forgiveness or granting it to someone else, your kids see that good choice in action.

A QUICK NOTE

The sooner an apology is extended or accepted, the better. If you've been waiting for the best time to do either, be assured—the time is now. There is no reason to hold on to the pain.

MARCH 17

Behave Yourself

Josiah was eight years old when he became king,
and he reigned in Jerusalem thirty-one years.
He did what was right in the eyes of the LORD and
followed the ways of his father David,
not turning aside to the right or to the left.

—2 CHRONICLES 34:1–2

There are some standard lines almost every mom has uttered, such as, "This is going to hurt me more than it hurts you." Or this one: "Behave yourself. Someone is going to know your mother."

I started saying that last one when my kids hit junior high school. Since we were from a small community, it was very true.

Years after my children had finished junior high and the older two boys were in college, I was preparing to speak at an event near the university they attended. A gentleman came up to me, introduced himself, and went on to say, "I am the assistant dean of the college of agriculture. I know your son."

Oh no, I thought. *Now* I *have to behave myself.*

JUST A THOUGHT

What if we give that parental phrase a twist? Here's what I'm thinking: "Behave yourself. Someone might want to know your heavenly Father." The way you live each day has the potential to draw others to the Lord.

MARCH 18

Choose Your Attitude

Although he had forbidden Solomon to follow other gods, Solomon did not keep the LORD's command. So the LORD said to Solomon, "Since this is your attitude and you have not kept my covenant and my decrees, which I commanded you, I will most certainly tear the kingdom away from you and give it to one of your subordinates."

—1 KINGS 11:10–11

I live on a farm. My husband is a retired military pilot who took over the family's farming operation several years ago. When that happened I became interested in the weather more than ever before.

Prior to that life change, my only weather concern was how to dress appropriately before leaving the house or if the church picnic would be cancelled because of rain. Now I find myself frustrated because the weather isn't cooperating with my agricultural needs. More rain, less rain, more heat, less heat—all beyond my control.

You may not have wanted to control the rain or the temperature, but chances are you've experienced other circumstances out of your control. Things don't always go the way you'd like or the way you planned. Occasionally it might feel like nothing is going right. Even when that is the case, remember: You can always choose your attitude.

IT'S SIMPLE BUT NOT EASY

Lord, help me choose the best attitude—whether I feel like it or not.

MARCH 19

Too Busy

Beloved, do not imitate what is evil
but imitate what is good.

—3 JOHN 11 NRSV

I walked into the living room and discovered that my youngest son, only a toddler at the time, had taken every toy out of the toy box and scattered them around the room.

"Wow," I exclaimed. "You have quite a mess here. You'll have to pick up all these toys and put them away."

That darling little boy looked up at me, and with the sweetest voice, said, "I'm not gonna pick up my toys nenny more times. I'm too busy."

I was surprised by his response and wondered where in the world he'd heard that excuse. Was there some character on *Sesame Street* who was too busy?

Almost immediately I realized that he had probably heard those words from me. Had I declared myself "too busy" so often that he was imitating me? Ouch, the truth can hurt.

LET'S PRAY

Lord, please help me. I don't want to be too busy for the important things in life—things like time spent with you or with my family. Let me use my time wisely and model that for my kids.

MARCH 20

Living on the Edge

If we are "out of our mind," as some say, it is for God;
if we are in our right mind, it is for you.

—2 Corinthians 5:13

I know a young man who leads climbing expeditions to Mount Rainier. He could be classified as someone who lives on the edge; every time he takes a climbing group up the mountain, he assumes a risk.

Personally I can't imagine choosing to climb a very steep, very dangerous mountain. Does that mean that everyone who doesn't want to make that climb is failing to live life on the edge? No, I don't think so.

I have a friend who is a mother of three, a grandmother, a teacher's aide at the local public school, and occasionally the caretaker of an elderly neighbor. To my knowledge she's never climbed a mountain and doesn't intend to, but her motto in life is this: "I want to do things for God that are *so big* they're bound to fail unless he intervenes." Now that's living on the edge.

HOW ABOUT YOU?

You don't have to climb a mountain either. Raising kids who love and obey God can be exhilarating and exciting, and it is definitely a pursuit where the intervention of God will mean success.

MARCH 21

Please Listen

My dear brothers and sisters, take note of this:
Everyone should be quick to listen,
slow to speak and slow to become angry.
—JAMES 1:19

There has been a great deal of research done on the topic of listening. Typically it's classified as a communication skill, and success and failure in many occupations is tied to one's ability to listen.

Being a mom is not an office job, but we both know it should be classified as work. Listening is important in the field of motherhood.

Moms who listen well are good role models for their children. When you look at your children as they speak to you and give them your attention, you're modeling good listening skills. Kneeling down to their eye level will help them listen to you. When it comes to older kids who might tower over you, having them sit down is helpful.

Listening to your child is important. Listening to your heavenly Father is more important, and you're modeling that for your child too. When you communicate with either one, remember to be quick to listen.

PRAY WITH ME

Father, help me be a better listener to you and to my children. Help me avoid distractions, and let me hear with my ears and my heart.

MARCH 22

Peach Pie

We have different gifts, according to the grace given to
each of us. If your gift is prophesying, then prophesy in
accordance with your faith; if it is serving, then serve;
if it is teaching, then teach;
if it is to encourage, then give encouragement;
if it is giving, then give generously;
if it is to lead, do it diligently;
if it is to show mercy, do it cheerfully.

—ROMANS 12:6–8

The phone rang. It was my friend Barb. "Are you going to the post office this afternoon?"

"I wasn't planning to. Can I help you with something?"

"I baked you a peach pie and I have to run to work. I thought if you were going to the post office you could come by my house and pick it up."

You've already guessed my response—I gladly scheduled that trip. Barb is a wonderful cook and she was generously sharing her talent, her gift, with me and my family.

God has given you and your children gifts you can share. Help your kids identify their God-given gifts and talents.

IDENTIFY THOSE GIFTS

As your children watch you encouraging or serving or teaching or giving or exercising the gifts God has given you, encourage them to use their gifts to build the kingdom.

MARCH 23

Be Kind

"Give, and it will be given to you.
A good measure, pressed down, shaken together and
running over, will be poured into your lap.
For with the measure you use, it will be measured to you."

—LUKE 6:38

"Be kind. Everyone you meet is fighting a battle." That quote caught my eye and more importantly caught my heart. It expands on the instruction to be kind by explaining why kindness is important: "Everyone you meet is fighting a battle."

Battles can take different forms. Sometimes the battles are obvious, such as battles with poor health, conflicts in families, unemployment, or struggles with drugs and alcohol, to name a few.

Some battles are less conspicuous, such as battles with depression or rejection, or unspoken personal concerns. But obvious or obscure, those in the midst of a battle need your kindness.

The battles of children vary somewhat from those of adults, but God's principles are the same. Be kind.

THINK ABOUT IT

What battle are you fighting? How about your kids? Sowing kindness into the life of someone else may be just what is needed for both of you. Model that behavior.

MARCH 24

Ashamed

"If anyone is ashamed of me and my words in this adulterous and sinful generation, the Son of Man will be ashamed of them when he comes in his Father's glory with the holy angels."

—MARK 8:38

Rumor has it that on occasion, preteens wish their mothers were invisible. It's not that your child is ashamed of you; it's simply the stage of life when he or she chooses to live in the fantasy world called "No Moms Necessary."

If you're in a home right now with someone experiencing that fairy tale, take heart: It usually doesn't last very long. Soon that young lady or gentleman will realize that you are not as strange or obnoxious as was once believed.

Being momentarily embarrassed by your mom is a feeling that may come and go, and there are very few ramifications; but being ashamed of the gospel has serious consequences, for kids and for the moms who love them.

God's Word is clear. Anyone who chooses to be ashamed of the Lord will find that the Lord is ashamed of them.

YOUR ASSIGNMENT

Model confidence in the Word of God and the gospel message. Don't be invisible. Unashamedly proclaim the truth.

MARCH 25

Older?

Likewise, teach the older women to be reverent in the way they live, not to be slanderers or addicted to much wine, but to teach what is good. Then they can urge the younger women to love their husbands and children.

—Titus 2:3–4

A musical evangelist was scheduled to visit our church. We'd been friends for years and decided it would be fun to spend some time together before she had to set up for the evening concert.

Because I am ten years her senior, I'd already experienced things that were presumably in her future. She asked me about being a wife and mother and listened intently as I answered her questions about both. Hours later she took the platform at church to begin the concert.

"I had a wonderful day today," she said as I smiled knowingly. "I spent time with an older Christian woman."

What? I was confused and looked around, wondering who she'd seen later that day. Then it hit me: I was the older Christian woman.

YOUR TURN

Young or old, you can be a blessing to other women. Ask the Lord who he wants you to mentor, and then schedule a time to have lunch with her soon.

MARCH 26

Gossip

A perverse person stirs up conflict,
and a gossip separates close friends.
—PROVERBS 16:28

I know you won't be surprised when I tell you that gossip is not a good thing. That's something you can read in the Scripture above and other places in God's Word.

"A gossip betrays a confidence, but a trustworthy person keeps a secret" (Proverbs 11:13).

"Without wood a fire goes out; without a gossip a quarrel dies down" (Proverbs 26:20).

It isn't hard to get the picture, is it? Too often in the Christian community gossip is masked as genuine concern. "I want to share something with you about so-and-so in order to help you pray more effectively."

You don't need gossip in order to pray effectively. All you need is the desire to speak to your heavenly Father. God already knows all the details, and he also knows the best answer to any circumstance or situation.

Let your children hear you praying, not gossiping.

A QUICK NOTE OR TWO

First: If someone begins to speak to you with the words, "I don't know if I should tell you this or not . . ." Quickly and gently suggest she not say anything. Second: If someone will gossip to you, they will gossip about you.

MARCH 27

Teach Your Children

Fix these words of mine in your hearts and minds;
Tie them as symbols on your hands and bind them on your foreheads. Teach them to your children, talking about them when you sit at home and when you walk along the road, when you lie down and when you get up.

—DEUTERONOMY 11:18–19

Sitting at home, walking along the road, lying down, and getting up are all a part of everyday life. They are also times when you can potentially connect with your children in a meaningful way and teach them truths from the Word of God. When those connections occur, "quantity time" turns into "quality time."

Teachable moments are not scheduled or planned. They don't always occur in the structure of family devotions or during Bible study or Sunday school class. They can pop up in the most mundane times and locations, when you and your children are busy doing ordinary things.

In preparation for those spontaneous moments you must fix his Word in your heart. When you take the time to read and meditate on the Word of God, his instruction and wisdom will be readily available.

YOUR ASSIGNMENT

Take time each day to fix God's words in your heart and mind, and look for wonderful opportunities to share God's truth with your children.

MARCH 28

Robbery

"Bring the whole tithe into the storehouse, that there may be food in my house. Test me in this," says the LORD Almighty, "and see if I will not throw open the floodgates of heaven and pour out so much blessing that there will not be room enough to store it."

—MALACHI 3:10

"When is the best time to teach children about giving to the work of the Lord?" That was the question presented to me by a young mother. My answer was simple, though probably not as specific as was desired: "It is never too early."

A preschooler can be a giver by donating her gently used toys to the church rummage sale. An older child, able to earn money by doing odd jobs, can be encouraged to give to a mission project.

When at a young age a child experiences the joy of giving, it's easier to carry that discipline into adulthood. Earning a dollar and putting a dime in the donation plate is great training for later years when that child's earning potential has risen.

FOOD FOR THOUGHT

Giving is a blessing. It's an opportunity to further the kingdom of heaven. Don't rob God or your children. Model giving.

APRIL 1

A Do-Over

Then he told them plainly, "Lazarus is dead.
And for your sake, I am glad I wasn't there,
for this will give you another opportunity to believe in me.
Come, let's go to him."

—JOHN 11:14–15 TLB

The Scripture from John 11 indicates that the disciples were given a second chance, a do-over, "another opportunity." I was introduced to the concept of a do-over when my boys were young.

We'd be playing a game, shooting baskets, and one of them would miss a shot and call for a do-over. That meant he wanted another chance to make the basket. Typically I granted the request and he'd try again.

In a game it's possible to obtain a do-over and get another opportunity to be successful. In life it's much more difficult. You might receive a do-over and you might not.

If you've failed to follow the Lord's instructions and you're hoping for a do-over, ask for his forgiveness and then ask him for another try to get it right. You might find you've obtained a divine do-over, a second chance from God.

TAKE NOTE

When you truly repent and ask God for forgiveness, he not only forgives you but also forgets. That doesn't mean the consequences are erased. Listen carefully to his voice to avoid needing another do-over.

APRIL 2

Availability

Then I heard the voice of the Lord saying,
"Whom shall I send? And who will go for us?"
And I said, "Here am I. Send me!"

—ISAIAH 6:8

God does not care about your abilities, nor is he interested in what you consider your inabilities. He merely cares about your availability.

Mary gave birth to Jesus and placed him in a manger. Why? Because that was the only space available for the newborn baby. The manger had not been designed to hold a child. It was constructed to hold hay for the livestock. It was essentially a feeding trough, not a cradle or bassinet, but no guest room was available; so the manger became an essential part of God's plan.

The Lord wants you to be an essential part of his plan too. He doesn't care about your abilities or inabilities; he is interested in your availability. He cares about your willingness to listen, learn, and respond to his call.

THE CHALLENGE

God doesn't want to hear great claims of what you can do. He doesn't want to hear excuses about the things you think you can't do. He wants to hear you say, "Here am I. Send me!"

APRIL 3

Practice, Practice, Practice

Share with the Lord's people who are in need.
Practice hospitality.

—ROMANS 12:13

Practice makes perfect. Many a coach, parent, and piano teacher has uttered that phrase. I practiced the piano for years and improved as time went on. I did not, however, reach perfection. Now it's been years since I've practiced the piano, and what little skill I had has diminished.

When the Lord instructs you to practice things such as hospitality, I don't believe it is to achieve perfection. I do believe, however, that as you do something over and over you will become more proficient. If you continue to practice things like hospitality, not only will that skill improve but you will also be able to successfully maintain it.

The Lord is not demanding perfection in hospitality or in motherhood, which should come as a relief. He just wants you to practice.

"As for God, his way is perfect: the LORD's Word is flawless; he shields all who take refuge in him" (Psalm 18:30).

LET'S PRAY

Lord, I want to do my best when it comes to being a mom. Help me diligently practice your instructions and relax as I miss perfection.

APRIL 4

Pleasing God

Without faith it is impossible to please God,
because anyone who comes to him must believe that he
exists and that he rewards those who earnestly seek him.

—HEBREWS 11:6

"Nothing I ever did pleased my parents," the young woman lamented. Her statement was one I'd heard before. The fact that she used the word *nothing* led me to believe she was exaggerating.

Even if the truth was she *seldom* did things that pleased her parents—or if her parents didn't *appear* to be pleased by what she did—those are still sad statements.

It's possible you feel or have felt that way, that as a child (or even as an adult) you were unable to please your parents. Maybe you had no idea how to do it.

The good news is that the Lord, your heavenly parent, has let you know how you can please him. His desire is for you to have faith, to believe he exists; and he'll reward you as you seek him.

IT'S TRUE

You may have found it difficult to please your parents because their expectations were unexpressed or constantly changing. If you are a woman of faith, God is pleased with you.

APRIL 5

Wisdom

If any of you lacks wisdom, you should ask God,
who gives generously to all without finding fault,
and it will be given to you.

—James 1:5

The Lord is willing to give you wisdom for your role as a mother; yet when a problem arises, praying for wisdom is many times the very last resort. It seems easier to rely on your own strength or problem-solving ability than to seek wisdom from God.

Wisdom, however, is an essential tool in parenting, and you can ask for it. When you do ask, you'll get a generous portion. There are also other ways you can gain wisdom.

Wisdom is found through ridding yourself of pride and instead having a teachable spirit: "When pride comes, then comes disgrace, but with humility comes wisdom" (Proverbs 11:2).

Wisdom comes from revering the Lord—respecting and trusting him completely: "The fear of the Lord is the beginning of wisdom; all who follow his precepts have good understanding" (Psalm 111:10).

IT'S TRUE

Wisdom is essential to good parenting, and the Lord is willing to give you wisdom. Just ask, listen, and follow through under his instruction.

APRIL 6

Win the Prize

Brothers and sisters, I do not consider myself yet to have taken hold of it. But one thing I do: Forgetting what is behind and straining toward what is ahead, I press on toward the goal to win the prize for which God has called me heavenward in Christ Jesus.

—PHILIPPIANS 3:13–14

Those two verses are packed to overflowing with truth. First, Paul admits that he hasn't "arrived" yet. The Christian life is a journey; it is not a destination reached while on this earth. Heaven is the final stop, and until then the best we can do is to move in that direction, pressing toward the goal.

After debunking the myth of perfection, he goes on to explain how you can continually move forward. First, forget what is behind; and second, strain toward what is ahead—the prize.

The goal is to move forward. Just like Paul, you are not perfect. Chances are you have regrets from the past and fears for the future. Both of those can keep you from progressing in your journey to win the prize of heaven.

LET'S PRAY

Lord, I know I haven't arrived, and I want to move forward on my adventure to heaven. Help me continually make progress.

APRIL 7

He Knows You

For you created my inmost being;
you knit me together in my mother's womb.
I praise you because I am fearfully
and wonderfully made;
your works are wonderful,
I know that full well.
—Psalm 139:13–14

As a high school youth leader for many years, I observed far too many teenagers who did not "know full well" that they were wonderfully made. Sadly, I witnessed young men and women who showed disrespect for themselves and others. They failed to live in the truth of Psalm 139.

God knew you from the moment of conception. He created you and your children, so there's no need for a class on self-esteem. Each of you can know beyond a shadow of a doubt that you were no mistake. You are fearfully and wonderfully made. God's works are wonderful. You can know that full well.

REMEMBER THIS

God knit you together in your mother's womb. From the moment of your creation, he knew you. He knew and loved your children too. It's recorded in Genesis that God, after each moment of creation, declared, "It is good." It's time to praise God.

APRIL 8

Justice and Mercy

"This is what the LORD Almighty said: 'Administer true justice; show mercy and compassion to one another.'"
—ZECHARIAH 7:9

I remember a specific time when, as a mom, I erred on the side of justice rather than mercy. I wasn't proud of my misstep and definitely wished it had never happened. I wished that I had been more like Jesus. He is perfect justice and perfect grace.

The good news is that when I realized my error, I didn't hesitate to apologize. I knew it was time to admit my mistake from earlier years and ask my son for forgiveness.

His comment in response to my admission of guilt and my appeal for forgiveness surprised me. "Don't worry, Mom. I forgave you for that long ago." He showed me mercy.

I couldn't undo the mistake I'd made, but I received grace. The Lord had given me a living illustration of the lesson I was trying to learn.

IT'S YOUR TURN

Never be afraid to admit your mistakes and ask for forgiveness. You just might receive a blessing from the Lord in the form of an amazing illustration of his perfect grace.

APRIL 9

Moms Need Rest

"Come to me, all you who are weary and burdened,
and I will give you rest."
—MATTHEW 11:28

There are times in motherhood when nothing sounds better than a long nap. Maybe it's been a day or two or maybe even a week of sleep deprivation. That's when I used to try to play "catch up" even though I'd learned in one of my classes in college that you cannot "catch up" on your rest. The professor also tried to convince me I couldn't "bank" sleep; however, I refused to believe the science of sleep. I was almost certain I could catch up and bank.

When preparing for a big week, I'd try to get extra sleep before the marathon began. When I finished an exhausting day or two, I'd get a little extra sleep to recover the hours I'd lost. Maybe I'm an anomaly or a freak of nature (or maybe I was fooling myself), but I was certain it worked.

IT'S TRUE

Being a mom is a wonderful, amazing, exhausting experience. The remedy for a weary body and soul is found in Matthew 11: Come to the Lord, and he will give you rest.

APRIL 10

Attitude Adjustment

For seven days they celebrated with joy the Festival of Unleavened Bread, because the LORD had filled them with joy by changing the attitude of the king of Assyria so that he assisted them in the work on the house of God, the God of Israel.

—EZRA 6:22

The king of Assyria had an attitude adjustment, compliments of the Lord. According to the verse above, this adjustment was a welcome relief for the people of Judah. It filled them with joy.

You may know someone who could use an attitude adjustment. Maybe it's your husband or your kids, the teacher across the hall, or your business partner. Maybe that someone is you.

God can do it! Nothing is impossible for him. He is able to change your attitude and your outlook. He's willing to make the necessary adjustments if you allow him to work in your life.

LET'S PRAY

Father, you and I both know that there are days when my attitude is pretty awful. I need your help to make the necessary adjustment. I can't do it alone. Give me the desire and the power to change.

APRIL 11

Modern Idols

Even while these people were worshiping the LORD,
they were serving their idols.
To this day their children and grandchildren
continue to do as their ancestors did.

—2 KINGS 17:41

Being able to do two things at once can be very productive. The people in the verse above, however, are examples of multitasking in the worst sense of the word. They are worshiping God and serving idols.

Can you imagine what their lives must have been like? I can almost visualize a picture of their behavior. They probably had an Asherah pole right next to the temple. How appalling!

Wait a minute. It's possible the same behavior is alive and well today. We may not have Asherah poles, but there are idols of a different kind. After all, they come in all shapes and sizes. Money can be an idol. So can drugs or relationships or status. Unfortunately, trying to worship God and idols is not a thing of the past.

A QUESTION FOR YOU

Take some time and examine your life. Are you worshiping or serving anything other than the Lord? Is there a modern, more socially acceptable idol in your life? Now is the time to rid your life of any idols you may have.

APRIL 12

Help My Unbelief

Jesus asked the boy's father,
"How long has he been like this?"
"From childhood," he answered. "It has often thrown him
into fire or water to kill him. But if you can do anything,
take pity on us and help us." "'If you can'?" said Jesus.
"Everything is possible for one who believes."
Immediately the boy's father exclaimed,
"I do believe; help me overcome my unbelief!"
—MARK 9:21–24

Faith isn't always characterized by bold action. Many times faith is the result of complete helplessness. Feeble stumbling and weakness can be the catalyst to turn you to God.

When you face the truth that in your own strength you can accomplish nothing, the door is open for your heavenly Father to work. As you surrender to him, his strength is manifested. God's "power is made perfect in weakness" (2 Corinthians 12:9).

Just as the boy's father said when he petitioned Jesus to intervene and save his son's life, "I do believe; help me overcome my unbelief!"

BELIEVE IT

God's love and grace are always available. He knows exactly what you need and what is best for you. You can trust your heavenly Father.

APRIL 13

Patience, the Elusive Virtue

I waited patiently for the LORD;
he turned to me and heard my cry.
—PSALM 40:1

Could I ever actually speak the words of Psalm 40:1 in truth? Do I ever wait patiently for the Lord?

My first reaction is to dodge that self-searching question. There are many ways to avoid answering. One common tactic is to counter with a different question. For example, "What is the definition of *patiently*?"

That, however, will do very little to distract anyone from seeking the honest truth. If forced to answer the question, I would have to say I only occasionally wait patiently for the Lord. That admission is pretty convicting, and so are these other verses from the Word.

"A person's wisdom yields patience; it is to one's glory to overlook an offense" (Proverbs 19:11).

"Therefore, as God's chosen people, holy and dearly loved, clothe yourselves with compassion, kindness, humility, gentleness and patience" (Colossians 3:12).

AN IMPORTANT VIRTUE

Some people believe it's a mistake to ask God for patience. They think they'll receive even more trials and tests demanding patience. I don't agree. Patience is a virtue God wants you to exhibit, so ask him to provide you with a sufficient amount.

APRIL 14

The Problem and Solution

Why, my soul, are you downcast?
Why so disturbed within me?
Put your hope in God,
for I will yet praise him,
my Savior and my God.
—Psalm 42:5

When you know the Lord, when you realize his great love and his amazing power, why are you ever downcast? I cannot answer for you, but I know that for me the answer lies, at least in part, in where I choose to focus my attention. I become distressed when my focal point is on my circumstances and not the love and power of God.

Years ago I learned that a dear friend was suffering from a serious illness. The news was shocking and saddening. When I heard the report, I took my eyes off the Great Physician and looked only at the problem.

"Put your hope in God," says the psalmist—but how? The key is in the Scripture above: "Praise him!" Circumstances change. The Lord, your Savior and your God, does not.

REMEMBER

When negative circumstances clamor for your attention, the quickest way to reset your vision is to praise your heavenly Father—your God who never changes.

APRIL 15

Recalculating

See to it, brothers and sisters, that none of you has a sinful, unbelieving heart that turns away from the living God.

—HEBREWS 3:12

A GPS is a wonderful navigational tool designed to help you find your way as you travel to unfamiliar locations. The very first one I owned was famous for its mechanical voice declaring "recalculating . . . recalculating . . ." each time I missed a turn or failed to take the correct exit.

There's a degree of comfort in the word *recalculating*. It's a guarantee that the GPS is doing its best to get you back on course. Admittedly there's also a bit of annoyance, knowing you've somehow failed to follow the original directions. Both of those emotions are valid.

In your spiritual walk you may find yourself "recalculating" and experiencing comfort *and* annoyance. On the one hand, you have to deal with the reality that you've somehow gotten off course. Conversely, you can take comfort knowing the Holy Spirit is gently guiding you back on track.

REMEMBER

Embrace the "recalculation" of the Holy Spirit and do your best to stay on course in the future.

APRIL 16

Make Time

For it is written: "Be holy, because I am holy."

—1 PETER 1:16

"Take time to be holy, spend much time in prayer." That's the refrain from an old hymn. It's repeated very often in the song written in the early 1800s.

Yes, the idea the hymn expresses is a good one, but it's possible you often decide to move along with your day rather than taking time. I'm just guessing, but it's likely that on occasion you promise you'll find time later to pray or read Scripture or meditate on God's Word. You'll find time later to be holy.

Now be honest. How often do you actually "find" the time even if in your earlier promise you were expressing a heartfelt desire? Taking time doesn't always work. Instead, *make* time.

SO

Rather than finding time, it's much better to make time. Making time means being intentional. Yes, on some days you might need to get up earlier than normal to make time, but that's what you do for something you consider important.

APRIL 17

Fix Your Eyes

But my eyes are fixed on you, Sovereign LORD;
in you I take refuge—do not give me over to death.

—PSALM 141:8

I travel quite often on a country road near my home. For years, two very large German shepherd dogs controlled this road. Each time I passed the home where they lived, the dogs would rush at my car and I would shift my attention to them.

I'd take my foot off the gas and grasp the wheel tightly, trying not to hit the dogs. They always managed to slow down my travel.

Then one day it dawned on me that focusing on the dogs was the wrong way to handle the situation. On my next trip, I stared straight ahead as the dogs attacked. I kept my foot on the accelerator and drove down the road, ignoring the growling and barking animals.

It was amazing! By not fixing my eyes on the dogs, I managed to maintain my speed and travel along smoothly.

A QUESTION FOR YOU

Where are your eyes fixed? Are you focused on your circumstances, regrets of the past, or fears for the future? Fix your eyes on the Lord.

APRIL 18

Feeling Hopeless

"When I had lost all hope, I turned my thoughts once more to the Lord. And my earnest prayer went to you in your holy Temple. (Those who worship false gods have turned their backs on all the mercies waiting for them from the Lord!)
"I will never worship anyone but you!
For how can I thank you enough for all you have done?
I will surely fulfill my promises.
For my deliverance comes from the Lord alone."

—JONAH 2:7–9 TLB

In the Scripture above we learn that Jonah had lost all hope. In his state of hopelessness, he turned his thoughts to the Lord and prayed. That was the remedy, the cure for his feelings of discouragement and despair.

Discouragement and motherhood occasionally go hand in hand. You can feel like a failure—incompetent, inept, and miserable. Admitting those feelings to yourself can make you feel even worse, more downhearted.

That's when you need to do what Jonah did: Turn your thoughts to the Lord. He is the One who can deliver you.

IF THIS IS YOU TODAY

If you're feeling hopeless right now, I want to challenge you to turn your thoughts to the Lord. Join Jonah and say, "How can I thank you enough for all you have done?" Now count your blessings and turn your hopelessness to hopefulness.

APRIL 19

Growing

Grow in the grace and knowledge
of our Lord and Savior Jesus Christ.

—2 PETER 3:18

I once heard it said that people fall into one of two categories. One: people who need to know the Lord, or two: people who need to know the Lord better. In other words, folks who have yet to come to a saving knowledge of Christ and those who have chosen to love and follow the Lord.

The instruction in 2 Peter is written to believers—to those who need to know the Lord better. It is up to you to do what it takes to know him better, or, as Peter wrote, to "grow in the grace and knowledge of our Lord." You can make the choice to become more spiritually mature. You can choose to become better acquainted with Jesus.

There are similarities between knowing the Lord better and knowing a friend better. To accomplish either, you need to invest your time and energy. Knowing Jesus better is well worth the effort.

TRY THIS

Take time right now to close your eyes and tell the Lord what is on your heart. Talk with him about the challenges you see in the day ahead. As you connect with your friend Jesus, you will grow in your knowledge of him and grow in the grace he freely offers.

APRIL 20

Equipped

Now may the God of peace, who through the blood of the eternal covenant brought back from the dead our Lord Jesus, that great Shepherd of the sheep, equip you with everything good for doing his will, and may he work in us what is pleasing to him, through Jesus Christ, to whom be glory for ever and ever. Amen.

—Hebrews 13:20–21

I grew up as the youngest of three children, so I had no younger siblings to learn from or enjoy. After my husband and I had been married for six years, our first son was born. Over the next six years I became the mother of two more sons. Not only were boys a mystery to me, but babies in general hadn't been a part of my life up to that point. I felt ill-equipped to do my job as a mom.

Ill-equipped or not, there were three little boys counting on me. God had given me an assignment: to do the best job I could as their mother. It was during those early years of parenting I heard these words: "God does not call the equipped; he equips the called."

A QUESTION FOR YOU

What has God called you to do? Do not be afraid to tackle the assignment. If he's called you, he'll equip you.

APRIL 21

Straighten Up

On a Sabbath Jesus was teaching in one of the synagogues, and a woman was there who had been crippled by a spirit for eighteen years. She was bent over and could not straighten up at all. When Jesus saw her, he called her forward and said to her, "Woman, you are set free from your infirmity." Then he put his hands on her, and immediately she straightened up and praised God.

—LUKE 13:10–13

Jesus did a powerful work in the life of the woman who had been crippled for so many years. The healing was obvious to everyone, for this woman went from being bent over to being erect and straight. When that happened, she didn't waste a minute; she straightened up and praised God.

God is still at work today. His power hasn't diminished over time, and he's able to help you "straighten up" in every sense of the phrase. Come to Jesus when he calls you—just as the woman did—and praise him when he touches your life.

I WONDER

What would God like to do in your life to help you "straighten up"? Is there a spirit that has been holding you back from being all he desires for you? Take some time to ponder that thought.

APRIL 22

Control

Like a city whose walls are broken through
is a person who lacks self-control.
—Proverbs 25:28

"I've got everything under control." Those words are laughable. There is no mom who has everything under control. Actually, no person could make that statement with a high degree of confidence.

Control of everything is out of your control! That statement is not meant to suggest that control is not desirable. Control is, in fact, what most people desperately want. As a believer, however, you can know that it's best if God is in control.

"Cast all your anxiety on him because he cares for you" (1 Peter 5:7).

"If anyone has caused grief, he has not so much grieved me as he has grieved all of you to some extent—not to put it too severely. The punishment inflicted on him by the majority is sufficient. Now instead, you ought to forgive and comfort him, so that he will not be overwhelmed by excessive sorrow" (2 Corinthians 2:5–7).

You guessed it; inevitably we lose control, even when we think we have it.

There is one thing, however, you can control. With God's help, you can control yourself.

LET'S PRAY

Lord, help me give up control to you and develop more self-control as you lead me.

APRIL 23

Ordinary Mom

When they saw the courage of Peter and John
and realized that they were unschooled, ordinary men,
they were astonished and they took note that
these men had been with Jesus.

—Acts 4:13

Peter and John were not special in any way. They were not highly educated. They had no power, prestige, or money. They were just ordinary men who had been with Jesus.

God had a plan and a purpose for these ordinary men, and he has a plan and a purpose for you. Your lack of education or training does not have to limit you. Ordinary people can do extraordinary things when they spend time with Jesus.

It's possible that you've said the words "I'm just a mom" when you've been asked what you do. Here's an idea for the next time you hear that question. Instead, say, "I'm a mom, a molder of young lives, a contributor to the pool of responsible adults of the future. I'm no ordinary woman. I spend time with Jesus."

IT'S TRUE

I'm not necessarily recommending you answer with those words, but as a mother who spends time with the Lord, there is nothing ordinary about you.

APRIL 24

Nourishment

Your own soul is nourished when you are kind;
it is destroyed when you are cruel.

—PROVERBS 11:17 TLB

When your children entered the world, they weren't capable of nourishing themselves. A newborn baby is totally dependent on you for nourishment.

Then as they matured, things began to change. By year one, babies have started to feed themselves the food you've provided. By the time they reach age eighteen, they're completely in control of their diets. The decisions about quantity and quality of food are all their choice. The nourishment of their bodies is their responsibility.

You might be wondering, *What about the nourishment of their souls?*

As a mom, you have a wonderful opportunity to teach and encourage your children to grow spiritually on the road to adulthood. Praying for them and with them when they are young, and then continuing those prayers as they reach adulthood, is a great way to contribute to their spiritual growth. Ultimately, the nourishment of your children's spirits is their responsibility.

THE PLAN

Step one: Take seriously the responsibility to nourish your own soul. Kindness is one component of that process. Step two: Encourage your child to grow spiritually.

APRIL 25

Eternal Guarantee

"The grass withers and the flowers fall,
but the word of our God endures forever."

—Isaiah 40:8

I have several products in my home that have a lifetime guarantee. With those guarantees come several nagging questions.

Whose lifetime? Is it mine, my children's lifetime, or perhaps the "life" of the product itself? This logically leads me to the next question: How can an inanimate object have a life? Finally: Do other people ask questions like this, or is it only me?

Assuming I will never have these questions answered adequately in my lifetime, I've decided to relax knowing that God's Word tells me of at least two things that have an eternal guarantee. They are man—living eternally in heaven or in hell—and God's Word, which stands forever.

I may not completely understand eternity, and I do have a few unanswered questions about it; but I know that believing the truth of those eternal guarantees is a very wise thing to do.

LET'S PRAY

Thank you for loving me and for giving me the opportunity to live in heaven with you for eternity.

APRIL 26

Perfect?

You will keep in perfect peace
those whose minds are steadfast,
because they trust in you.

—Isaiah 26:3

There is no perfect hairdo. There is no perfect little black dress. There is no perfect home. There is no perfect homemaker, and there is no perfect mother.

When you try to discover the aforementioned hairdo or black dress or home, or try to become the perfect homemaker or mom, you are bound to fail. The only One who is perfect is your heavenly Father.

The Lord, however, is willing to give you, an imperfect mom, his perfect peace. His Word is clear about what is necessary for you to receive that gift of peace. You must have your mind focused on God, reflecting his character. You're to trust in him completely, confident he will do what he has promised. He will give you peace.

IT'S TRUE

God's gifts are not limited to those who are perfect. You are not perfect and don't have to be to please your heavenly Father. He wants to give you peace—his peace that passes understanding.

APRIL 27

There's a Limit

To all perfection I see a limit,
but your commands are boundless.
—PSALM 119:96

There are certain things in life that are limited. No matter how hard you try, you will never be able to enjoy more than twenty-four hours in a day. That's the limit. There are 365 days in a year (366 every four years), and there's nothing you can do to change that. That's the limit. The days of your life are also limited.

The psalmist identified something else that is limited—something the average mom all too often fails to acknowledge. Perfection!

The fact that perfection is limited can be easily forgotten when you are in the throes of motherhood. As a mom, you want to do the very best you can, which is an admirable goal; but that goal is very different from the goal to be perfect. The first is attainable; the second is not.

Everyone is far from perfection, but the commands of God are boundless. That truth is a great reminder for moms everywhere. There is a limit to everything created by man—to every product of human ingenuity or ability.

REMEMBER

It is fruitless and unhealthy to strive for perfection as a mom. God does not demand it or expect it; nor is he pleased by it.

APRIL 28

Mary Poppins

He said to me, "My grace is sufficient for you,
for my power is made perfect in weakness."
Therefore I will boast all the more gladly about
my weaknesses, so that Christ's power may rest on me.

—2 Corinthians 12:9

My favorite movie of all time is *Mary Poppins*, the fictional story of the nanny who helped a family realize the importance of spending time together.

Upon meeting Jane and Michael Banks, the two children under Mary Poppins' charge, Ms. Poppins reaches into her amazing carpet bag and takes out her tape measure. After measuring each child, Mary Poppins measures herself and announces, "Mary Poppins: practically perfect in every way."

I have never felt that way—"practically perfect," I mean. Far from it, actually. Sometimes I grieve my imperfections, such as when I've hurt someone or failed in some other way to be a good representative of Jesus Christ.

I'm not perfect—not even "practically perfect." But God's Word states in 2 Corinthians that his grace is sufficient, that his power is made perfect in weakness.

LET'S PRAY

Father, thank you for your amazing grace. Thank you for loving me even when I have difficulty loving myself.

APRIL 29

God's Law

The law of the LORD is perfect, refreshing the soul.
The statutes of the LORD are trustworthy,
making wise the simple. The precepts of the LORD are right,
giving joy to the heart. The commands of the LORD
are radiant, giving light to the eyes.

—PSALM 19:7–8

It is impossible to be a perfect mom. Rather than weep over the truth of those words, rejoice over the perfect things of God.

God's law is perfect. Unlike the laws of our land, which are created, debated, and many times amended, God's law is flawless. His statutes can be trusted, and they mark the path for a wise mom.

The principles and guidelines established by God are guarantees of joy when they are followed in your home. His commands light your path—the path to righteousness.

The next time you feel the urge to lament the fact that you are not perfect, instead rejoice that you have God's perfect law to guide and direct you each day.

A SUGGESTION FOR YOU

As you read the Word of God and encounter a verse that speaks to you, take time to write it down and post it inside one of your cupboard doors. Then each time you set the table, each time you reach for a glass or plate, read that verse and remember that his Word is perfect.

APRIL 30

No Comparison

For what was glorious has no glory now in comparison
with the surpassing glory.
And if what was transitory came with glory,
how much greater is the glory of that which lasts!

—2 CORINTHIANS 3:10–11

When these verses in 2 Corinthians compare the law and the message of the gospel, they conclude there is no comparison. The gospel outshines the law, for it is eternal.

Comparison might not be possible between the law and the gospel, but comparisons are made on a daily basis. We compare prices to determine the most economical purchase. We compare products to determine what is needed in our home. Sadly, moms compare themselves to other moms.

When comparing yourself to another mom, the comparison is usually rigged. Either you're comparing your strength to another's weakness and you win, or vice versa and you are the loser.

God does not compare you to anyone else to determine a winner and a loser. He knows your heart and loves you unconditionally.

REMEMBER

Social media does not define you or anyone else. God does not evaluate your number of friends or the impressiveness of your posts. Don't fall into the trap of comparison online or anywhere else.

GOD DISCIPLINES THOSE HE LOVES

They disciplined us for a little while
as they thought best; but God
disciplines us for our good, in order that
we may share in his holiness.

—Hebrews 12:10

MAY 1

Safety and Security

"Whoever listens to me will live in safety
and be at ease, without fear of harm."

—PROVERBS 1:33

It was an experiment. They put a fence around the playground and watched as the kids played in every inch of the area. They ran and played tag. They hid behind the big trees and shot baskets on the court.

Then the fence was removed. The size of the playing area had not changed, yet the kids huddled in the center of the playground. No more games that stretched from one end of the fence to the other.

The absence of the fence didn't mean the kids ran and played in a larger area. The opposite was true. The researchers concluded that the boundaries provided safety and security.

God's Word provides boundaries for you and for your children. His instructions are there to act as a fence to keep you in a place of blessing.

FOOD FOR THOUGHT

Too often the Word of God is seen as restrictive and confining. "Why should I do that?" or "Why shouldn't I do this?" we ask. Rather than question, let us give thanks for the secure boundaries he's given.

MAY 2

Consequences

LORD our God, you answered them;
you were to Israel a forgiving God,
though you punished their misdeeds.
—PSALM 99:8

"I'm sorry, Mom."

You hear those words over and over, and you know there are times when your child is truly sorry, genuinely repentant for his wrongdoing.

By the same token, there are times when the words "I'm sorry" are simply used to avoid punishment. They're not heartfelt.

"Are you sorry for your misdeed or sorry you were caught?" That question has the potential to elicit an interesting response.

Even being legitimately remorseful for your actions does not mean you or your child will be protected from the ramifications of those actions. God was and is forgiving, but there are consequences for misdeeds.

As a mom, it's important to forgive your child. By the same token, if you've established and communicated a predetermined consequence for misbehavior, it's important to keep your word. There is only one way to avoid punishment: Avoid disobedience.

LET'S PRAY

Lord, thank you for being a forgiving God. Even though my desire is to be obedient to your instruction, I sometimes fail. Help me as a mom to be forgiving when my child fails. Help each of us learn from our disobedience.

MAY 3

Boundaries

It was you who set all the boundaries of the earth;
you made both summer and winter.
—PSALM 74:17

As a mom, you set boundaries for your children. That's a smart thing to do. You want to protect them from the dangers in their environment and in some cases, protect their environment from the dangers they can create.

When my kids were very little and we went on camping trips, they would play in an extra large playpen we constructed. That was much safer than playing near the river.

As they got older, as preschoolers, they were able to play in our fenced-in backyard. That fence, for the most part, kept them safe from harm. The more responsible they became, the more their boundaries expanded.

God tells his people to stay within the boundaries he's constructed. That's where you and your children will find safety and blessing.

MY PRAYER FOR YOU

Lord, help this sister of mine stay within the boundaries of safety you have established. Bless her abundantly for her obedience.

MAY 4

Guilty as Charged

"The LORD is slow to anger, abounding in love
and forgiving sin and rebellion.
Yet he does not leave the guilty unpunished."
—NUMBERS 14:18

All too often, the focus is placed on the first sentence of the verse above. Those words reflect wonderful, amazing truths about God. He is slow to anger. He is abounding in love. And he forgives both sin and rebellion. Those descriptions of God are very reassuring to everyone who knows the truth that we are all sinners saved by grace.

Wouldn't it be awful if your heavenly Father had anger issues? Don't worry, he doesn't. What if his love for you was halfhearted? Again, not a concern; it is abounding. I love the picture that is painted by that description.

Thank goodness he forgives the sin and rebellion of those who love him. Yes, the words in the first sentence of Numbers 14 are very comforting and very true.

The next sentence is also true. Your loving heavenly Father will punish those who are guilty, and his punishment is always fair and is never excessive.

SO

Do what you can to obey the Word of the Lord. That is the way to avoid his punishment.

MAY 5

Thinking and Feeling

"I thought, 'Now the Philistines will come down against me at Gilgal, and I have not sought the LORD's favor.' So I felt compelled to offer the burnt offering."
"You have done a foolish thing," Samuel said.
"You have not kept the command the LORD your God gave you; if you had, he would have established your kingdom over Israel for all time."

—1 SAMUEL 13:12–13

"Don't just *think* about it. Do it."

"It doesn't really matter whether or not you *feel* like being obedient. Do as you were told."

I heard those statements more than once when I was growing up. Who said them? My mom did when I was trying desperately to avoid doing what she'd instructed. Maybe you've found yourself telling your children the same thing.

Kids aren't the only ones ignoring instruction. Mom, it's possible you spend time *thinking and feeling* and disregarding the directives of God.

That was Saul's problem, as recorded in the Scripture above. He hadn't bothered to check with the Lord about the right thing to do; instead he used his own inferior intellect and did what he *felt* was correct. All of his thinking and feeling amounted to disobedience.

REMEMBER

It doesn't matter what you think or feel; God expects your obedience. When you've given your kids an important instruction, expect them to obey.

MAY 6

Who and What

They promise them freedom, while they themselves
are slaves of depravity—for "people are slaves
to whatever has mastered them."

—2 PETER 2:19

"Who is in control of this household?" As the adult, you know you should be the one in control; and yet occasionally you may wonder if the children have mysteriously taken charge.

Simply asking that question can help you refocus and regain the control you need to have as the mom. It can help you become the parent once again.

It's important to realize that it's not only your kids who can improperly gain control. That's why there's another question you should consider asking. As crazy as it may sound, it's also smart to ask: "*What* is in control?"

It can be easy to allow busyness to gain control. On the flip side, idleness can be ruling your home. So can anger or indifference. It's part of your job as a mom to be certain the proper person and the proper priority is in control of your home.

TWO IMPORTANT QUESTIONS TO ASK YOURSELF

First: Who is in control of my household? Second: What is in control of my household? Be honest with yourself and with the Lord as you answer. If the answer isn't pleasing to you or to God, make changes today.

MAY 7

Correction

Discipline your children, and they will give you peace;
they will bring you the delights you desire.
—PROVERBS 29:17

There is a big difference between correcting a child and teasing or abusing him. God gives you a model for correction. He disciplines you, his child, with love and with fairness. He does not correct you in anger or frustration, and he expects you, as a mom, to follow his lead.

Being a mom can be frustrating, and it can make you angry. Things don't go as planned. Children don't follow instructions. Other adults fail to give you the support they promised. These things happen. This is reality.

It's important not to act out and correct your child in anger or frustration. You are to discipline your child because of the bad behavior they display, not as a reaction to how their behavior makes you feel.

The Word says you'll be very glad you did because those same kids you've taken the time to correct will bring you peace. They will be a delight.

THINK ABOUT IT

Do you want your children to bring you joy? Being a mom can be tough. God will help you correct your children with love.

MAY 8

Prove It

If you refuse to discipline your son,
it proves you don't love him; for if you love him,
you will be prompt to punish him.

—Proverbs 13:24 TLB

I have three sons. I joke that when I only had one child and someone asked if they could hold the baby, I would inquire, "Are you a registered nurse?" (Okay, maybe that's a slight exaggeration.)

By the time the third son arrived, I was a great deal more relaxed. Then it was: "Can anybody get the baby?" Things tend to get more laid-back when you have to balance your time and energy with more than one child. Some of that is healthy, but things can get a little too lax.

Years later when my youngest son was a teenager, he lobbied for a later curfew. His great debating skills did not sway the decision. He was told to be home at the same time his older brothers always had to be home. After all, I didn't want him to think he was loved any less than the other boys.

JUST SO YOU KNOW

It takes time, energy, and a commitment of love to correct your children. Taking that time, energy, and commitment is essential to showing your love.

MAY 9

Never in Anger

"In your anger do not sin":
Do not let the sun go down while you are still angry,
and do not give the devil a foothold.

—EPHESIANS 4:26–27

Your child, no matter how adorable and creative and beautiful and amazing, will make you angry. The key is to be certain your anger is not out of control—that it doesn't govern your actions or dictate your words.

The word *let* in the Scripture above is significant. God knows you can control your anger. It's a choice. Will you permit your anger to control you? Anger can't overtake you without your permission.

When you're tempted to say you were "overcome with anger," remember that the Word instructs you not to *let*—not to allow—the day to end while you're still angry. Anger cannot take control of you.

THINK ABOUT IT

Anger is a human emotion experienced by young and old. God doesn't tell you not to be angry. Instead he tells you not to sin while angry. Count to ten. Take a deep breath. Give yourself a time-out. Or employ the most effective way to guard against expressing your anger: Pray and ask the Lord for help.

MAY 10

Little Red Wagon

[May God] equip you with everything good for doing his will, and may he work in us what is pleasing to him, through Jesus Christ, to whom be glory for ever and ever. Amen.

—HEBREWS 13:21

The words above are a prayer by the apostle Paul for the Hebrew people. The prayer isn't just a plea for God to equip believers; he specifically asks the Lord to equip them with "everything good."

Furthermore, he specifically asks God to equip them "with everything good for doing his will." Paul doesn't ask God to give them more fun, or more happiness, or more power to achieve personal success. No, he wanted them to be equipped for God's will.

If you only want to do your own will, you don't need the power of God. You don't need a locomotive engine to pull a little red wagon. You can do that on your own.

IT'S TRUE

In order to do the will of God, you will need him to equip you. He is able to work in you and help you each minute of your day.

MAY 11

To-Do List

And now, Israel, what does the LORD your God
ask of you but to fear the LORD your God, to walk in
obedience to him, to love him, to serve the LORD your God
with all your heart and with all your soul, and to observe
the LORD's commands and decrees that I am giving
you today for your own good?

—DEUTERONOMY 10:12–13

I am a list maker. Before I go to bed at night, I make a list of things I hope to accomplish the next day. As the day progresses, I make adjustments to that list, marking off the various tasks that have been completed and occasionally adding new ones.

The Scripture above is a to-do list created by your heavenly Father. The items on the list are not to be accomplished in a day and then crossed off the list; they are guidelines for every day.

You are to fear God, be obedient to him, love him, and observe his commands. Beyond that, you are to serve him—not halfheartedly, but with all your heart and soul.

IT'S TRUE

The chances are great you have told your child to do something "for his own good." That is precisely why God is giving you the instructions above. Put his words on your to-do list.

MAY 12

Relationship Guidelines

In Christ Jesus you are all children of God through faith.
—GALATIANS 3:26

Through faith, you are a child of God; you have a relationship with your heavenly Father. Undoubtedly you have other relationships too. Some are casual, like the people you've known for years and see occasionally at the grocery store.

Other relationships are deeper, like the ones you have with folks you worship with each week or see in your weekly Bible study. Then there's your family. You have a relationship with members of your immediate family and beyond, and you have a special relationship with your children.

Every relationship, whether it's formal, casual, or very close, operates within a set of guidelines. There are rules that have been established to keep the relationship healthy.

These rules may be cultural norms that are simply understood, such as shaking someone's hand when it is extended in greeting. Or they may be specifically agreed upon. For example, one partner in a relationship may assure the other that something said in confidence will not be repeated.

The Lord gives you guidelines in his Word for your relationship with him. Without them you would live in chaos. Giving your children rules and guidelines is important too. Relationship without rules leads to chaos.

TAKE NOTE

To build a healthy relationship with your children, it's important to give them reasonable guidelines for behavior.

MAY 13

Rules

No one serving as a soldier gets entangled in civilian affairs, but rather tries to please his commanding officer. Similarly, anyone who competes as an athlete does not receive the victor's crown except by competing according to the rules. The hardworking farmer should be the first to receive a share of the crops.

—2 TIMOTHY 2:4–6

In life there are certain guidelines—rules that must be followed. When a teenager enrolls in a drivers' education course, he or she is typically given a booklet entitled *Rules of the Road*. These are the important laws every driver must commit to memory and diligently obey. The guidelines are not optional; they are for the safety of everyone on the road.

The instructions God has given are not discretionary either. They are given to help you live an abundant life. They are perfect in every way.

Your household also has a set of rules that must be followed. They were determined with your family in mind, knowing the purpose of the guidelines was to make your home a safe and peaceful dwelling.

Just as God's rules are influenced by his love, it's important that your rules are established in connection with a loving relationship with your children. Rules without relationship lead to rebellion.

AN IMPORTANT NOTE

Rules with relationship lead to respect.

MAY 14

Lots of Fun

"I gave them this command: Obey me, and I will be your God and you will be my people. Walk in obedience to all I command you, that it may go well with you."

—JEREMIAH 7:23

According to the Scripture above, God didn't just give the Israelites rules and regulations. He let them know the benefit of obeying him. If they obeyed, he would be intimately connected with them. "I will be your God and you will be my people." He goes on to tell them that obedience will result in things going well.

Years ago I walked into my first teaching assignment and told my fourth-graders, "I am a very fun teacher. If you follow my rules we will have lots of fun while you learn. If you don't, we won't."

My message was simple, direct, and accurate. So is God's message. The fourth-graders had a choice to make, and so do you.

THE TRUTH IS THIS

The choice is simple, but simple is different from easy. The choice is straightforward and uncomplicated. It is not without effort, however, but God will help you obey.

MAY 15

Ears to Hear

"Whoever has ears, let them hear."
—MATTHEW 11:15

There's a quote from an old Jewish proverb that has delighted me for years: "A mother hears what a child doesn't say." It's true, isn't it? It's almost as if you have an amazing power, a sixth sense, when it comes to your child. You hear what isn't said and you know what you should do, all because you're that child's mother.

There's a question that many children might have on their minds but they aren't asking. I wonder if their mothers can hear it. "Do you love me enough to discipline me?" No child would utter those words, yet most kids want the answer. Do you hear what isn't being said?

God disciplines his children, the children he loves unconditionally. That's what kids are hoping their moms will do. They're not speaking those words or asking for discipline, but in their hearts the question exists: "Do you love me enough to discipline me?"

TO PONDER

A mother hears what a child doesn't say. Can you hear the heart of your children? Are you willing to love them as God loves you? He wants you to love them enough to correct and guide them.

MAY 16

Pain or Peace

No discipline seems pleasant at the time, but painful.
Later on, however, it produces a harvest of righteousness
and peace for those who have been trained by it.

—HEBREWS 12:11

Parents don't enjoy correcting their children; nor do children enjoy correction.

The writer of Hebrews speaks of discipline being painful rather than pleasant but goes on to note the great benefit that will be produced as a result.

For years I thought those words of encouragement only applied to the recipient of the discipline, but perhaps they also apply to the mom who administers the discipline.

It's not pleasant or fun to discipline your child. It does hurt you; it is emotionally painful. But you persevere because you know what that discipline will produce: a "harvest of righteousness and peace" not only for your child but also for you.

LET'S FACE IT

Mom, you have to think long-term. If your goal is for your child to enjoy peace and a right standing with the Lord, you have to endure the unpleasant task of correcting that child. It is worth the momentary pain both of you will experience.

MAY 17

I Love Him

"The Lord disciplines the one he loves,
and he chastens everyone he accepts as his son."
—Hebrews 12:6

Very often I'll hear a mom interrupting herself while describing a difficult situation she's having with one of her children. She breaks off her commentary and quickly adds these words: "You need to understand, I really love my child. I really do!"

No one has suggested there is a lack of love between this mother and her child, so I used to wonder why there was this compulsion to interject a disclaimer into the description of how the child had been misbehaving.

Then one day I understood, when a young friend of mine said: "Parents today believe a lie. They believe the opposite of love is discipline. And how do we know that's a lie? Because God disciplines those he loves."

NEVER EASY

God does not want to discipline you, but he is willing to do so because of his great love for you. It may not always be easy or pleasant for you to discipline your child, but it is the loving thing to do.

MAY 18

Yes and No

"All you need to say is simply 'Yes' or 'No'; anything beyond this comes from the evil one."

—MATTHEW 5:37

"Mom, may I go to the park with Michelle?"

"No, it's too close to lunchtime."

"Please, Mom. We're only going to be there for about fifteen minutes because Michelle has to go to piano lessons this afternoon."

"No!"

"But there's a new slide and it's amazing. It's really tall and really curvy!"

"Okay, but be back before lunch."

What is wrong with that exchange? Mom answered no more than once, but that didn't stop her daughter's demands. She knew her mom didn't really mean no. No just meant "maybe" or "give me more information" or "I'm really tired right now."

This mom's no was something that could be debated—and that's precisely what her daughter did. Mom's no did not necessarily mean no.

SOMETHING TO THINK ABOUT

If you don't want to debate and negotiate every time your child makes a request, take time to adequately consider her request before you answer. The correct response might be "yes" or "let me think about it."

MAY 19

Lies of the World

Everyone born of God overcomes the world. This is the victory that has overcome the world, even our faith.

—1 JOHN 5:4

Christ has overcome the world, but the world is still clamoring to have its lies and half-truths about parenting accepted and believed.

Here are a few that are popular today:

Your child *will* be difficult.

You *will* experience the terrible twos and the turbulent teens.

Your child *will* rebel.

All teenagers lie and drink and have sex.

All children disrespect authority.

Your children *do not need* loving correction.

Every one of those statements is untrue and is a distraction. They are lies of the world. Don't believe them. Instead, believe the truth in the Word of God; the truth that is available to equip and encourage you in your very important job as a mom.

JUST FOR YOU

Don't passively accept the lies of the world as the truth. Instead, become intimately familiar with the truth of God's Word. He wants you to know and live in that truth.

MAY 20

Restrain Your Child

And the LORD said to Samuel: "See, I am about to do something in Israel that will make the ears of everyone who hears about it tingle. At that time I will carry out against Eli everything I spoke against his family—from beginning to end. For I told him that I would judge his family forever because of the sin he knew about; his sons blasphemed God, and he failed to restrain them."

—1 SAMUEL 3:11–13

Eli knew his sons were making poor decisions, and he failed to discipline them. God did not respond to this by saying, "Boys will be boys." He didn't say, "Don't worry about it, Eli. All teenagers rebel." He didn't say, "No problem, Eli, you're a very important man, and I know priests are busy with other things and don't have time to correct their kids."

No, those were not the words of God. Instead, he reprimanded Eli for his failure to discipline his children. Eli knew about his sons' detestable behavior and turned a blind eye to it. He failed to restrain them.

Correcting your children is your responsibility. God doesn't want you to ignore that job.

TOUGH LOVE

The older children get, the harder it will be to remedy their poor behavior. Don't wait until that behavior is offensive to God.

MAY 21

No Emotion

"In your anger do not sin":
Do not let the sun go down while you are still angry.
—EPHESIANS 4:26

Emotions are an important part of who you are, and they run the gamut from delight to annoyance, from joy to sorrow. As a mom, there are times when you can't imagine ever feeling more than incredible love for your child. At other times, that little rascal can do something that makes you angry.

One of the cardinal rules when it comes to correcting a child is never to discipline in anger. Now I want you to think of an even more radical possibility. What if you disciplined your child with none of the other emotions moms sometimes feel? No pity, no sympathy, no frustration.

Disciplining without emotion doesn't indicate a lack of caring or love; instead it's a healthy detachment. You've given your child a boundary, and when she chooses to cross that boundary, you deliver the predetermined consequence. You're fulfilling the contract you made with your child. The only emotion you have is love.

THINK ABOUT IT

Love is the best motivation for correcting your child. It's the example set by God.

MAY 22

The Truth of the Word

The father of a righteous child has great joy;
a man who fathers a wise son rejoices in him.
—PROVERBS 23:24

The words of the verse above are true for the mother of a righteous child too. A child who is wise and in right standing with God is capable of bringing great joy to his mom.

"A wise son brings joy to his father, but a foolish son brings grief to his mother" (Proverbs 10:1).

Once again, the words of the proverb apply to both a mother and a father, a son or a daughter. A child who is wise will bring you joy, and a foolish child will make both father and mother grieve.

"Her children arise and call her blessed" (Proverbs 31:28).

These words are specifically addressed to a mother. Why did the woman in Proverbs receive praise from her children? The answer is found a few verses later in Proverbs 31:30: "Charm is deceptive, and beauty is fleeting; but a woman who fears the LORD is to be praised."

THE TRUTH OF THE WORD

A mom who chooses to discipline her children in love both loves and lives the Word. She is to be praised.

MAY 23

Consistent and Reasonable

Be careful to do what the LORD your God has commanded you; do not turn aside to the right or to the left.

—DEUTERONOMY 5:32

Your children depend on the assurance of your consistency. They want to know that the rules you've set and the consequences you've established will be fair and won't change on a whim. Your consistent, fair correction will foster their security.

Fair discipline also means that the consequences you've set are reasonable. At times you'll have to make a judgment call. For example, was your child's action based on disobedience or simple childish carelessness? Spilling a glass of orange juice at the breakfast table is likely an accident. If, however, your child lifts the glass of juice, looks you in the eye, and tips it upside down, that is defiance and your child should expect a consequence for this behavior.

In the same way that you want to "be careful to do what God has commanded," you also want your child to follow your consistent, fair instruction—not turning aside "to the right or left."

LET'S PRAY

Lord, I want to model obedience to your Word. I also want to duplicate the fairness and consistency of your commands as I administer loving correction.

MAY 24

React or Respond

One of those listening was a woman from the city of Thyatira named Lydia, a dealer in purple cloth. She was a worshiper of God. The Lord opened her heart to respond to Paul's message.

—Acts 16:14

Will you respond to your child's actions, or will you react? A reaction is like a knee jerk. It doesn't take any thought. It's automatic. But responding is a different matter. A response is a thoughtful reply.

Here's the scenario: You've told your teenager to be home by eleven o'clock or lose the car keys for a week. She walks through the door at 11:35, hoping you've already gone to bed—but you haven't.

Do you react and shout at her about the importance of being responsible and honoring the curfew you set for her? Do you react as a result of the horrible things you've imagined might have happened between 11:00 and 11:35?

Or do you take a deep breath and explain that 11:35 is thirty-five minutes late, and she'll be without the car keys for seven days? Do you continue to speak in a calm tone as she gives you several excuses or claims you're the meanest mom in the world?

A QUESTION FOR YOU

Responding isn't always as easy as reacting. God will help you. Are you willing to ask for his help?

MAY 25

Excuses, Excuses

Now we know that whatever the law says,
it says to those who are under the law,
so that every mouth may be silenced and
the whole world held accountable to God.

—ROMANS 3:19

"He made me do it!" I heard that statement more than once as my three sons were growing up. In the beginning I took those words at face value and assumed that the young man pleading his case had a valid excuse for whatever he'd done.

It didn't take me long to discover that casting the blame on a brother was just a way to avoid personal responsibility. Rather than reacting to the claim of innocence and turning to look for the newly accused culprit, I learned to respond.

"Your brother may have encouraged you to do it. He may have dared you or coerced you, and I'll talk to him in a minute. You, however, are the one who did it, and you are responsible for your actions."

In other words, the explanation is no excuse. That truth doesn't only apply to youngsters. The English teacher may be boring, but that explanation is no excuse for the teenager failing to do the assignment.

THINK ABOUT IT

Children and teenagers are not the only ones who try to explain away mistakes they've made. The explanation is no excuse when it comes to moms too.

MAY 26

The Transition

When I was a child, I talked like a child,
I thought like a child,
I reasoned like a child. When I became a man,
I put the ways of childhood behind me.

—1 CORINTHIANS 13:11

Motherhood is the only profession I know of where success is marked by no longer being necessary. As your children reach adulthood, they will be making the vast majority of their decisions without you. Your role will be that of a consultant—an *unpaid* consultant.

When on occasion they think you might have a good idea or some experience or knowledge in a particular area, you may be asked for an opinion; but as adults, your children will not have to act on the gem of wisdom you've shared. They do not have to take your advice.

If this seems rather sad as you look at your sleeping baby, keep in mind that one of the victories in being a mom is to see your children becoming independent individuals—no longer talking, thinking, or reasoning as children.

BEFORE YOU KNOW IT

The day will come when "Mom" is no longer your job description. Instead, it will be a term of endearment.

MAY 27

Eliminate the Vote

That is just what I did in Jerusalem.
On the authority of the chief priests I put many of the Lord's people in prison, and when they were put to death, I cast my vote against them.

—ACTS 26:10

It's important to listen to the members of your family and to treat each one with respect. In fact, modeling respect will potentially mean that your children will listen and respect you.

One mistake that can be made in the name of respect is to give an equal vote to every member of your family—young and old alike.

"Where should we go on vacation this summer? One, two, three votes for the exotic cruise we can't afford. And one additional vote for camping at the lake. (Thanks for voting with me, sweetheart.) It looks like the kids' votes win. I'll get that cruise booked right away!"

Ridiculous? Yes. It may be a good idea to listen and get input from every member of the family, but voting is unnecessary.

TAKE NOTE

When you're asking your kids for input, be certain they understand that you're merely gathering information that will be evaluated and considered. If your children are old enough, they can actually help you look at the pros and cons of each suggestion.

MAY 28

Resist the Rescue

"Anyone, whether native-born or foreigner, who eats anything found dead or torn by wild animals must wash their clothes and bathe with water, and they will be ceremonially unclean till evening; then they will be clean. But if they do not wash their clothes and bathe themselves, they will be held responsible."

—LEVITICUS 17:15–16

Decisions have consequences. In the Scripture above, the instructions were given and the consequences were outlined: Anyone failing to follow the instructions would be held responsible. No excuses.

You may experience the overwhelming temptation to rescue your children when they're found in a self-inflicted, preventable predicament. It can be difficult to resist the rescue, but consider what can result if you don't.

A child who is repeatedly rescued from his poor decisions will become dependent and have a very difficult time taking responsibility for his actions. Mom is always there repairing the damage, so it really doesn't matter what choices he makes.

Furthermore, because he doesn't have to be responsible for his mistakes, he soon determines that even his successes are not his own. Somehow Mom must have been the one to make those happen too.

DON'T DO IT

Don't rob your child of the enjoyment and encouragement of success by not allowing him or her to take responsibility for missteps. Resist the rescue.

MAY 29

Choose Today

"If serving the LORD seems undesirable to you, then choose for yourselves this day whom you will serve, whether the gods your ancestors served beyond the Euphrates, or the gods of the Amorites, in whose land you are living. But as for me and my household, we will serve the LORD."

—JOSHUA 24:15

The last sentence of the Scripture above is often featured on plaques in homes across our nation: "But as for me and my household, we will serve the LORD."

Those are powerful words of commitment and encouragement, but equally encouraging are these words in the first sentence of Joshua 24:15: "Choose for yourselves this day whom you will serve."

You make this choice on a daily basis, perhaps even from one hour to the next. God's Word gives you direction. The Holy Spirit gives you guidance. And the Lord will guide and direct your children too.

Teaching your children to choose each day whom they will serve and follow is an important responsibility. When the lesson is learned, you can proclaim with Joshua: "As for me and my household, we will serve the LORD."

A MOM'S DESIRE

As a follower of Christ, your desire is to see that your children follow and serve him too. Encourage them and let them know it's a daily choice.

MAY 30

Mom-Control to Self-Control

Like a city whose walls are broken through
is a person who lacks self-control.

—PROVERBS 25:28

When your child's life began, she was completely under your control. She ate when you fed her. She wore the clothes you chose for her, and she went where you decided she would go.

As she grew up, she had more control. Before long she was able to choose what she would eat, what she would wear, and where she would go. Many of the choices made were no longer your responsibility. She was no longer under "mom-control."

As she grows, will she exhibit self-control? In the biblical sense, self-control means much more than making decisions on your own. Self-control means mastery of one's actions and emotions in situations where there is temptation or extreme irritation.

Self-control is taught and caught. If your daughter has seen you exhibit godly restraint in difficult situations, and if you've allowed her to do the same by giving up more and more mom-control through the years, the chances are great she will display that fruit of God's Holy Spirit.

LET'S PRAY

Lord, please help me loosen my control on my child's life and tighten my grip on you, encouraging my child to develop godly self-control.

May 31

Discipline

Whoever loves discipline loves knowledge,
but whoever hates correction is stupid.
—Proverbs 12:1

Years ago I was on a live television show, and the host asked a question that could have been very difficult. Now remember, this was live TV. There was no follow-up editing to remove the missteps or stutters.

"What would you say is one of the most important characteristics a successful mother possesses?"

As the camera rolled, I took a moment to contemplate and then answered: "It's helpful for a mom to be teachable, to be willing to be disciplined, and to learn what it takes to do the job God's way. Being teachable is definitely an important attribute and one of the keys to success."

"And how would you define success?" Oh boy, another tough question.

"I would say it's raising a child who chooses to love God, obey God, and glorify God with his life. That doesn't mean the child has chosen to pursue a clerical occupation. It means that as an adult he or she has chosen to follow the Lord's direction and to learn to use the gifts and talents he's supplied."

Let's Pray

Dear heavenly Father, I want to learn from you and your Word. I want to love your Word and be disciplined enough to live within the boundaries you've set.

TEACH YOUR CHILDREN TO THINK LONG-TERM

Shadrach, Meshach and Abednego replied
to him, "King Nebuchadnezzar, we do not need
to defend ourselves before you in this matter.
If we are thrown into the blazing furnace,
the God we serve is able to deliver us from it,
and he will deliver us from Your Majesty's hand.
But even if he does not, we want you to know,
Your Majesty, that we will not serve your gods
or worship the image of gold you have set up."

—Daniel 3:16–18

JUNE 1

Even If

"We want you to know, Your Majesty, that we will not serve your gods or worship the image of gold you have set up."
—DANIEL 3:18

Shadrach, Meshach, and Abednego were thinking long-term when they found themselves in a situation that would require a big commitment. Here's the dilemma they were in.

King Nebuchadnezzar made a very large statue and told everyone under his command to bow down and worship that statue every time they heard music being played.

The three heroes in this passage of Scripture from Daniel were committed to worshiping no one but the one true God. That meant they were not going to obey the king—which, unsurprisingly, didn't sit well with him.

For those who refused to obey King Nebuchadnezzar's command to bow down, there would be consequences. Those who didn't do as the king demanded would "immediately be thrown into a blazing furnace" (v. 6).

With that gloomy fate before them, the three brave Jewish men stood strong in their commitment to follow God's law. Their decision was not based on the immediate outcome; it was rooted in faith. "But even if he does not [deliver us], we want you to know, Your Majesty, that we will not serve your gods or worship the image of gold you have set up" (v. 18).

LET'S PRAY

Lord, help me stand for and stand up for the truth of the gospel and teach my children to do the same.

JUNE 2

Making Choices

Choose my instruction instead of silver,
knowledge rather than choice gold.
—PROVERBS 8:10

"Mrs. Smiley," one boy in my fourth grade class began, "may our February book report be on a Choose Your Own Adventure book? Please?"

"Yes, please let us report on one of those books," added another pleading young man.

"Let me think about it," was my reply. After all, I had to decide if that type of book was really educational. Ultimately I acquiesced, and the boys let out a cheer. Their lobbying had paid off.

Years later, my own sons were reading those same books with an equal amount of enthusiasm. It was then that I realized the books, based on the premise that choices must be made on every page, were actually very educational.

Life is made up of choices, and the more good, godly choices you make and encourage your children to make, the better. Good choices give you opportunities to honor and glorify God with your life.

IT'S TRUE

In a sense you are able to "choose your own adventure," and so are your children. Making choices that are in line with the instructions in God's Word are more than good choices; they are the best.

JUNE 3

Expect It

Why, my soul, are you downcast?
Why so disturbed within me?
Put your hope in God,
for I will yet praise him,
my Savior and my God.
—Psalm 42:11

The psalmist is questioning the sadness and distress he is feeling. "Why? Why?" The questions that begin with the word *why*, especially when they are addressed to the Lord, usually do not have an easy answer.

It's interesting that the psalmist doesn't seem to wait for an answer to his questions. It's as though he knows that those answers may not come anytime soon. Instead, he chooses to do what he can do immediately; he decides to put his hope in God and praise him.

I know that being a mom sometimes means feeling discouraged. We wonder, *Why did that problem arise? Why do I feel so alone? Why am I supposed to solve everyone else's problems?*

Instead of waiting for answers that may never come, choose to put your hope in God and praise him. Teach your children to do the same.

REMEMBER

The "why" questions are often unanswerable. Instead of wasting precious time and energy waiting for those answers, look to the Lord and praise him.

JUNE 4

Diligence

Diligent hands will rule,
but laziness ends in forced labor.

—PROVERBS 12:24

There are times when I feel tired and lazy. It's not an "I'm absolutely exhausted" kind of tired. It's more of an "I'm really tired of all this responsibility" kind of tired. You may be feeling that way right now, or you might have a teenager in your home who can relate.

That's when you'll find me lying on the couch or in the hammock, purposely making very few decisions except whether I'd prefer a glass of iced tea or lemonade.

Everyone has moments like that, and some folks may even have whole afternoons. But if you're thinking long-term, lazy days don't come too often. The teenager who is hoping to go off to college and has agreed to earn a portion of his tuition by working in the summer will only choose a lazy day when it's already his day off.

The person—adult or teenager—who lives life in the tired and lazy mode, dodging responsibility and diligence, is also choosing to disobey God's instruction and the path to success as he defines it.

SO

Be a leader for the Lord by choosing to be diligent in all you do, and help your children see the benefit.

JUNE 5

Perseverance

Therefore, since we are surrounded by such a great cloud of witnesses, let us throw off everything that hinders and the sin that so easily entangles. And let us run with perseverance the race marked out for us.

—HEBREWS 12:1

Years ago I decided to train for a 5K. My goal wasn't impressive; it was to start and finish the race. If you're a serious runner, you're probably disappointed in me, but when the training began, I wasn't even a serious walker . . . so I decided my goal was a good one.

I can't report that the run was a delight, but I did enjoy reaching my goal. My success was the result of perseverance. More than once during the run I considered giving up. I wasn't having fun, wasn't feeling terrific, and definitely wasn't winning.

There are times in your child's life when she'll feel like giving up. Maybe her schoolwork or her job or other responsibilities are no longer fun. Maybe she isn't feeling great about showing up every day. Perhaps she's also realized she simply isn't winning.

That's when perseverance comes into play. God wants you and your child to persevere, to run the race he has marked out for you.

STAY STRONG

If you're on the path God designed for you, run with perseverance and encourage your child to do the same.

JUNE 6

Sowing Seeds

"But the seed on good soil stands for those
with a noble and good heart, who hear the word,
retain it, and by persevering produce a crop."

—LUKE 8:15

Many times Jesus used parables to teach, and many of his parables depended on the listeners having some degree of agricultural knowledge. In Luke 8 he told of a farmer sowing seed.

In the parable, the seed was the Word of God. That seed was sown on the path, on rocky ground, among thorns, and on good soil. The good soil, unlike the others, produced a bountiful crop.

Jesus went on to explain the meaning of his words. The seed planted in the good soil represented "those with a noble and good heart, who hear the word, retain it, and by persevering produce a crop."

As a believer, your life is capable of producing an abundant crop for the Lord—a crop of fellow believers who desire to follow Christ. Regardless of the age of your children, now is the time to sow into their lives. Keep in mind they will not be children forever.

IT'S TIME

As a mom, you have a strong influence in the lives of your children. Sowing seeds of faith into their lives now can result in a harvest of blessings in the future.

JUNE 7

Practice

This has been my practice:
I obey your precepts.
—Psalm 119:56

Your music teacher, your soccer coach, and your mother all reminded you to practice correctly! No matter how hard you practiced, if you weren't doing it correctly, the chances were great you would perform incorrectly. Practice done correctly has a strong possibility of improving your performance.

You practice your tennis swing and your gourmet cooking as correctly as possible in hopes you will improve. But in the long run, if you consider what will really matter twenty, thirty, or fifty years from now, will your tennis game or your culinary artistry come to mind?

I don't think those skills will matter. Instead, let me refer you to the Scripture from Psalm 119. The psalmist made it his practice to obey God's precepts—God's guidelines and instructions. He made it his habit and his routine. Obeying God's rules became second nature to him.

FOR YOUR TO-DO LIST

It's time to make obeying God's instructions a part of your daily routine. Encourage your kids to do the same.

JUNE 8

Fix Your Eyes

Therefore, since we are surrounded by such a great cloud of witnesses, let us throw off everything that hinders and the sin that so easily entangles.
And let us run with perseverance the race marked out for us, fixing our eyes on Jesus, the pioneer and perfecter of faith. For the joy set before him he endured the cross, scorning its shame, and sat down at the right hand of the throne of God.

—HEBREWS 12:1–2

The Bible verses above suggest two things that will help you and your child develop long-term thinking. The first is to surround yourself with "a great cloud of witnesses." In other words, associate with people who will encourage you to live a life pleasing to God. Peer pressure is a real thing for both children and adults.

The second suggestion has to do with focus. Just as a runner focuses on the finish line, we believers fix "our eyes on Jesus, the pioneer and perfecter of faith." As you look at the path you want to travel and focus on the final destination, you will be able to run the course successfully.

SO

Pay attention to the company your child keeps, and also be aware of the message you're sending by the company you keep. As you run the race of life, keep your eyes on Jesus.

JUNE 9

The Waiting Game

Wait for the Lord;
be strong and take heart
and wait for the Lord.

—Psalm 27:14

One aspect of thinking long-term is to develop the ability to wait without losing heart. When I was expecting my first child, I circled the due date on my calendar. I was sure that without fail, that was the day he would arrive. After all, Dr. Tanner had given me that information and he had delivered hundreds of kids.

The predicted day came and went. What I had assumed would be a monumental occurrence did not happen. How was that possible? Hadn't I waited long enough?

Then the next day passed and I foolishly imagined I would be pregnant forever. I don't need to tell you that my ridiculous thought did not come to pass. Two days after the circled date, the baby finally arrived.

I know that sounds silly to you; it sounds silly to me too. At that point in my life, I hadn't adequately developed the skill of waiting for God's timing. Waiting on God is important whether you are waiting for a baby or waiting for an answer to prayer.

LET'S PRAY

Lord, I want to trust your timing even if it means waiting. Please help me when I struggle.

JUNE 10

Now!

So that you may live a life worthy of the Lord and please him in every way: bearing fruit in every good work, growing in the knowledge of God, being strengthened with all power according to his glorious might so that you may have great endurance and patience, and giving joyful thanks to the Father, who has qualified you to share in the inheritance of his holy people in the kingdom of light.

—Colossians 1:10–12

Patience is a virtue. That's a familiar cliché, and it's also a virtue most children aren't interested in cultivating.

"But I want it now!"

My hope is that you read those words with an appropriate whine in your voice. Or maybe even a tear or two. Kids, and some adults, want what they want when they want it. Such impatience has never been considered a virtue.

Learning to be patient is a baby step toward learning to think long-term. If you can wait patiently for lunch when you're three, you might have a better chance of waiting patiently for the bus at age nine and waiting for the right man when you're twenty-five.

A QUESTION FOR YOU

Are you cultivating patience in your child, or are you responding immediately to her every demand? God is patient. Help your children learn patience.

JUNE 11

Saving for the Future

The wise man saves for the future,
but the foolish man spends whatever he gets.
—PROVERBS 21:20 TLB

An important aspect of thinking long-term is acknowledging that there is uncertainty in life. A foolish mom might see that fact as a free pass to do anything and everything, regardless of the consequences.

"Spend all you make; why save for a future that may never come? Spend more than you make; you won't have any difficulty getting more credit." This woman has decided she may be gone tomorrow, so her attitude is to live only for today.

A wise mom knows that no one can predict what the future will hold, but rather than squandering the wages she has earned or the gifts she's received from God, she uses them wisely. She invests her time and her resources in a way that is pleasing to God, knowing her future is in his hands.

A wise mom teaches her children to do the same: to invest in the kingdom of God and to use wisdom as they spend what they have earned.

COULD IT BE?

I heard it said that your check register is a reflection of your faith. Being wise with everything God has entrusted to you is a good example for your kids.

JUNE 12

Reality

We fix our eyes not on what is seen,
but on what is unseen,
since what is seen is temporary,
but what is unseen is eternal.

—2 CORINTHIANS 4:18

"You have to face reality."

I'm sure you've heard those words before. Maybe you've even said that very thing to someone. "You have to face reality!" But what is reality?

The dictionary would tell you reality is something real, a real or true situation—something that actually exists.

The world defines reality as what can be seen, heard, touched, tasted, or smelled. But is reality limited to what you experience with your five senses, or is it something more?

We are told in 2 Corinthians 4:18 to "fix our eyes": to focus on what is eternal and unseen. The reality of Christ is not always experienced with our senses. The spiritual world, the world beyond what our eyes can see, is real and something that actually exists. The eternal is very real.

HERE'S A THOUGHT

The next time someone challenges you to "face reality" when it comes to your walk with Christ, look for a God-given opportunity to share your faith in a grace-filled way.

JUNE 13

Detour

He has barred my way with blocks of stone;
he has made my paths crooked.

—LAMENTATIONS 3:9

I don't appreciate detours. They slow me down, confuse me, and typically add miles and minutes to my trip.

And that's just the traveling detours. There can be other, even more unpleasant detours in life.

You start down a pathway of life you think you should travel, and the next thing you know you're forced to make an unplanned, uncharted turn. Those detours can be unpleasant and a little unnerving.

Rather than lament the perceived loss of efficiency, try looking at detours as possibilities. They might provide an opportunity for service that you hadn't imagined. Maybe the change in direction will mean you can experience an important life lesson.

In retrospect, we can sometimes see the detours of life as God-ordained changes in direction. Detours can actually be blessings in disguise.

SO NEXT TIME

When you find yourself forced to take a detour, resist grumbling about the change of plans and look for the opportunities and the adventure God may be preparing for you.

JUNE 14

Flexibility

Do not conform to the pattern of this world,
but be transformed by the renewing of your mind.
—ROMANS 12:2

Are you flexible? I'm not interested in whether or not you can touch your toes or do a back bend. I'm talking about emotional flexibility. My answer to that question would be "sometimes."

Years ago I purchased a cute piece of artwork. It was a drawing of a little bird in a rather contorted position, yet the bird was smiling. The caption read, "Blessed are the flexible, for they shall not be bent out of shape"—followed by the verse from Romans 12:2.

When I brought the print home, I put it on my desk and propped it up by my light. One morning as I sat down to work, I noticed the picture was missing. I glanced around, wondering where it might possibly be, and found it under the roller of my big, heavy desk chair, a little worse for wear.

Now was my big chance. I could choose to be flexible or to be "bent out of shape." It's always a choice.

HOW ABOUT YOU?

It can be tough to take things in stride, but most annoyances are simply that: annoying. Don't be anxious. Keep your eye on the big picture, and present your requests to God.

JUNE 15

Long-Term Thinker

By faith Moses, when he had grown up, refused to be known as the son of Pharaoh's daughter. He chose to be mistreated along with the people of God rather than to enjoy the fleeting pleasures of sin.

—HEBREWS 11:24–25

Moses was a long-term thinker. He could have chosen to identify with Pharaoh's daughter, which would have made him the grandson of the ruler of all of Egypt—a pretty heady position! But Moses knew that the power and prestige associated with the royalty of Egypt would be short-lived. He didn't choose the "fleeting pleasures of sin."

Sin can be very enticing. It comes in different forms, increasing its ability to attract adults and children too. Sin can be subtle, with its consequences masked by its appeal. It can draw you or your child in and camouflage the truth of the consequences—inhibiting your ability to think long-term.

TAKE ACTION

If there is some beguiling sin that's been tempting you, be honest with yourself and with God and think of the consequences. Look for teachable moments to help your kids do the same.

JUNE 16

Not a Sprint

Those who hope in the LORD will renew their strength.
They will soar on wings like eagles;
they will run and not grow weary,
they will walk and not be faint.

—ISAIAH 40:31

For the most part I enjoy walking, and it's also good for my health. One day my oldest son, then in college, joined me as I walked. He was riding a bicycle and at times had trouble keeping it upright because our pace was so slow.

After a mile or so he challenged me. "Mom, you're capable of going much faster than this."

He was correct. I was capable of increasing my speed, but there was something he didn't understand. "Yes, I could go faster, but the point of my walking isn't to set any speed records. The point is to still be walking years from now."

I knew that if I jogged, I would not enjoy the outing and it wouldn't be long before I talked myself out of even putting on my tennis shoes. The goal was longevity—not speed.

Longevity is also a goal in the Christian walk. Maybe that's why you never hear it called the Christian sprint.

LET'S PRAY

Lord, I want to walk with you each day and let you determine the speed. Help me not rush ahead or fall behind but instead keep pace with you.

JUNE 17

What's Your Goal?

I will praise you, Lord my God, with all my heart;
I will glorify your name forever.
—PSALM 86:12

There are certain things that were repeated again and again in our family. One was actually a question: "What is your goal?"

For example, if one of my sons was trying to decide whether or not to join a certain school-related organization, I'd ask, "What's your goal?" If the goal was as simple as having fun, and that organization was deemed as fun, then he could see that joining it might help him reach the goal.

That one simple question can be helpful for children and for adults. It can help you identify your motivation and choose the right path.

What is your goal? If you can honestly identify one of your goals as living a life that glorifies God, you're well on your way to making choices that will support that goal.

THINK ABOUT IT

The question "What is my goal?" can apply to many areas of your life and your child's life. Teach your son or daughter to ask and answer that question honestly.

JUNE 18

Building Adults

In this way they will lay up treasure for themselves
as a firm foundation for the coming age,
so that they may take hold of the life that is truly life.

—1 TIMOTHY 6:19

For many years I've had a framed print by the door of my home office. I chose to put it in that specific location so that I would be able to read the words each time I left the room. The words are simple and so very true: "It's easier to build children than to repair adults."

That print was there to remind me that even though the investment I made in my children today might seem tiring, I was making an investment in their future. Building into the lives of your children is essentially preparing them for the time when they're adults.

Every builder knows that a house needs a good foundation. It's easier to build a secure foundation in the beginning than to repair the crumbling foundation of an older home.

It's the same idea with raising children. They need a good foundation—a strong foundation of faith—and you can help build it. With a firm foundation, fewer repairs will be required in the future.

LET'S PRAY

Father, help me think long-term by diligently building the lives of my children.

JUNE 19

Remember

[Joshua] said to them,
"Go over before the ark of the LORD your God
into the middle of the Jordan. Each of you is to take up a
stone on his shoulder, according to the number of the tribes
of the Israelites, to serve as a sign among you. In the future,
when your children ask you, 'What do these stones mean?'
tell them that the flow of the Jordan was cut off before
the ark of the covenant of the LORD. When it crossed the
Jordan, the waters of the Jordan were cut off. These stones
are to be a memorial to the people of Israel forever."

—JOSHUA 4:5–7

As instructed by the Lord, Joshua gave the twelve men he'd chosen the orders God had given him. These men were to construct a memorial, a reminder of what God had done.

For me, my journal is a reminder. I've recorded both prayer requests and the answers to those requests. They are a reminder of many things: joys, heartbreaks, concerns, surprises, and divine intervention. Looking back on those journal entries reminds me to look to the future and the continued faithfulness of God.

IT'S TRUE

A journal can become a collection of your memories of God's love and faithfulness, encouraging you in your faith walk.

JUNE 20

Don't Burn Bridges

Those who guard their lips preserve their lives,
but those who speak rashly will come to ruin.
—PROVERBS 13:3

There are times when it can be difficult to hold your tongue. When someone mistreats you or someone you love, it takes a great deal of willpower to guard your lips. It is, however, the best decision. Exercising willpower is a little like practicing patience; it's a way of thinking long-term.

I heard the story of a young man who was preparing to leave his current job and was asked to do an exit interview with his boss. There were many things he could have said about his experience with the company, but the great majority would not have been complimentary and wouldn't have facilitated any positive changes.

Instead of speaking rashly, the young man honestly shared the positive aspects with his soon-to-be-former employer. They parted ways amicably, and the young man went on to search for employment.

It didn't take long before he had a new job, and after nine months on the job, his new boss told him that one of the reasons he had been asked to interview was the sterling recommendation he received from his former employer.

THE LESSON

Help your kids understand that speaking in haste without guidance from the Lord can unnecessarily burn bridges.

JUNE 21

The Fine Line

Even as fools walk along the road,
they lack sense and show everyone how stupid they are.
—Ecclesiastes 10:3

Let's take a look at the definition of two very common words. *Fun*: enjoyment, amusement, or lighthearted pleasure. *Stupid*: lacking intelligence or common sense.

Now that you have those definitions in mind, I want to share something a young man recently said.

To quote eleven-year-old Nathan: "There's a fine line between fun and stupid."

Ah, those words were incredibly well-spoken.

I'm not sure what Nathan had witnessed in order to come up with such a brilliant and accurate observation, but it was obvious to me he had a pretty good idea about the importance of long-term thinking.

Anyone who chooses not to cross that line—be it someone in grade school, a teenager, or even a mom—acts wisely.

YOUR ASSIGNMENT

Nathan's keen observation is very true. Do your best to teach your children to avoid stepping over that fine line between fun and stupid. That lesson will serve them well throughout life.

JUNE 22

Stand for Christ

"If you do not stand firm in your faith,
you will not stand at all."
—Isaiah 7:9

When my kids were growing up, there was a poster on the wall where the middle school kids met each Sunday. It said, "If you don't stand for something, you'll fall for anything," followed by the Scripture reference above. In other words, you must know the truth so you're not deceived.

The kids in our church had good Sunday school teachers, but I knew it was the job of every parent to see to it that the children God had given them learned to "stand firm" in their faith.

The older kids get, the more temptation there is for them to become chameleons—the lizard that changes color in order to camouflage itself and blend into the environment. Teenagers generally don't want to stand out from the crowd. That reticence can result in decisions that are counter to the Word of God . . . or can result in "not standing" for what is right.

LET'S PRAY

Lord, I know how difficult it is to go against the crowd and stand up for you. Help me give my kids confidence to do just that so they won't be deceived.

JUNE 23

Each Day

Teach us to number our days,
that we may gain a heart of wisdom.
—Psalm 90:12

My father died when I was twenty-two years old. I graduated from college in May, and he died in August. My father-in-law died after I had been married for many years and had three adult sons, three daughters-in-law, and several grandchildren.

It was after my father-in-law's death that I found myself doing the best I could to live in the truth of Psalm 90:12 each day. Perhaps at age twenty-two when my own father died, I was too young to realize that each day was precious. I was too naïve, too immature to recognize that the days we have on this earth are numbered.

That concept is difficult for a young person to grasp, but the promise of a heart of wisdom makes it a great lesson for everyone. God is willing to be your teacher, and the sooner you learn to number your days, the better.

LET'S PRAY

Lord, help me invest my time in the things that are truly important. Teach me to number my days. Thank you for your promise to give me a heart of wisdom.

JUNE 24

From Suffering to Hope

Through [Jesus] we have gained access by faith into this grace in which we now stand. And we boast in the hope of the glory of God. Not only so, but we also glory in our sufferings, because we know that suffering produces perseverance; perseverance, character; and character, hope.

—Romans 5:2–4

When you are able to think long-term, you are better able to handle the trials of life. When you teach your children to think about the future, it helps them put suffering, hardship, and mistreatment in perspective.

No one is exempt from suffering, although the degree of suffering can vary greatly. No one goes through life without distress, and no one is eager to repeat the experience that may have led to those painful times.

The Word is very clear, however, that those trials and suffering produce perseverance, character, and hope. When your children face suffering in any form, listen to them carefully. Let them know you understand that they are hurting. Then encourage them to trust God, who sees and controls the bigger picture.

IT CAN BE HARD

Sometimes as a mom you may want to fix things right away and protect your children from any suffering or pain. That might be your desire, but it's not best for your kids. Pray that they will be filled with hope.

JUNE 25

Strong and Courageous

"Be strong and very courageous. Be careful
to obey all the law my servant Moses gave you;
do not turn from it to the right or to the left,
that you may be successful wherever you go."

—JOSHUA 1:7

God knew Joshua had big shoes to fill after the death of Moses, so he offered words of encouragement. He told Joshua about the land he had promised the Israelites and the success they would have against their enemies; and he promised that no one would win a battle against them. The Lord promised to be with Joshua as he had been with Moses.

God continued to speak words of encouragement, promising to be with Joshua every step of the way. Next he told Joshua to be "strong and courageous" (v. 6). The Lord repeated that command again and again because he wanted Joshua to get the message: "Be strong and courageous."

It can take courage to think long-term, but God will always keep his promises to you. You can entrust your future to him.

IT'S TRUE

The Lord wants you to be strong and courageous and to think long-term. He will be with you every step of the way, just as he was with Moses and Joshua. Encourage your child as God encouraged Joshua.

JUNE 26

Face the Target

We make it our goal to please him,
whether we are at home in the body or away from it.
—2 Corinthians 5:9

When the kids were growing up, we played darts at Grandma's house. The dartboard was on a wall in the back corner of the recreation room. Undoubtedly that location had been selected because it was: (a) far from any chairs that might be occupied, and (b) on an unfinished wall.

The importance of being far from the chairs was obvious; it was for the protection of anyone who might be in a chair. And the unfinished wall provided an appropriate place for darts that missed the mark.

The goal of darts is to hit the bull's-eye. On occasion, I achieved that goal. More often than not, my dart landed on one of the outer rings or on the wall.

Rather than feeling bad about my poor performance, I'd laughingly announce that my personal goal had been to throw my darts at the right wall.

Thinking long-term won't always mean you hit the bull's-eye, but it will mean you're facing the right direction.

IT'S TRUE

When your child is doing his best to think beyond the moment, applaud those decisions. He doesn't have to hit the bull's-eye to be successful.

JUNE 27

It's Not Fair

Appoint judges and officials for each of your tribes
in every town the Lord your God is giving you,
and they shall judge the people fairly.
—Deuteronomy 16:18

"It's not fair! It's just not fair!" said a teenage girl between her sobs. She had made it as far as her Sunday school teacher's home, looking for someone with an understanding ear and a tender heart. When her teacher opened the door, the young girl found what she wanted and needed and she sobbed unashamedly.

This girl had been abandoned by her biological parents and was now feeling mistreated by her foster parents, who expected her to watch the younger children in their home.

"It's not fair," was her cry. Was it fair? At that point fairness was not the most important question the teacher had on her mind. Instead it was, "How can I comfort this sweet girl?"

"Life is not fair," her teacher began. "There is trouble that can't be avoided, but Jesus cares about you. When you walk with him you can overcome the injustice. Let's pray together."

NOW JOIN ME IN PRAYER

Father, help me continually hold your hand. Help me teach my children to do the same so they can be victorious when troubles arise.

JUNE 28

Exceeding Abundantly

Now unto him that is able to do exceeding abundantly above all that we ask or think, according to the power that worketh in us, unto him be glory in the church by Christ Jesus throughout all ages, world without end. Amen.

—Ephesians 3:20–21 KJV

How big is God Almighty? How powerful is he? What is he capable of accomplishing in your life? Those questions are all answered in the verse above. He is able to do "exceeding abundantly above . . ." Above what? Above *all* you ask or think. In the New International Version, the answer is "all we ask or imagine."

I love this promise from God's Word. Our God is not limited by time or space or by your ability to ask, think, or imagine.

So how should you respond to this truth? Clearly the answer is to give glory to him forever and ever. Amen—so be it!

IT'S TRUE

God's plans for you and for your child are bigger and better than any you could imagine. Because they are God's plans, they are perfect—unlike the imperfect plans of man or mom.

JUNE 29

The Solid Rock

"Therefore everyone who hears these words of mine
and puts them into practice is like a wise man who built his
house on the rock. The rain came down, the streams rose,
and the winds blew and beat against that house;
yet it did not fall, because it had its foundation on the rock."

—MATTHEW 7:24–25

Thinking long-term means that a disappointment or setback doesn't signify all is lost. A child or an adult who is a long-term thinker has learned to look beyond the "if onlys" of life. The wise man who built his house on the rock didn't spend time whining about the rain that came down, the streams that rose, or the winds that blew and beat against his house.

Why? Because in spite of those negative circumstances, his house did not fall. When that house was constructed, the man made certain it had a firm foundation that would last. The home was built on the rock—the rock of faith in Jesus.

REMEMBER

Every child and every adult could make a list of "if onlys," but that list would not change reality. It's more beneficial to make a list of blessings and thank God for them.

JUNE 30

Think

Brothers and sisters, stop thinking like children.
In regard to evil be infants, but in your thinking be adults.

—1 Corinthians 14:20

A newborn baby doesn't have the ability to think long-term. That's a skill that comes with age and training, and the training falls under your job description—Mom.

"Do you want to buy a better bicycle? Think long-term and start to save your money today."

"Do you want to make the basketball team? Today is the day to start practicing."

"Do you want to go to college? Now's the time to study and do a good job in school."

Too often children want something but do not understand the idea of doing what it takes to receive it. They are thinking like children. That can also be true for adults.

"I want to grow closer to Christ. What do you mean I should read the Word and pray?"

Thinking long-term is thinking like a responsible adult. It's not a factor of age.

LET'S PRAY

Lord, I want to encourage my children to learn to think responsibly and look long-term when they make decisions. Please, Father, help me do the same.

YOU ARE HIS CHILD

For those who are led by the Spirit of God
are the children of God.
—Romans 8:14

JULY 1

Christ's Ambassadors

We are therefore Christ's ambassadors,
as though God were making his appeal through us.
We implore you on Christ's behalf:
Be reconciled to God.

—2 Corinthians 5:20

I was sitting in church one Sunday and noticed a young mom trying to corral her preschooler. The little boy was pointing and whispering, and she was patiently whispering in his ear—probably answering the many questions he was asking.

All at once he forgot about using his "whisper voice." Pointing to the pastor, he blurted out, "Is that Jesus?"

Blushing, his mom gently put her hand over his mouth and again whispered to him. My guess is she was answering the question and maybe telling him no more questions for a while.

"No, that isn't Jesus," would be the easy answer, but perhaps she explained that the man up front was an ambassador for the Lord. You are also his ambassador if you've come to faith in Christ and you have the privilege of sharing his message of grace and truth in your own home and beyond.

LET'S PRAY

Lord, please give me the words to speak so I can fearlessly and confidently present the gospel message.

JULY 2

Masterpiece

For we are God's handiwork,
created in Christ Jesus to do good works,
which God prepared in advance for us to do.

—EPHESIANS 2:10

Years ago, before we had any children, my husband and I traveled to Europe to visit my brother who was living there at the time. We spent several days in Paris, and on the last day in the city we planned to see the *Mona Lisa*. I couldn't imagine actually seeing that masterpiece!

Well, I still can't imagine it. When we arrived at the museum, we discovered it was closed because they were filming an American movie inside. What bad timing on our part!

While attempting to comfort one another in our disappointment, these words were spoken: "I guess we'll just have to save that for next time." (By the way, I'm not actually anticipating a "next time.")

I missed seeing that particular masterpiece, but I have been privileged to see many others. When you see a child of God, you're viewing a masterpiece created by the Master himself.

REMEMBER

You are a masterpiece created by God to do good works. You are his child, and he has wonderful plans for you.

JULY 3

Humility

When pride comes, then comes disgrace,
but with humility comes wisdom.
—PROVERBS 11:2

Humility is valued in the Word of God and in the Christian community. References to it are found throughout the Bible. Proverbs 11:2 is an example from the Old Testament; and from the New Testament, Philippians 2:3: "Do nothing out of selfish ambition or vain conceit. Rather, in humility value others above yourselves."

Have you heard the story of the youngster who earned a lapel pin in Sunday school for exhibiting humility? The first time he wore the pin, they took it away from him. Obviously he was not displaying humility! Perhaps that silly story illustrates how difficult it can be to be humble.

Not too long ago I heard a very good, legitimate explanation of what humility is and what it is not. And I quote: "Humility is not thinking less of yourself; it is thinking of yourself less."

IT'S TRUE

Every mother can use a big dose of wisdom, and the Word tells you that with humility comes wisdom. Thinking of yourself less and thinking of others more is the first step.

JULY 4

Calling on Him

The LORD is near to all who call on him,
to all who call on him in truth.
—PSALM 145:18

Have you ever noticed what happens when a young person yells "Mom!" at a gathering with several mothers present? Heads turn, ears perk up, and almost without fail, every mother there will momentarily respond to the call, just in case it is her child calling. Even moms whose children aren't there will temporarily forget that the child they hear could not possibly be hers.

I've done it, and I'm guessing you have too. We've turned to answer the call only to remember our kids were at Grandma's house.

Kids call and moms answer. That's just the way it is; and that's the way it is with God too. He's right there—ready, willing, and able to answer when one of his children calls to him. That is a promise that is incredibly reassuring.

LET'S PRAY

Thank you, Father, for hearing my cry. Knowing you listen, you hear, and you respond in love to me is amazing and reassuring. Let me always call to you in truth.

JULY 5

The Guest

When Jesus reached the spot, he looked up and said to him, "Zacchaeus, come down immediately. I must stay at your house today." So he came down at once and welcomed him gladly. All the people saw this and began to mutter, "He has gone to be the guest of a sinner."

—LUKE 19:5–7

The last statement in the Scripture above always makes me smile. You might think that's odd, but let me explain.

The townspeople had been disgusted with Zacchaeus for a long time. He was a tax collector, and not only that—according to the crowd he was a crooked one, taking more than was owed.

Now to add insult to injury, Jesus declared he was going to stay in the home of this scoundrel. The people were outraged.

That portion of Scripture is not where I find the humor. I smile when I remember that indeed, Jesus chose to be the guest of a sinner. Think about it; unless he was completely alone, he was always with a sinner.

The words of the townspeople are actually very reassuring. If Jesus was willing to be the guest of the sinner Zaccheaus, he is open to being my guest and yours.

LET'S PRAY

Lord, thank you for showing me over and over in your Word that you love and forgive. Thank you for caring about a sinner like me.

JULY 6

Tyranny of the Urgent

Let people and animals be covered with sackcloth.
Let everyone call urgently on God.
Let them give up their evil ways and their violence.

—JONAH 3:8

The buzzer on my dryer went off and I jumped out of the chair. I was eager to take out the clothes because it was a load of no-iron shirts, and you can only take that label guarantee so far. I had learned that if I retrieved the shirts before the buzzer completed its alert and then immediately put them on hangers, I could save myself the nuisance of ironing.

The dryer buzzer is an example of the "urgent." Some say they are victims of the tyranny of the urgent as they scurry from one buzzer to the next. And when we only give our immediate attention to the buzzers of life, the urgent overshadows the important—hence the tyranny.

SOME QUESTIONS TO PONDER

Do you feel an urgency to follow the biblical instruction the Holy Spirit has been whispering in your ear? Do you jump out of your chair when you are prompted and eagerly follow God's direction, or do you imagine that the prompting of the Lord can wait?

JULY 7

Expectations

In the morning, LORD, you hear my voice;
in the morning I lay my requests before you
and wait expectantly.

—PSALM 5:3

Expectations—we all have them. I can still remember meeting my first college roommate. I had certain expectations for our relationship and, for the most part, those were met. Through the years, however, reality hasn't always lived up to my thoughts or imagination.

At times I've set my expectations so high they were bound to fail. Other times I've purposely chosen low expectations so I wouldn't face disappointment.

From the verses above, we have no idea what requests the psalmist has made. Were they realistic? Were they outlandish? Perhaps the more important question to ask is: Was God able to meet those requests?

We don't know the nature of what he was requesting, but the answer to that final question is yes: "God is able to bless you abundantly, so that in all things at all times, having all that you need, you will abound in every good work" (2 Corinthians 9:8).

God is able. Will he do precisely what you have asked? Only if it is best!

KEEP THIS IN MIND

God loves you and hears your requests, and his answers are always what is best for you.

JULY 8

Open My Eyes

Open my eyes that I may see
wonderful things in your law.

—PSALM 119:18

The verse above from Psalm 119 brought an interesting thought to mind. What if I began each day by praying that God would open my eyes to see the wonderful things he had for me in his Word?

It can be too easy to sit down with your Bible, read the Word, and cross that task off your to-do list. You have another of the day's chores finished! It is also possible to read with your eyes closed—not literally, but figuratively. Your eyes can be closed to the true message. If that's the case, you could be missing the wonderful things in God's law.

What's the solution? Instead of simply reading the verses that come next in your study plan or devotional, instead of hurrying through God's word, take time to pray the words of Psalm 119:18. Ask the Lord to open your eyes, and then be prepared to learn and grow for he *will* answer your prayer.

LET'S PRAY

Father, too many times I rush through my quiet time, treating it like a chore and not a divine appointment. Please forgive me and let me see the wonderful things in your Word.

JULY 9

Do These Things

LORD, who may dwell in your sacred tent?
Who may live on your holy mountain?

—PSALM 15:1

David asks God two questions in Psalm 15:1. Then he goes on in verses 2 through 5 to give the answers.

The one whose walk is blameless.
who does what is righteous,
who speaks the truth from their heart;
whose tongue utters no slander,
who does no wrong to a neighbor,
and casts no slur on others;
who despises a vile person
but honors those who fear the LORD;
who keeps an oath even when it hurts,
and does not change their mind;
who lends money to the poor without interest;
who does not accept a bribe against the innocent.

These are portions of the law, and they're followed with the promise that whoever follows the law will not be shaken. That was true before the sacrifice of Jesus. He fulfilled the law. Knowing him allows you to live with God eternally.

IT'S TRUE

Jesus paid it all because of love.

JULY 10

Anything Worth Doing

"For I myself am a man under authority,
with soldiers under me. I tell this one,
'Go,' and he goes; and that one, 'Come,' and he comes.
I say to my servant, 'Do this,' and he does it."

—MATTHEW 8:9

"Anything worth doing is worth doing well." Recently I heard that adage with a little twist: "Anything worth doing should be done. Period!" That version reminded me of a lovely older woman I had the privilege of worshiping with every Sunday for over thirty years.

Mary was a practical woman who wasn't afraid to share ideas, answers, and helpful hints with the younger women in the congregation. One of those hints has stayed with me for years.

Mary said that when the Lord brings to mind something kind you can do for someone, do it! Don't wait for the perfect time or until you've analyzed all the aspects of the deed. If you feel he has given you an idea that would bless someone, do it!

Mary's words remind me that good deeds should be done sooner rather than later.

FOOD FOR THOUGHT

Has the Lord been prodding you to do an act of kindness that you've been postponing? Now is the time to deliver that blessing.

JULY 11

Hearing from God

He says, "Be still, and know that I am God;
I will be exalted among the nations,
I will be exalted in the earth."

—Psalm 46:10

God can silently communicate with you as you read his Word. The Bible is a love letter from him filled to overflowing with instructions and assurances of his everlasting love.

Being still and listening to the still small voice of God as you pray is another important component in your communication with the Lord. The whisper of God's voice is heard more clearly when you quiet yourself and turn your ears, your heart, and your mind to him.

Your heavenly Father speaks through his Word, in a still small voice, and on occasion he seems to shout. Those are the times when there is no doubt about the direction you are receiving from him. It is loud and clear, and there is no uncertainty about what he expects from you.

LET'S PRAY

Lord, you know what is happening in my life and you know precisely how I should handle the situation. Please make your way clear to me as I read your Word, pray, and wait for your direction.

JULY 12

A Friendship

Just as you received Christ Jesus as Lord,
continue to live your lives in him, rooted and built up
in him, strengthened in the faith as you were taught,
and overflowing with thankfulness.

—Colossians 2:6–7

There was a time in your life when you chose to receive Christ Jesus as Lord. You may have known about him for years before you made that decision. There is a difference, however, between knowing about someone and actually meeting that person.

There are people I know something about and have never met, and there are people I might recognize if our paths crossed once again. We have not developed a friendship. A casual meeting doesn't guarantee that person is now more than an acquaintance.

As a believer, your relationship with the Lord goes well beyond acquaintance. It is a friendship that will grow stronger each day as you continue to live in him, rooted and built up, strengthened in faith, and overflowing with kindness.

YOUR FRIENDSHIP

The Lord wants to have an intimate, growing friendship with you. Do your part to nurture that friendship.

JULY 13

The Basics

One of them, an expert in the law, tested him with this question: "Teacher, which is the greatest commandment in the Law?" Jesus replied: "'Love the Lord your God with all your heart and with all your soul and with all your mind.' This is the first and greatest commandment. And the second is like it: 'Love your neighbor as yourself.' All the Law and the Prophets hang on these two commandments."

—MATTHEW 22:35–40

I remember hearing the story of a famous professional football coach who decided his players' fundamentals of performance were in need of some attention. His noted lecture began with these words: "Gentlemen, this is a football." Now that's an example of really getting down to the basics.

Jesus reminded people of the basics too: the greatest commandment in the Law. He told them to love the Lord with everything they had. Then moments later, he told those listening and all of us who read his words today, to "love your neighbor as yourself" (v. 39).

The basics? The greatest commandment? Love!

LET'S PRAY

Father, I want to follow your commands, the basics of the faith. Lord, I want to love the way you love.

JULY 14

Perfect Timing

Wait for the LORD;
be strong and take heart
and wait for the LORD.

—PSALM 27:14

Sometimes God says yes. Sometimes he says no. Sometimes he says to wait. Of those three answers, I believe that waiting is the most difficult for me to accept. Even a no seems better. Yes or no brings closure and finality. Wait does not.

Waiting for the Lord can be a very long and lonely process. Waiting for something is also rather countercultural. We are told that we must be proactive in all we do. Getting down to business is not only expected, but also applauded. Waiting on God is not *proactive* in the traditional sense.

Waiting until the Lord directs you means giving up control and—well, just waiting. Waiting for the Lord is not being lazy. It is a courageous, faith-filled trust that God will respond. Remember, your heavenly Father is never early, and he's never late. Waiting on him does not ruin your timing. It perfects it!

LET'S PRAY

Patience is not easy, Lord. Waiting for you to respond can take more patience than I seem to have. That's when I need and want to remember that you see the big picture and you will answer me when the time is right.

JULY 15

Your Desires

Take delight in the LORD,
and he will give you the desires of your heart.
—PSALM 37:4

The verse above has two important parts. It begins with the instruction to "delight in the LORD," followed by the outcome that will result from following the instruction: "he will give you the desires of your heart."

To some that verse may sound like a formula for getting something you really, really want. All you have to do in order to get the desires of your heart is to claim delight in the Lord. A person can formulate his own desires and then expect the Lord to fulfill those desires. Right?

Wrong! Wrong unless God places those desires in your heart. When you truly delight in God that is exactly what occurs. His desires become yours.

THERE'S NO DOUBT

All of God's promises are true. Delighting in the Lord and letting God place his desires in your heart guarantees you will receive those desires from him. What an amazing promise.

JULY 16

Abba, Father

The Spirit you received does not make you slaves,
so that you live in fear again;
rather, the Spirit you received brought about
your adoption to sonship.
And by him we cry, "Abba, Father."

—ROMANS 8:15

Abba is an intimate term for God as Father. As a believer, God is not some distant acquaintance or long-lost relative. God is your Father, and you can cry to him.

That knowledge is reassuring, but for some it can be difficult to understand. Perhaps you have fond memories of a loving father—a "daddy" who was always there for you, teaching you about the Lord and telling you that you were lovable, capable, and beautiful. Knowing your earthly father's love may have helped you understand God's love.

Or you may have had an absent father—physically or emotionally. You may not know your earthly father or think of him with fond memories.

It doesn't matter which description is more accurate when it comes to your personal history because you've been adopted into the family of God. By the Spirit you can cry, "Abba, Father."

IT CAN BE DIFFICULT

Relating to God as a loving father is hard if your earthly father didn't fit that description. No dad is perfect. Now is the time to claim your new family and let the Lord embrace you with his perfect love.

JULY 17

Love You

The LORD appeared to us in the past, saying:
"I have loved you with an everlasting love;
I have drawn you with unfailing kindness."

—JEREMIAH 31:3

The words "Love you!" seem to be spoken with much more frequency today than in the past. The "Good-bye!" that was traditionally used to end a phone conversation has been replaced with a questionably sincere "Love you!" Perhaps the absence of the word *I* at the beginning of that statement keeps it more lighthearted and less committed—which leads me to ask: What does "Love you!" actually mean?

In some cases, maybe it is simply a shortened version of the statement declaring love for an individual. At other times, it is probably a throwaway remark. I suppose it's up to every individual to interpret those two words.

In contrast, the words in Jeremiah 31:3 are very clear. God states that he has "loved you with an everlasting love."

From the beginning until the end, he can truthfully say the words: "I love you."

ONLY GOD

The love of one person for another cannot be described as an everlasting love. Only God's love will endure forever, throughout all eternity. His love is a precious gift.

JULY 18

Nothing

For I am convinced that neither death nor life,
neither angels nor demons, neither the present nor
the future, nor any powers, neither height nor depth,
nor anything else in all creation, will be able to
separate us from the love of God
that is in Christ Jesus our Lord.

—Romans 8:38–39

The apostle Paul was absolutely sure that nothing could separate a believer from the love of God. In the Scripture above, he made an impressive list of things that might try and fail. And in Romans 8:35, he suggested a few other things that might do their best to separate you from God's love: "Shall trouble or hardship or persecution or famine or nakedness or danger or sword?"

It's unlikely you've faced famine, nakedness, or the sword, but it's very possible you've encountered trouble, hardship, persecution, or danger. No matter what you've gone through or what you're experiencing this very moment, God loves you. No perils known to man can separate you from his love.

KNOW THIS

You may not feel loved; you may not feel like loving him; but that does not change the fact that God loves you. Remember: "Jesus loves me, this I know; for the Bible tells me so."

JULY 19

An Overcomer

"I have told you these things, so that in me you may have peace. In this world you will have trouble. But take heart! I have overcome the world."

—JOHN 16:33

"In this world you will have trouble." Those are the words of Jesus—the accurate, precise, truthful words of Jesus. He didn't make this uncontroversial statement to depress or overwhelm you; the Word says he "told you these things so that in [him] you may have peace."

Being a child of God does not mean you are exempt from the troubles in this world, but you can have peace in spite of the difficulties of life. You can be confident and undaunted because you are filled with the Spirit of the One who has overcome the world.

In order to live in the incredible peace that only God can provide, you must heed the words found in Isaiah 26:3: "[God] will keep in perfect peace those whose minds are steadfast, because they trust in [him]."

LET'S PRAY

Lord, my desire is to keep my thoughts and mind on you and your goodness. I trust you and your Word, and I long for your peace. Help me on the days when my confidence and trust waver.

JULY 20

Love Is

Love is patient, love is kind. It does not envy,
it does not boast, it is not proud. It does not dishonor
others, it is not self-seeking, it is not easily angered,
it keeps no record of wrongs. Love does not delight
in evil but rejoices with the truth. It always protects,
always trusts, always hopes, always perseveres.

—1 Corinthians 13:4–7

You are God's child, a woman who knows that God loves her. He has chosen you to love him. His word tells you that he is love (1 John 4:8).

Typically, there is some resemblance between a child and her parent. The Scripture from 1 Corinthians describes love; it describes God. Take a minute and see if you can replace your name in that description. Fill in the blanks.

________ is patient, ________ is kind. ________ does not envy, ________ does not boast, ________ is not proud. ________ does not dishonor others, ________ is not self-seeking, ________ is not easily angered, ________ keeps no record of wrongs. ________ does not delight in evil but rejoices with the truth. ________ always protects, always trusts, always hopes, always perseveres.

HOW DID YOU DO?

Choose one description of love where filling in the blank with your name made you uncomfortable. Ask God to help you in that specific area to make you resemble him more completely.

JULY 21

A Peculiar People

But ye are a chosen generation, a royal priesthood, an holy nation, a peculiar people; that ye should shew forth the praises of him who hath called you out of darkness into his marvelous light.

—1 PETER 2:9 KJV

If you were to call someone peculiar, chances are it would be considered an insult. That person would presume you find them weird or odd or at best curious. Yet in the verse above, you and all believers are classified as "peculiar people."

The writer of 1 Peter isn't trying to insult you, so don't be offended by his words. He means that as a child of God, you are not like the crowd. You don't react the way the majority of the people react. You are not easily angered and you're quick to forgive. Let's face it; that's just not normal.

Spending time with other "peculiar people" is a good idea. Finding others who refrain from anger and forgive even when the offender hasn't extended an apology will encourage you to welcome that label. There could be no better position than to be "a chosen generation, a royal priesthood, an holy nation, and a peculiar people."

YOUR JOB

Let it show; let others know!

JULY 22

He Makes Me Crazy

Because the LORD had closed Hannah's womb,
her rival kept provoking her in order to irritate her.

—1 SAMUEL 1:6

It was the middle of the day when I received a phone call from one of my sons. Since my kids reached adulthood, I've never hesitated to permit them to speak into my life. There are times, however, when I question the intelligence of encouraging them to do just that.

I answered the phone and engaged in a few minutes of entertaining chitchat. When his tone became more serious, I knew he had things on his mind. My feeling was confirmed as he began to point out something I needed to be aware of and potentially change.

He had permission to speak into my life with candor and honesty. I was willing to listen and take action if I felt it was best. In this particular case, I didn't—and I'll admit I found his words rather annoying.

Rather than disagreeing, I told him I'd take his recommendation under prayerful consideration. After saying good-bye I sighed and uttered these words: "Sometimes he makes me crazy!"

Then I smiled, turned my face heavenward, and asked the Lord; "Do you ever say that about your kids?"

SO

Whether the answer is yes or no, God never stops loving his kids, and their moms don't stop either.

JULY 23

His Kids

Do everything without grumbling or arguing, so that you may become blameless and pure, "children of God without fault in a warped and crooked generation." Then you will shine among them like stars in the sky.

—PHILIPPIANS 2:14–15

I have friends from childhood who are no longer a part of my life. Even with the advent of social media and things like Facebook and Twitter, I really don't know them anymore. We no longer talk together every day or even once a year.

Those same people may have no idea I have three sons. They don't know my children or my grandchildren and they really don't know me.

As a Christian, you are a child of God and there are people in your life who don't know or understand who you really are because they don't know *whose* you are.

God calls you his child because of the love he has for you and because of your decision to love him back. His desire is that the people in your life will also become his children.

You can help them get to know your heavenly Father by demonstrating his attitude and being prepared to tell others about him.

LOOK FOR OPPORTUNITIES

God will give you openings to demonstrate his love. Let him guide your words.

JULY 24

The Motivation

For God so loved the world that he gave his one and only Son, that whoever believes in him shall not perish but have eternal life.

—John 3:16

I was sitting quietly as the morning message began with the reading of a familiar Scripture, John 3:16. The words of that Scripture were well-known, but I had never heard them read quite like they were that day.

"For God sooooooo loved the world that he gave his one and only Son." Those words, with the emphasis on the vastness of God's love, his motivation for the sacrifice, definitely caught my attention.

I'm a mom with sons, not one, but three. I wondered, was there anyone I loved sooooooo much that I'd give one of my sons as a sacrifice. I couldn't think of anyone.

And the sacrifice of Jesus was not for a good friend or a close relative; it was for "the world."

"Very rarely will anyone die for a righteous person, though for a good person someone might possibly dare to die" (Romans 5:7).

For God so loved you; for God so loved your children; for God so loved the ones who would never choose to love him back; that he gave his one and only Son.

GOD SOOOOOOO LOVED

God so loved ________ that he gave his Son. Fill in the blank with the name of someone who needs to experience that love.

JULY 25

The Right Combination

By faith Abraham, when called to go to a place
he would later receive as his inheritance, obeyed and went,
even though he did not know where he was going.
By faith he made his home in the promised land
like a stranger in a foreign country;
he lived in tents, as did Isaac and Jacob,
who were heirs with him of the same promise.
For he was looking forward to the city with foundations,
whose architect and builder is God.

—Hebrews 11:8–10

Abraham is a man whose faith was clearly illustrated by his actions. God called him to leave his home, to leave the familiar, and to travel to a foreign land. Because of his faith in the Lord, he obeyed. His actions and his faith went hand in hand.

There are several examples in Hebrews 11—examples of others whose faith and works were intertwined. God wants each of his children to walk by faith and do good works for the kingdom. That's his desire for you, and the importance of combining faith and works is underlined by Hebrews 11:6: "And without faith it is impossible to please God, because anyone who comes to him must believe that he exists and that he rewards those who earnestly seek him."

SO

Make it your goal to please God—believing he exists, seeking him, and doing good works for his glory.

JULY 26

Direction

We have confidence in the Lord that you are doing
and will continue to do the things we command.
May the Lord direct your hearts into
God's love and Christ's perseverance.

—2 THESSALONIANS 3:4–5

One of the responsibilities of a mom is to guide, direct, and teach her children. That responsibility begins when kids are very young. Just think of the many things you have taught or will teach your children.

Before they leave your home, you'll have the opportunity to teach them everything from manners to math; and even more important than those lessons is the privilege you'll have of teaching them what you have allowed God to teach you. Ultimately your children will make the choice to live out the things you have taught them or to ignore your teaching.

You are God's child, he is able to direct your heart "into God's love and Christ's perseverance." It is your choice, however, to take his direction and learn from him. Both you and your kids will make the choice to either follow in the direction of God's love or take a more perilous route through life.

LET'S PRAY

Lord, help me to effectively share your love with my children. Help me direct their paths in the way of righteousness.

JULY 27

A Safe Place

Dear friends, by building yourselves up in your most
holy faith and praying in the Holy Spirit,
keep yourselves in God's love as you wait for
the mercy of our Lord Jesus Christ
to bring you to eternal life.

—JUDE 20–21

When my children were young, I enforced rules for their well-being. "You need to hold my hand. We're in a parking lot, and running to the door on your own could be very dangerous. You're still little, and it's difficult for drivers to see you."

In Jude 20–21, God provides different instructions for the well-being of every believer. As God's child you are reminded to "keep yourself in God's love." You are to stay in the safety and security of the boundaries of that love.

Just as you set boundaries for your children, God does the same. They are not arbitrary and they are not motivated by anything but love. He loves you so much that he has given you his Word and his Holy Spirit to guide you and keep you from danger.

YOUR CHILDREN AND GOD'S CHILDREN

There are many parallels between the boundaries God sets for you in love, and the boundaries you set for your children to keep them from harm.

JULY 28

His Representative

No one who is born of God [deliberately, knowingly, and habitually] practices sin, because God's seed [His principle of life, the essence of His righteous character] remains [permanently] in him [who is born again—who is reborn from above—spiritually transformed, renewed, and set apart for His purpose]; and he [who is born again] cannot *habitually* [live a life characterized by] sin, because he is born of God *and* longs to please Him.

—1 JOHN 3:9 AMP

I'm not sure what you have on your résumé, but as a Christian, as one reconciled to God, you can include this: "God's child, renewed and set apart for His purpose." In that role, your job is to represent him as accurately and effectively as possible. He wants to use you to encourage others to accept his gift of love.

It can be difficult to share the truth of God's saving grace with people who know you well. Take your own children, for example. They know many of the mistakes and missteps you've made as a believer and maybe even the ones that occurred before you were born of God.

But have courage! Encouraging others to recognize the love of Jesus and to choose to love him too pleases God.

REALIZE THIS

Being Christ's representative is a high calling. The Lord trusts you to carry his message to a hurting world.

JULY 29

Favoritism

As for those who were held in high esteem—
whatever they were makes no difference to me;
God does not show favoritism—
they added nothing to my message.

—Galatians 2:6

God doesn't show favoritism. His love for you is not based on your performance or your usefulness. He loves you because that is his nature. You don't deserve his love, and you can't earn it. God loves you—*period.*

Your love for your children is a flawed replica of God's love. When you're on your game, you show no favoritism. Other times one child may move up the ranks a bit. This lack of perfection does not specifically define you; it defines the human race.

The good news is that God is perfect! He is perfect in all of his ways, and his love knows no bounds. He will not compare you to the mom down the street. You know the one—she's the mom who undoubtedly makes fewer mistakes than you; the one who hardly ever favors one child over another.

Showing favoritism isn't God's nature. You are his child and therefore his favorite.

IT'S TRUE

There is no competition in the family of God. Everyone there is a winner!

JULY 30

Thank You

Always giving thanks to God the Father for everything,
in the name of our Lord Jesus Christ.

—Ephesians 5:20

Most mothers do their best to teach their children to say please and thank you at an early age. Kids learn that asking, "May I please have another cookie?" is much more effective than simply shouting, "Cookie!" Likewise, saying thank you for a cookie is bound to make a mother smile. Children are well on their way to developing grateful attitudes when those words are a part of their vocabularies. The goal is to teach them to give thanks to God.

More than anything or anyone else, God is worthy of your praise. As a child of God who is living her life in him, you are to be thankful. Wait—not just thankful, but overflowing with thankfulness!

IT'S TIME

Now is the time to give the Lord thanks for loving you as his child; for giving you grace you do not deserve; and for allowing you to spend eternity with him in heaven. Praise God!

JULY 31

God's Children

See what great love the Father has lavished on us,
that we should be called children of God!
And that is what we are!
The reason the world does not know us
is that it did not know him.

—1 John 3:1

You are God's child. Take a minute and let the truth of those words sink into your very being. He loves you and he chose to make you a member of his family. This is not a temporary arrangement.

Those around you who don't understand the reality of God or his love will not know why you are so thankful to be a part of the family of God. That's because they haven't officially met your heavenly Father . . . yet.

Perhaps you'll have an opportunity to make the introduction. Be on the lookout for that possibility. You never know what God will do, but his Word says he doesn't want anyone to perish.

"The Lord is not slow in keeping his promise, as some understand slowness. Instead he is patient with you, wanting everyone to come to repentance" (2 Peter 3:9).

LET'S PRAY

Father, I want to be able to hear your voice telling me it's the perfect time to share the story of your love. Give me listening ears and the courage to speak.

GOD LOVES YOUR CHILD MORE THAN YOU DO

"If you, then, though you are evil,
know how to give good gifts to your children,
how much more will your Father in heaven
give good gifts to those who ask him!"

—MATTHEW 7:11

AUGUST 1

No Secrets

"Come, see a man who told me everything I ever did. Could this be the Messiah?"

—JOHN 4:29

In the book of John, we read about the woman at the well. After she had a life-changing encounter with Christ, she went back to her village to tell others about him. The woman encouraged those she saw to "come, see a man who told me everything I ever did."

How could Jesus do that? Where did he get his information? I'm sure that was what the woman and the people in her village were wondering.

The answer is simple. Christ could tell her everything she had ever done because God knows everything. He knows everything you and your children have ever done too; there is nothing that is kept secret from him.

That fact might be startling to grasp, but it's true. You might be able to think of one or two things you wish he didn't know. Your kids might have a secret or two that you don't know, but none of their secrets are hidden from God.

JUST THE FACTS

Nothing is hidden from God, and he loves you and your children unconditionally. But God demonstrates his own love for us in this: "While we were still sinners, Christ died for us" (Romans 5:8).

AUGUST 2

Now What?

"Our God, will you not judge them? For we have no power to face this vast army that is attacking us. We do not know what to do, but our eyes are on you."

—2 CHRONICLES 20:12

The words from 2 Chronicles 20:12 are the words of Jehoshaphat, the king of Judah. The people in his command, the people for whom he was responsible, were under attack; so Jehoshaphat turned to God for answers.

At first he questioned the Lord, asking him why he wasn't simply striking the enemy down. Jehoshaphat explained the dilemma they were in, and he admitted his helplessness and his inability to solve their problem. Then he turned his eyes to the Lord for direction.

What situation are you facing today? Do you feel powerless to solve the problems of your son or daughter? Keep in mind the great love God has for your child and join the king of Judah. Admit you don't know what to do and focus your eyes on the One who does.

IT'S TRUE

There is no one who can give you better guidance and direction. You may not know what to do, but God does. Keep your eyes on him and wait for his answer.

AUGUST 3

God's Will

Do not conform to the pattern of this world,
but be transformed by the renewing of your mind.
Then you will be able to test and approve what God's
will is—his good, pleasing and perfect will.

—ROMANS 12:2

The words of the pastor pierced my heart. He was speaking of praying for his daughter as she traveled overseas on a mission trip. As he talked about praying for her safety and well-being, I immediately thought of the times I had prayed the same prayer for my children. Then he said something that was a startling wake-up call.

He said that in the midst of his prayer he changed his thinking and began to pray for his daughter to be in the center of God's will. He prayed this, trusting that God Almighty loved his daughter even more than he did.

I had to think. Was I willing to give up *my* desires for my children, *my* hopes, *my* dreams for them? Was I willing to put my children into the hands of the Lord who loves them with an everlasting love?

THE CHALLENGE

God wants to hear the concerns on your heart. He also wants you to know of his great love for your children. Pray for them to be in the center of God's will.

AUGUST 4

Peace

Now may the Lord of peace himself give you
peace at all times and in every way.
The Lord be with all of you.
—2 THESSALONIANS 3:16

The words from 2 Thessalonians are a benediction, a prayer asking for God's blessing. Paul, Silas, and Timothy asked God to give the Thessalonians peace "at all times and in every way." That would be a pretty amazing thing to receive—God's continual peace.

Motherhood is not typically characterized by unwavering peace. There are ups and downs of emotion. Yes, at times things are peaceful, but there are also times of chaos and disappointment.

It's not that God is withholding his peace in those times of turmoil. Perhaps the lack of peace has to do with you refusing to receive the gift God is offering. Could it be that on occasion you've allowed the circumstance you are in to rob you of the peace God has to offer?

That question is simply food for thought delivered to you by someone who has allowed certain situations to steal her peace and consequently the peace of those around her.

LET'S PRAY

Father, you offer peace to those who love you. Help me receive your gift of peace and share it with my children.

AUGUST 5

Sleep Soundly

I lift up my eyes to the mountains—
where does my help come from?
My help comes from the LORD,
the Maker of heaven and earth.
He will not let your foot slip—
he who watches over you will not slumber;
indeed, he who watches over Israel
will neither slumber nor sleep.

—PSALM 121:1–4

I'm a very sound sleeper. Most of the time it takes something pretty spectacular to wake me up. I can sleep through all the normal "night noises" at our home. My kids used to be required to report in when they arrived home after a ball game or an outing, and the next morning they'd laughingly ask me if I even remembered them telling me good night. The truth was I seldom did.

Being a sound sleeper isn't all that bad, although I'm certain there were times I should have been a little more alert. What a blessing it is to know that the Lord never sleeps; he is on duty at all times, watching over you and the ones you love. He is paying attention to all that is happening and doesn't need you or your kids to report in.

REMEMBER

The Lord, the Maker of heaven and earth, the One who loves you and your children, never sleeps. You can sleep well, for he is wide awake.

AUGUST 6

Somebody!

The eyes of the LORD are on the righteous,
and his ears are attentive to their cry.

—PSALM 34:15

Years ago my brother was surprised to hear the cry of a young child coming from outside his home. He glanced out the window and saw a little girl about three years old sitting on the sidewalk by her tricycle. The little bike was overturned, and it was obvious she and the tricycle had experienced some trouble.

As she sat and wept, she was also yelling as loudly as she could, "Somebody! Somebody!"

My brother decided he fell into the category of "somebody," and ran outside to see if he could help. He heard her cry and went to her rescue. Just as he reached the little girl he saw her mother rushing to the scene. This mom had also heard her daughter's frantic cry for help and came running.

Mom, you aren't always there to hear the cry of your children, but you can be assured that as the psalmist said, the Lord hears the cry of the righteous. He is ready, willing, and able to be the "Somebody!" for you and for your child.

IT'S TRUE

Your limitations are not God's limitations. That fact can be incredibly comforting and reassuring. God's eyes and ears are on the righteous.

AUGUST 7

Day and Night

Blessed is the one
who does not walk in step with the wicked
or stand in the way that sinners take
or sit in the company of mockers,
but whose delight is in the law of the LORD,

and who meditates on his law day and night.

—PSALM 1:1–2

Being a mom can lead to many a sleepless night. Moms aren't limited to sleep deprivation exclusively during the first year of their child's life, nor does the loss of sleep only come when that son or daughter reaches adolescence.

A mom with kids at any age can find herself in bed at night reliving a problem from earlier in the day. The next thing she knows, she has lost priceless, irreplaceable minutes or even hours when she could have been sleeping.

The truth is, it does almost no good to contemplate, reflect, or meditate on a difficult situation when it's time to get some sleep. Instead of pondering the problem, do what's recommended in Psalm 1: Meditate on the Word of God.

THE ULTIMATE CURE FOR INSOMNIA

When you or anyone you love is going through a difficulty, big or small, don't lose precious sleep worrying. Your time is better spent pondering, contemplating, reflecting, and meditating on God's Word.

AUGUST 8

Awesome God

Who among the gods is like you, LORD?
Who is like you—majestic in holiness,
awesome in glory, working wonders?
—EXODUS 15:11

I find some humor in the fact that when I pray and request a miracle from God, I'm truly amazed when I witness the answer to that prayer. Maybe you've had that same experience. You have a specific concern that you bring to God; you truly believe he is capable of responding to that request; and when he does, you find it overwhelming!

Why is it so surprising and amazing when—by his awesome power, might, and love—God responds? If it weren't possible for him to intervene in the situation, why would anyone even ask for his help at all? Is the problem a lack of faith? Is that why it is so astonishing when God answers prayer?

Being overwhelmed by the fact that God cares about every aspect of my life and the lives of my children is not a lack of faith. It is, in fact, an appropriate response, for our God is an awesome God!

HOW ABOUT YOU?

My hope, my prayer, my expectation is that I will always be overwhelmed by God, who is "majestic in holiness, awesome in glory, working wonders."

AUGUST 9

Upside Down Thinking

He said to them, "You are the ones who justify yourselves in the eyes of others, but God knows your hearts. What people value highly is detestable in God's sight."

—LUKE 16:15

I heard a mother tell her son they needed to start doing some upside down thinking. Beforehand, the young boy had been very upset and disappointed, and his mother was trying to help him see beyond the obvious—to see that God could turn an unfortunate incident around for good.

In this mom's view, "upside down thinking" meant thinking more in line with God than with the world. Many of the things valued by the world are unimportant in God's eyes. Some are even detestable.

When this boy was able to give his disappointment to God and trust him with the outcome, he was able to relax. He joined his mom in some upside down thinking and did his best to value what the Lord values.

FOOD FOR THOUGHT

Many things that are highly valued by mothers or by children have little or no value in the eyes of God. Maybe it's time to introduce a little upside down thinking in your home.

AUGUST 10

Next Right Choice

The prayer of a righteous person
is powerful and effective.

—JAMES 5:16

When my children were little, we prayed together every night. Many times they would share a concern with me. "Mom, we need to pray for Gordon. He didn't feel good at school today." They would share what was on their hearts and we would pray.

Then as the years went by, the boys no longer needed me to pray with them at night. That meant I wasn't typically aware of their concerns or the challenges they were facing. They may not have needed my guidance with bedtime prayers, but they were still in need of prayer. That was when I began to pray for each one by name, asking God to help him make the next right choice.

I didn't need to know what choices they were facing because God was with each one of them and knew what they would deal with throughout the day. I knew that God would be available to help each of my kids make the next right choice, then the next right choice, then the . . .

HE'S WITH YOUR CHILD

God is with your children and is able to help them make the next right choice. He loves them even more than you do.

AUGUST 11

Love You More

And I pray that you, being rooted and established in love, may have power, together with all the Lord's holy people, to grasp how wide and long and high and deep is the love of Christ,

—Ephesians 3:17–18

"Love you!"

"Love you more!"

The degree, the amount of love you have for a person, is very difficult to measure. I've always been confused by the dialogue above. How can someone know if his or her love is more or less than someone else's?

When my youngest son was born, his older brothers were very pleased and excited. It was fun to watch their reactions and listen to their words of love directed at their little brother.

I remember my second son, only a week away from his fourth birthday, looking at his baby brother and declaring, "I love him so much I could just squeeze his guts out!" Believe me, I made certain that declaration of love never came to pass.

I'm certain he still loves his brother today, maybe even more than he did years ago, but this truth remains: God loves each of your children more than anyone could.

GOD'S LOVE

His love for you and for your children cannot be measured, and it never fails.

AUGUST 12

Whatever It Takes

I want to know Christ—yes, to know the power of his resurrection and participation in his sufferings, becoming like him in his death, and so, somehow, attaining to the resurrection from the dead.

—PHILIPPIANS 3:10–11

The writer of Philippians is expressing his deep desire to know all there is to know about Christ. He's willing to do whatever it takes. Those words—"whatever it takes"—are difficult for a mother to pray concerning her children, even when the desired result is that child's salvation.

The tendency is to pray, "Whatever it takes . . . but keep him safe, healthy, and out of trouble." Most moms want to add multiple disclaimers to "whatever it takes."

It's easy for a mom to think God might need her help. "Lord, this is what you need to do in order for my child to accept the love you offer."

It's also easy to think that as the mother, you know what is best for your child. But when you are honest about your abilities compared to God's, you realize he definitely knows best. You love your child more than words can express, and God loves your child more than you do.

LET'S PRAY

Lord, I want my child to know you personally—not just know about you. My prayer is that you'll do whatever it takes to bring my child to a saving knowledge of you.

AUGUST 13

Challenges

They seldom reflect on the days of their life,
because God keeps them occupied with gladness of heart.

—ECCLESIASTES 5:20

I have a friend who gave birth to a child who is mentally disabled. Needless to say, that is a challenging situation. For many years I have admired this woman's attitude in regard to her circumstances.

I once heard her say that her responsibility was to help her daughter "be the best she could be." Her child cannot walk and can only say three words, but the mother has chosen not to be complacent. She is, however, content. She has chosen not to reflect on the difficulty of her days and instead to keep her eyes on the Lord—the one who knew her daughter even before she was born.

Every mom has challenges, and every mom can learn to be content in spite of those challenges. The key is to allow God to keep you "occupied with gladness of heart."

FOR YOU TO DO

Today is the day to begin the habit of focusing on the blessings of God that have made and continue to make your heart glad. With pen in hand, begin the list and do your best to continually add to it, allowing your heart to be filled.

AUGUST 14

It's a Boy!

"Before I formed you in the womb I knew you,
before you were born I set you apart;
I appointed you as a prophet to the nations."

—Jeremiah 1:5

I can still remember when the physician delivering my second son announced, "It's a boy!" I can also remember my naïve yet enthusiastic reply: "Oh good! I already know how to do boys."

My doctor, the father of five sons, probably rolled his eyes. More than anyone in the room at the time, he understood that having one son did not mean I knew all there was to know about being a mom to little boys.

It didn't take long for me to realize that too. After having three sons, all with the same father, the same grandparents, living in the same community, attending the same church, and on and on, let me be the first to declare that they are three very different individuals.

God created each one of my children and each one of yours. Even identical twins who share the same DNA are unique individuals—fearfully and wonderfully made by God who knew them even before they took their first breath.

JUST IMAGINE

Before your children were born, God already knew and loved them. That mind-boggling thought is true.

AUGUST 15

You've Got a Problem

"Ah, Sovereign Lord, you have made the heavens and the earth by your great power and outstretched arm. Nothing is too hard for you."

—Jeremiah 32:17

As a mom, you may have encountered a problem or two with your child that seems absolutely impossible to solve. At one point it occurred to me that the difficulties that appear to be so insurmountable and difficult are not really mine to solve.

Even though that may be the case, I can still find myself laboring and stressing to come up with a solution. It's quite possible I am neither capable nor competent, yet I choose to waste my time and effort. When I finally realize the truth, I also realize it would be much better if I simply relinquish control to God.

When that happens, I no longer have an impossible problem. Granted, there might still be a problem, and it might still seem impossible; but it will be God's problem to solve. I simply admit, "God, you've got a problem."

His reply, if indeed I could hear his voice from heaven, would be: "Don't worry. I've got it. Nothing is too hard for me."

MY PRAYER FOR YOU

Giving your problems to God, the One who is more than able, is a choice. I pray that you will make that very good choice.

AUGUST 16

Joy, Patience, and Faithfulness

Be joyful in hope,
patient in affliction, faithful in prayer.

—ROMANS 12:12

For years I had a little ornament hanging on the knob of my breadbox. It had the word *Pray* in the middle in bold letters, and surrounding that word was the aforementioned verse: "Be joyful in hope, patient in affliction, faithful in prayer."

The three directives in that verse work together as one important path for you, Mom. In order for you to be joyful in hope, joyful as you wait for the unseen promise of God, you must be patient in affliction, in hardship or difficulty, and also faithful in prayer.

Prayer puts your focus where it belongs—not on the affliction, but on your heavenly Father. He is the One who is more than able and who loves your children even more than you do. Prayer will help you remember that any suffering your children might be experiencing is only temporary. Being faithful in prayer is essential to being joyful and patient.

LET'S PRAY

God, I know you are capable of giving me both joy and patience. That is my prayer.

AUGUST 17

Join in Prayer

I urge you, brothers and sisters, by our
Lord Jesus Christ and by the love of the Spirit,
to join me in my struggle by praying to God for me.
—Romans 15:30

When your children grow up and leave your home, there will probably be times when you'd like to be helpful, but the distance between you makes that impossible. You usually cannot drop everything and hop on an airplane or drive for hours at the drop of a hat.

So does that mean you're no help at all? Absolutely not! You can pray. Your prayers can reach around the country and around the world.

If your child is struggling, you can join in the fight by praying. You are never too far removed from those you love to offer real help, anywhere at anytime. Just pray. Prayer makes a difference.

LET'S PRAY

Lord, you know the struggles my kids are facing. I'm not even sure how to pray. Father, surround them with your love. Give them divine wisdom and keep them in the center of your will.

AUGUST 18

God's Love

I pray that you, being rooted and established in love,
may have power, together with all the Lord's holy people,
to grasp how wide and long and high and deep is the love of
Christ, and to know this love that surpasses knowledge—
that you may be filled to the measure of all the fullness of God.

—EPHESIANS 3:17–19

It's funny the things we moms remember from being pregnant. My oldest son was two and I was expecting again. More than once I remember wondering if I would have enough love for a second child.

It was as though I imagined I had a finite number of love units. My concern was that I might have used up too many on child number one. Would I have any love left for this second child of mine?

You know the answer to that silly question. Love is not stored in units, and no one is limited when it comes to either giving or receiving love. I had just as much love for my second son, my second gift from God, and also for my third child. Love never runs out.

That fact is illustrated beautifully when you consider the love of God. His love is beyond measure.

IT'S TRUE

God's love is available to all and is freely given. It is wide and high and long and deep and surpasses knowledge, confounding even the wise. He will always have enough love to share.

AUGUST 19

Peek-a-Boo

Nothing in all creation is hidden from God's sight.
Everything is uncovered and laid bare before the eyes
of him to whom we must give account.

—HEBREWS 4:13

Playing peek-a-boo with a young child is an interesting experience. The child hides his eyes behind his hands or another barrier and assumes he is completely invisible. He can't see you, so it's obvious (at least to the child) you can't see him.

Many times, older children and young adults make a similar assumption. They cannot see the Lord, so they believe he can't see them. It's clear that they are mistaken in that belief too.

Mom, you can't always be with your child to guide his actions and decisions. It wouldn't be healthy if you could. But God, your heavenly Father who loves your child even more than you do, will be there. Nothing is hidden from his sight, and he will be expecting an account of all he has seen.

IT'S TRUE

There is no hiding from God. He is able to see all we do and hear all we say. Rather than feeling frightened by that truth, you can choose to rejoice that God is always with you and with your children.

AUGUST 20

More Than These?

When they had finished eating, Jesus said to Simon Peter, "Simon son of John, do you love me more than these?"

—JOHN 21:15

I love marinated, grilled chicken breasts. It's undoubtedly one of my favorite foods. There are several factors that push that dish to the top of my list. First of all, it's easy to prepare, especially when someone else is in charge of the grill. More importantly, it tastes good.

I also love my husband and all our kids and their families. More than I love grilled chicken? Of course! The word *love* is used to describe several different feelings. As good as that chicken is, I love my family much more.

Jesus asked Peter an interesting question in John 21. "Do you love me more than these?" The "these" were the fish in Peter's net. Jesus wanted to know if Peter loved his occupation, his fish, more than he loved the Savior.

HERE'S A QUESTION FOR YOU TODAY

Is there anything you love more than Jesus? Do you love your children or your home or your husband or your job or [you name it] more than Christ? Rather than answering quickly, ask the Lord to help you make an honest evaluation.

AUGUST 21

Your Story

For we know that if the earthly tent we live in is destroyed, we have a building from God, an eternal house in heaven, not built by human hands.

—2 CORINTHIANS 5:1

Above the coat closet near the entrance to my home, there is a plaque that says, "Home is where your story begins." How true! Your story and the stories your children have may be happy, sad, or somewhere in between, but they probably began at home.

I've always thought there needed to be an addendum to those words—a little extension to add another thought. The perfect message would be: "Home is where your story begins . . . but it doesn't have to end there." Regardless of the quality of the memories you have from your youth and your original home, you can move forward and establish new ones.

More importantly, when you have a relationship with the living Lord, your story has a remarkable ending. "Home is where your story begins, and it goes on in heaven for eternity!"

IT'S POSSIBLE

Maybe your growing-up years were difficult. There can be countless explanations for the tough situation. Maybe you would rate them above average. Regardless of the past, your future home can be an upgrade, and your eternal home with Christ will be amazing!

AUGUST 22

Good Gifts

"If you then, though you are evil,
know how to give good gifts to your children,
how much more will your Father in heaven
give the Holy Spirit to those who ask him!"

—LUKE 11:13

"If you think *that* was good . . ." You've heard that phrase before, and you've probably said it too. The words, "If you think *that* was good . . ." are usually followed by a statement or a performance that has been deemed "even better."

Mom, you do your best to give your children good gifts. You love them, nurture them, encourage them, and correct them; but all those good gifts do not come close to the gift of God's Holy Spirit—the gift your Father in heaven will give "to those who ask him."

Jesus said, "The Advocate, the Holy Spirit, whom the Father will send in my name, will teach you all things and will remind you of everything I have said to you. . . . When the Advocate comes, whom I will send to you from the Father—the Spirit of truth who goes out from the Father—he will testify about me" (John 14:26; 15:26).

IF YOU THINK *THAT* WAS GOOD . . .

God's extraordinary gift of his Holy Spirit is even better!

AUGUST 23

God Is Smarter

Oh, the depth of the riches of the wisdom and knowledge of God! How unsearchable his judgments, and his paths beyond tracing out!
—ROMANS 11:33

Shortly after I came to know Jesus as my Savior, I found myself in a difficult situation. At the time, my knowledge of the Word of God was spotty at best. I had memorized a few verses, but let's face it: I was a beginner. Looking back, I understand why organized revivals encourage new Christians to get in an environment where they can study and learn, but I didn't come to Christ as the result of an "organized revival." When I found myself in this troubling situation, I was unprepared except for these two things: I knew God loved me, and I knew he was with me.

I prayed, asking the Lord to change the situation; but as I waited for him to do what I had asked, I sensed that he wanted to change me and not the situation. It didn't take long for me to agree, and I realized that even as a baby Christian I actually knew *three* things—not two. In addition to knowing God loved me and was with me, I knew he was smarter than me.

Today I know more about God's Word; we've walked together for decades. Even though my knowledge has increased, my hope is to never forget the fact that he is smarter than me.

AND

God is smarter than you. Trust him to do what is best, even if it means changing you.

AUGUST 24

If or Because

May your unfailing love be with us, LORD,
even as we put our hope in you.
—PSALM 33:22

God's love is unconditional. It is not based on your performance or the performance of your children. It is unwavering and unfailing. He does not love you because you are worthy of his love. He does not love you because you go to church each Sunday or volunteer at the youth center. He does not love you or your children "because."

His unconditional love also means it is not based on expectations. He does not love you if you continue to go to church each Sunday and volunteer at the youth center. He does not love you if you spend an hour each day in his Word. He does not love you or your children "if."

God loves you—period! God loves your children—period! His love is like no other. His love is unconditional and constant. No earthly love can match the love of your heavenly Father. He wants you and your children to choose to love him and live with him eternally.

LET'S PRAY

Father, it's difficult to even imagine a love like yours. I know I will never be able to match it. My prayer is simply that I may reflect it in my interactions with others, especially my own family.

AUGUST 25

Delightful

He brought me out into a spacious place;
he rescued me because he delighted in me.
—PSALM 18:19

Undoubtedly there are days when your child is absolutely delightful. She is pleasant and helpful and affectionate. I'm sure you can remember a day like that or at least a portion of a day.

By the same token, I know there are days or at least moments when you have been delightful. You've been lovely and charming and wonderful—at least for a while. We all have been; some for a longer time than others.

Personally, I know I'm much easier to love on those good days: those portions of a day when I'm being delightful. But God doesn't wait for those moments to love me, to love you, or to love your child.

Why? Because his love is not based on our changing behavior or attitudes; it is based on his unchanging nature. "Every good and perfect gift is from above, coming down from the Father of the heavenly lights, who does not change like shifting shadows" (James 1:17).

IT'S TRUE

God delights in you and will rescue you. His love for you is grounded in his very nature and will never change.

AUGUST 26

Don't Underestimate

Jonathan said to his young armor-bearer,
"Come, let's go over to the outpost of those uncircumcised men. Perhaps the LORD will act in our behalf. Nothing can hinder the LORD from saving, whether by many or by few."

—1 SAMUEL 14:6

In the Scripture above, it's easy to see that Jonathan didn't underestimate the power of God. He told his young armor-bearer that "nothing" could hinder the Lord from saving. He did not doubt the Lord's power or might but instead exhibited complete confidence in the One who can save.

That same confidence is reflected in the words of Zephaniah 3:17: "The LORD your God is with you, the Mighty Warrior who saves. He will take great delight in you; in his love he will no longer rebuke you, but will rejoice over you with singing."

The writer of Hebrews also echoes that confidence and calls Jesus the "author and finisher of our faith" (Hebrews 12:2 KJV).

You can have that same degree of assurance and confidence. Don't underestimate what the Lord can do. He has not changed, and neither has his love for you and for your child.

SO

Allow the Lord to work in your life and the life of your children, trusting that his ways are perfect and he is mighty to save.

AUGUST 27

Trust in the Lord

Trust in the LORD with all your heart
and lean not on your own understanding;
in all your ways submit to him,
and he will make your paths straight.

—PROVERBS 3:5–6

"What's a mother to do?" That was the opening line of a commercial for . . . Hmmm, I don't remember the product. Today I don't watch many TV ads, but that quote from the past is still in my memory: "What's a mother to do?"

Since I don't remember the answer that was given to that question, I'd like to suggest one myself—an answer from God's Word. What *is* a mother to do when she is concerned about her child? When that child is making poor decisions, or when she seems to be walking away from God rather than running to him, what is Mom supposed to do?

The answer is found in Proverbs 3:5–6. Trust in the Lord! This is not a call for some lighthearted, casual trust; you are to trust in him with *all* your heart instead of relying on what you can understand.

Trusting can be more difficult than doing, but it is what a mother should do. Then as the Lord makes your path straight, it will be time for doing what he directs.

HE SAID

First: Trust me. Second: Do as I say.

AUGUST 28

No Fear

There is no fear in love.
But perfect love drives out fear,
because fear has to do with punishment.
—1 JOHN 4:18

When your first baby arrived, chances are you got more than just an adorable little child. Typically it's a package deal. You get a cute, cuddly baby, and you get concern, apprehension, nervousness, and maybe even fear.

If you were the oldest child in your family, you may not have the slightest idea what I'm suggesting. You probably entered motherhood with more hours of practice than the workers at the daycare center.

Yet even if you began your new role with confidence and courage, there is something different about a child who is yours. He's your child to love and nurture and protect from the dangers of this world. That can be a daunting assignment, and occasionally you might find yourself teetering on the brink of fear.

That's because your love for your child, regardless of how strong and deep it is, is imperfect. God's love, in contrast, is perfect. He loves you and your child with perfect love.

HIS LOVE

It's wide and long and high and deep. It is perfect!

AUGUST 29

Comfort

"As a mother comforts her child,
so will I comfort you;
and you will be comforted over Jerusalem."
—Isaiah 66:13

God knows your heart. He knows that you love your child and that your desire is to comfort him.

A young child wants to hear his mother's calming voice when something has upset him. An older child may need you to console him after a disappointment or defeat. A teenager needs the reassurance that he will be fine and that his frustration will pass. You are there to encourage your child at every age and stage of his life, and so is the Lord.

God will comfort you and will comfort your child perfectly. He knows the struggle and he knows the enemy who is on the attack. "For our struggle is not against flesh and blood, but against the rulers, against the authorities, against the powers of this dark world and against the spiritual forces of evil in the heavenly realms" (Ephesians 6:12).

And God will win! "Ye are of God, little children, and have overcome them: because greater is he that is in you, than he that is in the world" (1 John 4:4 KJV).

AMEN!

Knowing that God will comfort your child in a more perfect way than you could ever imagine is a promise that brings peace.

AUGUST 30

God Is Always Near

What other nation is so great as to have
their gods near them the way the LORD our God
is near us whenever we pray to him?

—DEUTERONOMY 4:7

My children had just gotten to the age where I could allow them to be out of my direct sight in a store. With their newfound freedom came two very important rules.

Number one: You must stay together and not wander around on your own.

Number two: If anyone tries to grab one of you, I want both of you to yell, "Jesus!" at the top of your lungs.

The first rule probably makes perfect sense to you, but you might be wondering about the second. My thought was this: By crying, "Jesus!" as loud as they could, I would be able to hear them. More importantly, they would be praying—calling on the One who was right there!

I might be more than one aisle away, but the Lord God was nearer to them and would hear their cry. He is always near to you too.

BLESSED ASSURANCE

You are never alone, and neither are your children. God is always as near as a whispered (or shouted) prayer.

AUGUST 31

He Leads

The LORD is my shepherd; I shall not want.
He maketh me to lie down in green pastures:
he leadeth me beside the still waters.
He restoreth my soul: he leadeth me in the paths
of righteousness for his name's sake.

—PSALM 23:1–3 KJV

It's time for Follow the Leader, and God is "it." He promises to lead you "beside still waters" and "in the paths of righteousness for his name's sake." The Lord makes that same promise to your children. He will lead and guide them and give them strength.

Even if you wanted to give them rest, restore their strength, and help them do what honors God, you wouldn't be completely successful. That's why it is so incredibly wonderful that God loves you and every one of your children.

At this point you may still be praying for one of those kids to come to a saving knowledge of Christ. Don't stop praying, because God has not stopped loving your child.

He desires to walk with your child and comfort him. God wants to see that he dwells in the house of the Lord forever.

LET'S PRAY

Father, I want to see all my children holding your hand, walking with you here on earth and into eternity. Help me to avoid discouragement and instead to pray fervently.

GOD'S NOT KIDDING!

Whoever fears the LORD has a secure fortress,
and for their children it will be a refuge.
—PROVERBS 14:26

SEPTEMBER 1

Fear God

He said in a loud voice, "Fear God and give him glory,
because the hour of his judgment has come.
Worship him who made the heavens,
the earth, the sea and the springs of water."

—REVELATION 14:7

The room was crowded with teenagers, and we were doing a Bible study together. It was early in my lesson and a hand went up.

When I called on the teenage boy, he asked, "What in the world does it mean to 'fear God'? Is it like being afraid of snakes or spiders or rabid dogs?"

Another teenager was quick to offer his take on the phrase. "It means to respect God."

More comments followed.

"You mean like saying excuse me?"

"Or telling God please and thank you?"

It was my turn, and I did my best to answer the original question. "Fearing God means knowing he's not kidding. He's not kidding about his love, his grace, or his mercy. He's not kidding about his justice."

They sat quietly for a minute or two, evidently doing their best to understand my explanation. God is not kidding.

NOW IS THE TIME

If you have never taken the opportunity to help your own children understand the fear of the Lord, today might be the perfect day. Be certain you include the attributes of mercy and justice.

SEPTEMBER 2

Please God

As for other matters, brothers and sisters,
we instructed you how to live in order to please God,
as in fact you are living. Now we ask you and urge you
in the Lord Jesus to do this more and more.
For you know what instructions we gave you
by the authority of the Lord Jesus.

—1 THESSALONIANS 4:1–2

More than one teenager has operated under the premise that asking for forgiveness is far superior to asking for permission. "If I ask Mom, she might say no. If I do it and she's mad, I'll just ask for forgiveness."

That's an interesting strategy, but it isn't very bright.

God possesses all knowledge, and the Bible is a book of loving instruction and wise counsel. Following his guidance can protect both you and your child from suffering the consequences of poor decisions.

There are consequences for failing to follow his instructions, but God is willing to forgive his children: "In him we have redemption through his blood, the forgiveness of sins, in accordance with the riches of God's grace" (Ephesians 1:7).

SET AN EXAMPLE

Living "in order to please God," seeking his permission, is a choice. Ask God before you take action; then go, stop, or wait according to his direction.

SEPTEMBER 3

Obedience

But Samuel replied: "Does the LORD delight
in burnt offerings and sacrifices
as much as in obeying the LORD?
To obey is better than sacrifice
and to heed is better than the fat of rams."

—1 SAMUEL 15:22

God has given you incredible abilities that truly bless your life. Now you might be thinking, "Who, me?" Yes, you!

Here is one I know you possess. God has blessed you with the ability to be obedient to his instructions. It's important to note that he doesn't force you to be obedient or expect you to be perfectly obedient.

He has simply equipped you to do what he's asked you to do. You can choose to be obedient.

Being obedient to God isn't always easy, and it isn't necessarily comfortable or popular; but it always pleases God. "To obey is better than sacrifice." Obedience is a choice—a very good choice that you are more than able to make.

YOU CAN DO IT!

God knew from the very beginning that the instructions in his Word would not be easy to follow. That did not keep him from setting down guidelines that will help you lead an abundant life. Don't get discouraged when you fall short; ask him for forgiveness and carry on. You can do it!

SEPTEMBER 4

Please Listen

"If my people would only listen to me,
if Israel would only follow my ways,
how quickly I would subdue their enemies
and turn my hand against their foes!"
—PSALM 81:13–14

Have you ever been speaking to someone who obviously wasn't listening to you? That can happen when you're competing with the TV or a cell phone or iPad for someone's attention. The "listener" seems to be completely oblivious to your attempt to communicate.

I've been guilty of not really listening. In fact, when my kids were toddlers, each one did the same thing when he figured out that I wasn't listening. He would put his sweet, chubby, typically dirty little hands on my cheeks and turn my face to his. Once we were eyeball-to-eyeball, he would repeat his request or ask the question on his mind, knowing I was now truly listening.

Hmmm . . . I wonder if at times the Lord would like to put his hands on my cheeks and turn my face to his, just to be certain I am really listening. Has he ever wanted to do the same thing to you?

IT'S TRUE

Listening to God, truly listening, can bring great rewards. Listening and following his instruction will be more than worth the effort.

SEPTEMBER 5

Pay Attention

Then Jesus said,
"Whoever has ears to hear, let them hear."
—MARK 4:9

It is significant that God gave Adam and Eve two ears and only one mouth. It can be difficult to use those two senses in the right proportion—listening twice as much as you speak. Nevertheless, it is the wise thing to do.

More than once God challenges those reading his Word to listen—to use the ears they possess.

"Whoever has ears, let them hear" (Matthew 11:15).

"Whoever has ears, let them hear what the Spirit says to the churches" (Revelation 2:11).

Those words might seem like an unusual directive. Most people have ears, and most of those ears function well. The emphasis seems to be not on the ears themselves but on the choice everyone has to listen adequately and accurately to what the Lord is saying.

It might have been easier to understand if he had said, "Please focus," or "Work with me now," or "Pay attention." He didn't—but upon examination, it is easy to see that his words were just as clear: "Whoever has ears, let them hear."

LET'S PRAY

Lord, I don't always do a good job of listening. Sometimes I'm actually making up excuses to avoid following the instructions you're giving me. I have ears; let me hear from you.

SEPTEMBER 6

The Majesty of God

LORD, our Lord,
how majestic is your name in all the earth!
You have set your glory
in the heavens . . .
When I consider your heavens, the work of your fingers,
the moon and the stars,
which you have set in place,
what is mankind that you are mindful of them,
human beings that you care for them?
You have made them a little lower than the angels
and crowned them with glory and honor.

—PSALM 8:1, 3–5

God and only God can be described with such powerful words and images. He is truly an awesome God! It stretches my mind to realize that God, the almighty Creator, actually cares for me, for you, and for our children. Who are we? Mortals and mere humans, the psalmist says.

Not only does God care for you, but he has "crowned" you with "glory and honor." There is no doubt that your heavenly Father deserves your praise!

PRAISE HIM

Join the psalmist in his call to praise: "Let every thing that hath breath praise the LORD. Praise ye the LORD" (Psalm 150:6 KJV).

SEPTEMBER 7

Courage

"So keep up your courage, men,
for I have faith in God that it will
happen just as he told me."
—Acts 27:25

It can be easy to get the wrong idea about courage. Courage is not the lack of fear; it is fear rightly placed. As a courageous woman, a courageous mom, you know that it takes courage to fear God and keep his commands.

Keeping the commands of God is not an easy task, and living within the boundaries of love he has set is countercultural. It is, however, the logical result of fearing God, of knowing that he is not kidding about his mercy or his justice.

Fearing God and keeping his commandments might mean you stand for something your neighbor despises. Fearing God and keeping his commandments might mean you don't get the promotion you honestly deserve.

And let me be perfectly clear: Fearing God and keeping his commandments does not look like mindlessly correcting others or serving as judge and jury when it comes to someone else's actions.

God calls you to lead with grace without compromising the truth—to have the courage to stand for what is right.

IT'S TIME TO . . .

Lead with grace without compromising the truth.

SEPTEMBER 8

Obey God

Peter and the other apostles replied:
"We must obey God rather than human beings!"
—ACTS 5:29

I have a question for you. Do you obey God? If you answered yes, here's another question. Why do you obey God?

Years ago, one of my sons asked me that second question. I thought about it for a minute and then answered, "Because I love him."

His response surprised me. "Come on, Mom. I think you obey God because you're afraid of what might happen if you don't."

He presented an interesting challenge. After a moment I decided he was probably right, and so was I. When I first realized God loved me, I probably obeyed him strictly out of fear.

Then as I began to understand that my actions and decisions had nothing to do with his love—and that his was an everlasting love—my motivation for obedience changed. At that point I wanted to obey God because of love.

In truth, the Lord is to be feared and loved.

YOUR TURN

Do your best to answer honestly: Do you obey God, and why? Consider your answers, and ask: Is it time to make some adjustments?

SEPTEMBER 9

Uncomfortable

Then a voice told him, "Get up, Peter. Kill and eat."
"Surely not, Lord!" Peter replied. "I have never
eaten anything impure or unclean."
The voice spoke to him a second time,
"Do not call anything impure that God has made clean."

—ACTS 10:13–15

"Drive for the comfort of your passengers." That was my subtle, or not so subtle, way of telling my teenage sons to slow down, to stop tailgating, or to quit changing lanes. I was one of the passengers, and I wanted to feel comfortable.

You probably won't find this hard to believe, but the boys were not always overly concerned about my comfort. Interestingly enough, neither is God. In fact, obedience to him can oftentimes make you uncomfortable.

In the Scripture above, Peter has seen a sheet filled with animals and he hears the command to "get up, kill, and eat."

He replies to the command defensively because the animals are unclean. God rebukes Peter, instructing him to refrain from calling anything created by God "impure."

Those words made Peter uncomfortable, but he chose to obey God's command. There will be times when God's Word will make you uncomfortable and you will have a choice to make.

SO

Comfortable or not, choose to obey.

SEPTEMBER 10

That's Familiar

You, therefore, have no excuse,
you who pass judgment on someone else,
for at whatever point you judge another, you are
condemning yourself, because you who
pass judgment do the same things.

—Romans 2:1

Did you catch that last phrase? Let me repeat it for you: "because you who pass judgment do the same things." That's what it says.

It would seem the human race is quick to recognize and pass judgment because the one who judges is intimately familiar with the poor behavior in question. That is a sobering thought.

Think about the last time you passed judgment on someone else. I don't expect you to share it with me or with anyone else, but think for a minute.

Is it possible that you do exactly the same thing that you were condemning? God's Word seems to make a pretty good case for that possibility. No one but you and the Lord need to know your answer to that question. If you claimed there was absolutely, positively no chance you were guilty of the same offense you were condemning, just keep that possibility in mind for the future.

IT'S TRUE

It is always a good idea to think before you speak. Don't forget that judging is God's job.

SEPTEMBER 11

In Conclusion

Now all has been heard;
here is the conclusion of the matter:
Fear God and keep his commandments,
for this is the duty of all mankind.

—ECCLESIASTES 12:13

"And now in conclusion . . ." I've heard more than one speaker begin wrapping up a session with those words. On a few occasions, that phrase has brought me great relief knowing that the end was in sight. Other times I've found myself wishing there was time to hear more.

The last chapter of the book of Ecclesiastes ends at verse 14, but verse 13 actually mentions "the conclusion." Solomon is wrapping up his message. Truthfully, the chapters and verses prior to the conclusion have not been very uplifting, Solomon having concluded that everything is meaningless—wisdom, pleasures, toil, folly, advancement, riches—all things he has personally experienced. His concluding remarks are these: "Fear God and keep his commandments, for this is the duty of mankind."

THAT'S IT!

Solomon has condensed many words into a simple sentence. It is short and to the point. Beyond that, it is accurate. In the conclusion of life on this earth, what a blessing it would be to have lived out Solomon's concluding words.

SEPTEMBER 12

Search Me

Search me, God, and know my heart;
test me and know my anxious thoughts.
See if there is any offensive way in me,
and lead me in the way everlasting.

—PSALM 139:23–24

Can you imagine someone being able to look deep within you? The thought might be a little frightening. The contents are usually not open for others to explore.

The psalmist may have protected his thoughts from others, but he clearly invited the Lord to search his heart. His desire was for God to know his thoughts, to identify anything offensive, and to lead him in the path of life.

Even when you don't specifically extend an invitation to God to examine your heart, he's still able. "You know when I sit and when I rise; you perceive my thoughts from afar" (Psalm 139:2).

You might imagine that with God being able to access all your thoughts, it would color his opinion of you. Here's the scoop: He created you, he loves you, and he knows all about you. "You discern my going out and my lying down; you are familiar with all my ways" (Psalm 139:3).

THIS IS A GOOD THING!

It is freeing to be loved by someone who knows everything about you and still chooses to love you!

SEPTEMBER 13

Partial Obedience

For he who said, "You shall not commit adultery," also said, "You shall not murder." If you do not commit adultery but do commit murder, you have become a lawbreaker.

—JAMES 2:11

Many children have probably heard the words "Sit down and eat your vegetables." You may have spoken them when your six-year-old hopped up from the table with green beans still on his plate. You caught him before he could escape.

"Sit down and eat your vegetables," you say again, and your son knows you mean business. So he sits down in his chair, picks up his spoon, and stirs the beans around on his plate. (That's the old "mess up your food and mom will think you've eaten it" trick.)

When he attempts to escape again and he's caught in the act, he explains that he *did* sit down at the table. Was he obedient? Only partially; he sat down but didn't eat his green beans. Partial obedience is not enough. Partial obedience is disobedience.

The same is true when you or your child choose to obey a portion of God's instructions. You may be sitting at the table, but you're refusing to eat your vegetables—and that combination is disobedience.

THINK ABOUT IT

You want your children to obey. God wants his kids to do the same.

SEPTEMBER 14

I Hear You

For it is not those who hear the law
who are righteous in God's sight,
but it is those who obey the law
who will be declared righteous.

—ROMANS 2:13

Has this ever happened to you? You have to make a quick trip to the grocery store for that one ingredient you don't have and can't do without. The kids are all in the family room watching a movie, so you stick your head in the door and let them know where you're going and that you'll be right back. You also tell them to listen for the timer and take the meat loaf out of the oven when it rings. Then you head out the door.

No more than thirty minutes later you're back home, and as you open the front door you are greeted by an unwelcome aroma. Could it be? Yes, it's the charbroiled meat loaf, still in the oven.

After taking the remains of the meat loaf out of the oven and turning on the exhaust fan, you head for the family room.

"Didn't you hear me earlier?"

They sheepishly look at one another and nod.

"If you heard me, why didn't you do what I asked?"

HMMM . . .

Has God ever wanted to ask you the same question: "If you heard me, why didn't you do what I asked?"

SEPTEMBER 15

No Excuses

For since the creation of the world God's invisible qualities—his eternal power and divine nature—have been clearly seen, being understood from what has been made, so that people are without excuse.

—ROMANS 1:20

For several years I was the music director at church. For the record, I had that position by default; it was not because of my musical ability. I think my enthusiasm and willingness landed me the job.

The choir was made up of people of all ages, but it was predominately high school students. In retrospect, I realize my willingness to take the job was actually a reflection of my love for teenagers.

On occasion, one of them would miss practice or be absent on Sunday. The next time I saw that teenager, he knew what to expect. I'd tell him he was missed and ask where he had been.

Regardless of his answer, my response was always to smile and say, "That's no excuse." I tried to pretend there was absolutely no legitimate reason for missing something as important as practice. He knew I was kidding, but that I'd genuinely missed him.

There is one time, however, when there actually *is* no excuse. There's never a legitimate reason for not realizing the eternal power and divine nature of God.

REMEMBER

The Word says, "No excuses!"

SEPTEMBER 16

My Heroes

The king of Egypt said to the Hebrew midwives,
whose names were Shiphrah and Puah,
"When you are helping the Hebrew women during
childbirth on the delivery stool, if you see that the
baby is a boy, kill him; but if it is a girl, let her live."
The midwives, however, feared God and did not do
what the king of Egypt had told them to do;
they let the boys live.
—Exodus 1:15–17

Throughout the Bible you learn of godly men who exhibited great courage. You can also read about women of courage. Two of my favorites are the Hebrew midwives Shiphrah and Puah.

These two women received orders from the king of Egypt. He was the ruler of the land, the man who could order the death of innocent people. In this case the innocent ones were newborn babies—specifically baby boys.

Even though the orders came from the top, the Hebrew midwives chose to disobey. This decision to refuse to comply, their choice to ignore a direct command, took a great deal of courage. Though they had plenty to fear, they did not fear the king of Egypt; they feared God.

HAVE COURAGE!

"In God I trust and am not afraid. What can man do to me?" (Psalm 56:11).

SEPTEMBER 17

God's Timing

He who testifies to these things says,
"Yes, I am coming soon." Amen. Come, Lord Jesus.
—REVELATION 22:20

It doesn't matter where you're going or how long you've been on the road: If you're traveling with children, it's inevitable you will hear the question, "Are we there yet?"

"Soon."

These days it is unnecessary to open a can in order to make a vegetable for dinner. You don't even have to tear open a plastic container. You can just pop the whole bag in the microwave and wait a few minutes. It will be ready soon.

I send a text and then wonder why I haven't heard a reply immediately. I expect everything to happen soon, within a matter of moments.

Jesus said he was coming *soon*, and you know his words are true. You don't know when, but most assuredly, you are closer to his arrival today than yesterday.

"Is Christ coming today?" No one knows, but using God's timeline, he will be here soon.

LET'S PRAY

Father, your Word is true. You have told me that you would soon come again. I want to live each day knowing that truth, and teach my children to do the same. Soon you will return.

SEPTEMBER 18

Thinking of You

How precious to me are your thoughts, God!
How vast is the sum of them!
Were I to count them,
they would outnumber the grains of sand—
when I awake, I am still with you.
—Psalm 139:17–18

No one in my car was surprised when I asked them to think about something they had learned in the past two days. My van was filled with teenagers who had been at a Christian conference for youth and, as tired as they should have been, they were still excited about the music they'd enjoyed and the speakers they'd heard.

A boy clear in the back spoke up first. "I liked what that last speaker said about God thinking about me. I know my mom thinks about me quite a bit because she always reminds me to grab my baseball uniform when we have an away game right after school. She's also thinking about me when she's at the grocery store. I know that because she buys the stuff I like. But God? Wow! He thinks about me constantly—twenty-four seven."

He went on, addressing the other teenagers in the car. "I don't know how he does it, but I do know he's not kidding. And he's thinking about all of you that much too!"

IT'S TRUE

You're on God's mind all the time, and so are your children.

SEPTEMBER 19

Staying or Leaving?

"You do not want to leave too, do you?"
Jesus asked the Twelve. Simon Peter answered him,
"Lord, to whom shall we go? You have the words
of eternal life. We have come to believe and
to know that you are the Holy One of God."

—JOHN 6:67–69

Earlier in John chapter 6, Jesus was teaching a truth that was very difficult for the people to accept. Some of those who were considered followers of Christ turned away from him because of what they heard. At that point, Jesus asked the Twelve, his disciples, if they were going to leave too.

These men had a decision to make—the same decision everyone must make. God's Word is true. He's not kidding. At times, the pleasures of this world may seem more desirable than following Christ. Those pleasures beckon young and old, and for an instant, it may seem that the better choice is to leave.

The response of Simon Peter is the only one that is acceptable to God. God's Word is true, and Jesus alone has "the words of eternal life."

IT HAPPENS

When you feel the temptation to walk away from the truth of God's Word to pursue the pleasures of this world, stop and pray. Remember, Jesus alone has the words of eternal life.

SEPTEMBER 20

Free Gift

The Spirit and the bride say, "Come!"
And let the one who hears say, "Come!"
Let the one who is thirsty come;
and let the one who wishes take the free gift
of the water of life.

—REVELATION 22:17

The young man returned from the sports camp very enthused about all he had learned. He liked the instructors, the scrimmages, and the Bible lessons. He even liked the food. As he went on and on about the week, he mentioned that he had been given a free T-shirt.

Free? That's unlikely. I'm certain the price of the shirt had been figured into the price his mom paid for his camp registration. Regardless of that fact, it seemed like a gift to the teenager.

At the grocery store you "buy one, get one free"—but is the second one really free? Is anything really free?

The answer to that question is yes. Salvation through Jesus Christ is a free gift. You can't earn it. God—who gave his only Son, the water of life—has paid the price.

LET'S PRAY

Father, thank you for the free gift of eternal life. Thank you for your Son, Jesus, who paid the price. Let me never take for granted the sacrifice that was made.

SEPTEMBER 21

Deserve? Appreciate!

He will not always accuse,
nor will he harbor his anger forever;
he does not treat us as our sins deserve
or repay us according to our iniquities.

—Psalm 103:9–10

I wouldn't use the word *sketchy* to describe my technological understanding, but I wouldn't be offended if someone did. Understanding the what, why, and how of all the devices that serve me so well somehow doesn't seem important. As long as I'm able to do what I need to do, I rarely consider how my laptop or cell phone actually work.

That is, until something goes wrong. Then I vacillate between panic and annoyance, neither of which is helpful. There is, however, someone who is incredibly helpful when it comes to understanding and remedying the problem. He troubleshoots for the business he manages and, remarkably, he's always happy to help me.

He doesn't accept pay for his services but always smiles when I tell him, "I don't deserve your kindness, but I really do appreciate it!"

No one deserves the goodness of God, but you can choose to appreciate it.

A THANKFUL HEART

When you think of what Jesus has done for you—motivated only by his amazing love—feel free to express your appreciation.

SEPTEMBER 22

Faithful

God is faithful,
who has called you into fellowship with his Son,
Jesus Christ our Lord.

—1 CORINTHIANS 1:9

I wish I always followed through with commitments. It's not that I say something and don't do it to be mean or irritating. What usually gets me in trouble is when I say I will do something and then forget I've said it. In fact, I've been known to ask someone to "watch me write this down so I won't forget."

When I don't write down the task or ask to be monitored while I make a note, the odds are I'll forget to do what I've promised. I realize that's a sad commentary on my ability to be faithful and keep my word, but I know my limitations and my dependence on sticky notes.

That's not like God at all. He doesn't need a sticky note or any other reminder. His promises are recorded in the Bible—written down so you can remember.

THE KEY

You can know exactly what God has promised by reading his Word. You can know this too: He is faithful to do what he's said he will do.

SEPTEMBER 23

How Much?

Your love, LORD, reaches to the heavens,
your faithfulness to the skies.
—PSALM 36:5

I saw the poster near the door of the bookstore. It was a picture of Jesus on the cross. The words written near the bottom of the poster were simple and yet incredibly meaningful: "I asked the Lord, 'How much do you love me?' 'This much,' he said. And he stretched out his arms and died."

Can you see the picture in your mind's eye? The Lord Jesus stretched his arms along the horizontal section of the cross, as far as they would go. "How much?" was the question. "This much" was his answer.

Measuring God's love is impossible. Is love even measurable? Does it come in units or in increments or in gallons or pounds? Is it available by the yard or by the meter or the acre or rod?

In Psalm 36:5, the psalmist made a valiant attempt to answer the question, "How much does God love you?" The conclusion is that his love and faithfulness are beyond measure.

HE'S GOD

It is difficult to measure and comprehend the love of God because, as a human being, you cannot duplicate the vastness of his love. Don't struggle to understand it; just rest in his love.

SEPTEMBER 24

In My Opinion

In those days Israel had no king;
everyone did as they saw fit.
—JUDGES 21:25

Did you do what you were supposed to do? Maybe you thought you did. Did you make a good choice? Maybe you thought so. Was it a wise decision? It felt like one.

You may have asked your teenager that series of questions, or you may have posed them to yourself. Regardless of the situation, how do you know when your decisions are the right ones?

When it comes to making choices, it's too easy to fall into the rut of doing what you *think* is right; what you *imagine* is a good decision; what you *feel* is wise. That said, doing what is right and fit in your own eyes may simply be another name for disobedience.

ANOTHER PLAN

Instead of doing what you hope is right, or what feels like a wise decision, go to the Word of God for direction. Do what is right in God's eyes, and not what you see fit. He knows what is best.

SEPTEMBER 25

His Powerful Word

For he spoke, and it came to be;
he commanded, and it stood firm.

—Psalm 33:9

The word of God is very powerful. He spoke and the world came into existence. "And God said, 'Let there be light,' and there was light" (Genesis 1:3). Several verses later we read, "God said, 'Let us make man in our image, in our likeness,'" and Adam was created (v. 26). God's Word is creative.

Consider the fact that Jesus raised his friend Lazarus from the dead. "When he had said this, Jesus called out in a loud voice, 'Lazarus, come out!'" (John 11:43). He spoke and Lazarus moved from death to life. God's word is life-giving!

In Hebrews 4:12, God's word is described as "alive and active." God's word is living and will minister to each person according to their needs.

Finally, one of my favorites: "Your word is a lamp for my feet, a light on my path" (Psalm 119:105). God's word will illuminate your path.

YOUR RESPONSIBILITY

"Therefore encourage one another with these words" (1 Thessalonians 4:18). God's word is powerful, creative, life-giving, and alive. Be encouraged!

SEPTEMBER 26

Simon Says

Whoever claims to live in him must live as Jesus did.

—1 John 2:6

"Simon says: Touch your head. Good job!"

"Simon says: Jump up and down. All right!"

"Simon says: Stand on one foot. Great!"

"Stand on two feet. Gotcha! Simon didn't say to stand on two feet."

In the game of Simon Says, you're supposed to do everything that Simon says, and when Simon doesn't order it, you're not supposed to do it. Simon's words are your guide.

In life, having Simon as your guide won't really do you much good. Simon Says is a fun game, but instead of following Simon you need to mimic the Lord Jesus Christ—to live as Jesus did.

Jesus says, "Love your neighbor."

Jesus says, "Be kind to one another and tenderhearted."

Jesus says, "Forgive."

AS A FOLLOWER OF CHRIST

The longing of every believer is to hear the Lord say, "Good job! All right! Great!" "His master replied, 'Well done, good and faithful servant! You have been faithful with a few things; I will put you in charge of many things. Come and share your master's happiness!'" (Matthew 25:21).

SEPTEMBER 27

My Rock

The Lord is my rock, my fortress and my deliverer;
my God is my rock, in whom I take refuge,
my shield and the horn of my salvation, my stronghold.
—Psalm 18:2

Years ago when the basement was dug for our new home, the man operating the backhoe discovered something rather surprising. At the south end of the future basement, a portion of rock was uncovered. Even though it wouldn't actually be in the way of the basement walls, the excavator recommended he dig it out so there would be no danger of it shifting and pushing against the wall in the future.

That seemed like a prudent plan, so he began to dig and dig and dig—but the rock was much larger than anyone had imagined.

The portion that he spotted first was about one twentieth of what was later unearthed. When the entire rock was removed, the man doing the job announced that he would put it anywhere I wanted it, but he would only move it once!

I chose the location and he moved the boulder. Years later I can report that thankfully, I'm happy with the location I chose so many years ago. The rock is there to stay.

IT'S TRUE

The Lord wants to be the immovable rock in your life, your shield, the horn of your salvation, and your stronghold.

SEPTEMBER 28

What's in a Name?

Therefore God exalted him to the highest place
and gave him the name that is above every name,
that at the name of Jesus every knee should bow,
in heaven and on earth and under the earth,
and every tongue acknowledge that Jesus Christ is Lord,
to the glory of God the Father.
—PHILIPPIANS 2:9–11

Names are very important and can be very persuasive. Where would you rather spend your hard-earned money—dining at a "Five Star" restaurant or at the "Not Too Bad in a Pinch" restaurant?

Regardless of the menu or the quality of the food, you would probably choose the first spot as the place to eat dinner. The initial impression left by the "Not Too Bad in a Pinch" name isn't very positive. I doubt that diner would draw a crowd.

The Scripture from Philippians tells of the importance of Jesus' name. His name is above every other; at his name "every knee should bow . . . and every tongue acknowledge that Jesus Christ is Lord."

Names are important, and the name of Jesus Christ is the most important name you can ever speak.

HIS NAME

The name of the Lord is wonderful!

SEPTEMBER 29

Wiser and Stronger

For the foolishness of God is wiser than human wisdom,
and the weakness of God is stronger than human strength.

—1 Corinthians 1:25

Do you remember learning about comparisons in elementary school? There are some describers, called "irregular adjectives," that require a whole new word for comparison. An example would be: *bad*, *worse*, and *worst*.

Then there are comparisons like big, bigger, and biggest or simple, simpler, and simplest. As an elementary student, these are easier to learn. But both types of adjectives help serve the purpose of comparing one thing to another.

You may know someone who, in your estimation, is wise, but the Word clearly states that God is wiser. The truth is that even the foolishness of God is wiser than that wise person who came to your mind. You may know someone who is very, very strong, but God is stronger.

As you let that truth sink into your heart and mind, it is clear whom you should follow. Do not depend on human wisdom or strength. Instead, listen to the One who is wiser and stronger.

SO

Put your trust in the One who is wiser and stronger—the One who is the wisest and strongest!

SEPTEMBER 30

Just the Beginning

The fear of the LORD is the beginning of knowledge,
but fools despise wisdom and instruction.

—PROVERBS 1:7

One of your responsibilities as a mom is to help your kids gain both knowledge and wisdom. Understanding that God's not kidding is an important step in that direction.

God's not kidding about these things.

He *is* love: "Whoever does not love does not know God, because God is love" (1 John 4:8).

His grace is sufficient: "He said to me, 'My grace is sufficient for you, for my power is made perfect in weakness.' Therefore I will boast all the more gladly about my weaknesses, so that Christ's power may rest on me" (2 Corinthians 12:9).

He is merciful: "He saved us, not because of righteous things we had done, but because of his mercy. He saved us through the washing of rebirth and renewal by the Holy Spirit" (Titus 3:5).

He is also serious about his justice: "For he has set a day when he will judge the world with justice by the man he has appointed. He has given proof of this to everyone by raising him from the dead" (Acts 17:31).

And he's not kidding about loving discipline: "Those whom I love I rebuke and discipline. So be earnest and repent" (Revelation 3:19).

YOUR JOB?

Teach your children the truth in God's Word.

TRANSFER YOUR FAITH

I have no greater joy than to hear
that my children are walking in the truth.

—3 John 4

OCTOBER 1

Don't Forget

Only be careful, and watch yourselves closely so
that you do not forget the things your eyes have seen
or let them fade from your heart as long as you live.
Teach them to your children and
to their children after them.

—DEUTERONOMY 4:9

When I spent some time with a friend from high school, a large part of our conversation began with the words, "Do you remember when . . .?" Then one of us would follow that phrase with some funny story we remembered from years ago.

Do you remember when . . .?

It can be amusing to remember things that occurred in the past. It can also be difficult—not because your memory might be fading, but because not all memories are good ones.

God wants you to remember the things he's done, and is doing, in your life. You are to "be careful" and "not forget the things your eyes have seen." His Word includes the instruction to "teach them to your children and to their children after them."

REMEMBER

God has been at work in your life since before you were born. When you share about what you have seen him do, those memories stay alive. Take the time to teach your children—and one day your grandchildren—about the things God has done. That is a powerful way to transfer your faith.

OCTOBER 2

An Enthusiastic Fan

"Be very careful to keep the commandment
and the law that Moses the servant of the LORD gave you:
to love the LORD your God, to walk in obedience to him,
to keep his commands, to hold fast to him
and to serve him with all your heart and with all your soul."

—JOSHUA 22:5

Are you a fan of baseball, golf, or football? Maybe you're a fan of a television show or a particular musician. I once wrote a letter of appreciation to a Christian recording artist, so I'd say that makes me a fan.

Here's another question for you. Are you an enthusiastic fan? I have to admit, I am. When I see a great play in basketball—or any other sport, for that matter—I've been known to cheer as though the players can actually hear my clapping and be encouraged by my enthusiasm.

A few more questions: Are you a fan of God? Do you enthusiastically cheer for the things you see him doing? Are you excited as his plan begins to unfold and you realize you're going to have the opportunity to be a part of it?

God calls you to be his enthusiastic servant! To love him, serve him, and be obedient to him with "all your heart and with all your soul."

THE WORD

"Never be lacking in zeal, but keep your spiritual fervor, serving the Lord" (Romans 12:11).

OCTOBER 3

Enduring

"All people are like grass,
and all their glory is like the flowers of the field;
the grass withers and the flowers fall,
but the word of the Lord endures forever."

—1 Peter 1:24

Some friends of mine returned from a ten-day trip to Scotland. On the Sunday they were overseas, they went to church in a building that had been constructed in the early 1600s. That building had obviously stood the test of time.

It's probable that through the years the church had received regular maintenance. Maybe it had also experienced extensive refurbishing. Things had been repaired and restored as much as possible. That's what is required to keep something that old in shape and useful.

It's incredible the church is still standing and holding worship services each week after hundreds of years. Perhaps it will be standing for another five hundred years; maybe it won't. There is no guarantee.

There is a guarantee, however, when it comes to the Word of God. It will still be standing five hundred years from now, a thousand years from now, and forever.

THINK ABOUT IT

God's Word does not require regular maintenance or an overhaul of any kind. When all else is gone, God's Word will endure.

OCTOBER 4

Exaggeration

The king said to him,
"How many times must I make you swear to
tell me nothing but the truth in the name of the LORD?"

—1 KINGS 22:16

I have a magnet on my refrigerator that sports a cute but unsuccessful excuse. The magnet reads: "It's not that I exaggerate. I just remember big." That little piece of humor is aimed at no one else but me!

"Remembering big" is something I try to avoid; but because exaggerating was a habit I developed in my early years, changing my ways was a challenge.

The truth of the matter is that you can actually substitute the word *exaggerate* with the word *lie*: "It's not that I lie. I just remember big." You *can* do the substitution, but who would want to display a magnet with those words on it?

In truth, there is no excuse for exaggerating. My father used to say that his younger brother "never ruined a story by sticking too closely to the truth." Yikes! That's not really a compliment.

TRANSFERRING YOUR FAITH

In the words of Mark Twain: "If you tell the truth, you don't have to remember anything." The Lord and your children want to hear the truth from you.

OCTOBER 5

Sweet Perfume

Thanks be to God, who always leads us as captives in Christ's triumphal procession and uses us to spread the aroma of the knowledge of him everywhere.

—2 CORINTHIANS 2:14

I was on the seventh floor of the hotel when I stepped into the elevator. There were already several people on board, and we picked up three more as we stopped at the next floor.

The newcomers entered the elevator and I immediately identified a specific brand of perfume. I avoid that particular fragrance because it is capable of giving me a headache almost immediately.

Unfortunately, not only were at least two of the elevator passengers wearing the perfume; but they had applied it with complete abandon. Before we made it to the first floor, I was already doing my best to fight off the inevitable headache. The fragrance was overwhelming, and in my opinion, very unpleasant. Thank goodness our trip together didn't begin on the twenty-second floor!

The aroma of perfume can be unforgettable, either in a good or bad way—but nothing compares to the unforgettable, sweet, and powerful aroma of the knowledge of Jesus Christ.

HERE'S A QUESTION

Are you spreading the aroma of the knowledge of Christ? That sweet smell can draw your children and others to Jesus.

OCTOBER 6

But How?

How can a young person stay on the path of purity?
By living according to your word.
I seek you with all my heart;
do not let me stray from your commands.
I have hidden your word in my heart
that I might not sin against you.
—Psalm 119:9–11

As the mother of three children, I was very interested in the answer to the question posed in Psalm 119:9: “How can a young person stay on the path of purity?”

I’m guessing that’s the desire of every mom who knows Christ and the importance of staying on that path. It’s the longing every believing mom has for her sons and daughters.

The world is filled with impure things that are constantly tugging at the hearts, minds, and lives of your children, so how can each one of them stay on the path of purity?

Verse 9 goes on to answer the question: “By living according to your word.” Verses 10 and 11 shine even more light on the answer. God encourages you to seek him with all your heart—a halfhearted effort won’t do.

REMEMBER

Hide his word in your heart and don’t stray from his commands. Encourage your kids to do the same.

OCTOBER 7

The Mission Field

"For a long time now—to this very day—you have not deserted your fellow Israelites but have carried out the mission the LORD your God gave you."

—JOSHUA 22:3

One of my former youth group kids spent several years on the mission field in South America. She was a teacher—a blessing to her students and to everyone whose life intersected hers. God had called her to serve others on the foreign mission field.

At one point many years ago, my husband and I thought that God might be calling us to do the same. I can vividly remember the period of prayer and then the act of obedience as we filled out forms and applied for teaching positions overseas. Ultimately God closed the door on that possibility, but the process we had gone through provided a wonderful lesson in faith and trust.

Our mission field proved to be one a little closer to home. In fact, we strategically placed a sign where we could read it as we left our bedroom and started each new day. The words were simple and true. "You are now entering the mission field." Our mission field was in our home and in our community.

YOUR MISSION FIELD

God has given you as a mother, an important mission in your own home. Serve there with gladness.

OCTOBER 8

Team Effort

What, after all, is Apollos? And what is Paul?
Only servants, through whom you came to believe—
as the Lord has assigned to each his task.
I planted the seed, Apollos watered it,
but God has been making it grow.
—1 CORINTHIANS 3:5–6

Maybe you've read an account of some particular sporting event and learned that So-and-So scored the winning goal, basket, or touchdown.

More than once I've wondered, *What is the "winning goal"?* I understand that the "winning goal" refers to the one scored in the last moments of the game, but what about the points scored previously? What about the defense that prevented points from being scored? Didn't they all contribute to the win?

A team sport is just that: a game where several players are involved with everyone having a common goal. Raising children has some parallels to a team sport. Typically, the cocaptains are Mom and Dad, but there are other folks who help with the win—teachers, youth leaders, grandparents, and the list goes on and on.

SO

As the team works together to achieve success, be certain to give credit to God for the win.

OCTOBER 9

Can't Stop

"As for us, we cannot help speaking about what we have seen and heard."

—ACTS 4:20

There are times when a child, or even an adult, can be so excited about something that they just can't stop talking about it. I am picturing an exchange I had recently with a young boy. He was telling me a story and was so excited that he barely stopped to breathe.

The funny thing is, as he went on and on about the incredible adventure he had just experienced, I started to get excited too. It was contagious! Before long, I felt as though I had been there myself and had seen and heard all of the things he was sharing with me.

In the Scripture above from Acts 4, Peter and John cannot stop speaking about what they've seen and heard. They have been commanded by the Sanhedrin not to speak or teach in the name of Jesus. Obviously these two disciples of the Lord did not intend to follow that order. They refused to stop telling others about Jesus.

HOW ABOUT YOU?

Are you excited about Jesus? What have you seen and heard that you can share with your children? Very often simply hearing of God's faithfulness and his power will change a life forever.

OCTOBER 10

Your Story

This is the account of Noah and his family.
Noah was a righteous man, blameless among
the people of his time,
and he walked faithfully with God.

—GENESIS 6:9

Genesis chapter 6 marks the beginning of the amazing story of Noah. The account of his obedience and faithfulness to God was recorded so that it would be available to bless, inspire, and instruct future generations.

I love to hear the stories of how another mom came to faith, how she listened to the Lord, and how God directed her life. Every believer has a story to tell, and everyone's story is unique.

God wants everyone to have a story. "The Lord is not slow in keeping his promise, as some understand slowness. Instead he is patient with you, not wanting anyone to perish, but everyone to come to repentance" (2 Peter 3:9).

The "everyone" in 2 Peter includes your children. On more than one occasion I've learned of a person who came to repentance and faith after hearing the story of someone else. Be certain your children know yours.

IT'S TRUE

"So then faith cometh by hearing, and hearing by the word of God" (Romans 10:17 KJV). Share your story, your faith, and the truth of the Word of God.

OCTOBER 11

Hope

Why, my soul, are you downcast?
Why so disturbed within me?
Put your hope in God,
for I will yet praise him,
my Savior and my God.

—Psalm 42:11

Why are you discouraged and upset? Maybe it's because of the current state of affairs in your home. Maybe it's because your prayers for your child seem to bounce off the ceiling and never reach God's ears.

Perhaps the hope you have that your faith will transfer to your child is based on all you've done. Maybe you're hoping your talent, hard work, strength, or commitment will be sufficient to bring your child to a saving knowledge of Christ.

The truth is that *your* hard work, strength, and commitment are things of the flesh. Instead of counting on your abilities, put your hope in God. He is able. Don't be discouraged and give up; expect him to listen and to act. And while you wait in hope, praise the One who is your Savior!

IT'S NOT EASY

When you've already prayed for two months or two years or twenty years and it seems as though nothing has happened, put your hope in God. The Word assures you he will act. It is always too soon to give up on him.

OCTOBER 12

Knowing God

But you, LORD, are a shield around me,
my glory, the One who lifts my head high.
I call out to the LORD, and he answers me from his holy mountain. I lie down and sleep; I wake again, because the Lord sustains me. I will not fear though tens of thousands assail me on every side. Arise, LORD! Deliver me, my God!
Strike all my enemies on the jaw;
break the teeth of the wicked.
From the LORD comes deliverance.
May your blessing be on your people.

—PSALM 3:3–8

Many times the world paints a distorted picture of the Lord. In order for your child to get a clear picture of God, he must hear and read God's Word. The Bible gives an accurate representation of who God is and what he desires.

Read again the words of Psalm 3. Read them aloud. Each sentence paints a true and accurate picture of God. He is Deliverer, Sustainer, Protector, the One who answers prayers and blesses his people.

As both you and your child internalize these and other truths about God, your knowledge will grow . . . knowledge of who he is and how his love, mercy, grace, and justice impact your lives.

SO

Read the Bible for your learning and for your child's. Get a true and accurate picture of God.

OCTOBER 13

Excuses!

"Another said, 'I have just bought five yoke of oxen, and I'm on my way to try them out. Please excuse me.'"

—Luke 14:19

Luke 14 features the parable of the Great Banquet. Talk about excuses! The folks who had initially been invited came up with all sorts of explanations as to why they couldn't possibly attend the banquet Jesus had prepared.

One had just bought a field and had to go see it. Another had purchased five yoke of oxen and was on his way to try them out. Then there was the man who announced that he'd just gotten married and couldn't come.

What a bunch of flimsy excuses. Wait a minute: That's a lot like the flimsy excuses that might be made today.

I just purchased a big screen TV and I have to go watch it. I just bought a car and I'm on my way to try it out. I just got married and my new wife would never understand.

YOUR EXCUSES TODAY MIGHT BE . . .

I'm too busy. I don't have time. My work is demanding. My kids are demanding. Stop! When the Lord invites you to spend time with him, don't look for an excuse. Go to his banqueting table, praying for yourself and your family and praising your heavenly Father.

OCTOBER 14

Should

"Woe to you Pharisees, because you give God a tenth of your mint, rue and all other kinds of garden herbs, but you neglect justice and the love of God. You should have practiced the latter without leaving the former undone."

—LUKE 11:42

I must admit, there are certain vocabulary words that I know exist, but I never intend to use. I find those same words offensive when I hear them on television or in a movie.

There's another category of words I call my "*try* not to use them" words. This group of words is not necessarily shocking or offensive to the general public; it is simply a collection of words I make a concerted effort to avoid.

The number-one word on that list is *should*. I don't like to say, "I should," "You should," "He should," "She should," or "They should." And here's my reasoning. The word *should* is a guilt-producer, and I do my best to refrain from using guilt as a motivator.

So instead of "I should exercise more," say, "I could exercise more." Instead of "You should make your family a priority," it's, "You could make your family a priority." My choice is substitute the word *could* for *should* whenever possible.

SO

It's something you could think about (and maybe even choose) to do.

OCTOBER 15

Whatever It Takes

I want to know Christ—yes, to know the power of his resurrection and participation in his sufferings, becoming like him in his death, and so, somehow, attaining to the resurrection from the dead. Not that I have already obtained all this, or have already arrived at my goal, but I press on to take hold of that for which Christ Jesus took hold of me.

—PHILIPPIANS 3:10–12

The writer of Philippians had a deep desire to know Christ intimately. He was willing to press forward toward that goal regardless of the path he might have to take.

As a mom and a follower of Jesus, you might be able to echo the words of Philippians 3:10–12 with complete sincerity—in essence, praying, "Whatever it takes, Lord."

It can be a very different matter to pray those words with your children in mind. "Whatever it takes to bring this child to you, Jesus. Whatever it takes." Even as those words are spoken you hope the "whatever" is painless or at least only slightly uncomfortable.

BUT

You know that anything capable of bringing your child closer to Christ is the best. The key is to keep your eye on the true treasure and teach your child to do the same.

OCTOBER 16

Looks Good

There is a way that appears to be right,
but in the end it leads to death.

—PROVERBS 14:12

I get a real kick out of eating at a fancy restaurant. Probably what amuses me most is how the food is presented. When you are the mother of three sons, the presentation of a meal is not considered incredibly important. Quantity is much more significant, followed closely by quality. The truth is, presentation isn't even considered.

On the rare occasions when I've actually eaten at a "fine dining" establishment, and on the even more uncommon occasion when I was joined by my sons, I've heard them wondering aloud why someone drizzled the raspberry sauce all over the plate instead of pouring it directly on the dessert.

Presentation might be enjoyable, but if that is the extent of your faith, it will be difficult to transfer it to your children. In some cases you can hide your heart behind a good presentation, but it's usually not hidden from your children. They see you too often and in too many situations to be fooled.

BE REAL

Make every effort to display quantity and quality when it comes to your faith.

OCTOBER 17

Feed 'Em

The third time he said to him, "Simon son of John, do you love me?" Peter was hurt because Jesus asked him the third time, "Do you love me?" He said, "Lord, you know all things; you know that I love you." Jesus said, "Feed my sheep."

—John 21:17

"I'm hungry!" I'm guessing those are words you've heard from your children before. Just minutes before dinnertime you've probably held them off with the reassuring words that the food will be on the table very soon.

If the claim of hunger is made shortly after you've cleared the table, the chances are great you'll remind them about the opportunity they just had to fill their stomachs. That's when your kids learn that timing is critical.

You don't want a child to go hungry in your house. You want your kids to be well-fed; that's why you do your best to provide delicious, nutritious meals. It's part of your job description whether you do the actual cooking or not.

You never let your children go without food to nourish their bodies, but have you considered what they need to nourish their souls? Jesus asked Peter to feed his sheep. You have the privilege of feeding his little lambs.

YOUR JOB

Take the time to encourage and model a healthy diet of God's Word.

OCTOBER 18

Every Opportunity

So then, while we [as individual believers] have the opportunity, let us do good to all people [not only being helpful, but also doing that which promotes their spiritual well-being], and especially [be a blessing] to those of the household of faith (born-again believers).

—Galatians 6:10 AMP

Years ago I started praying for God to make me aware of the opportunities he had given me. I was pretty sure I was missing openings to witness for him, to encourage others, and to pray and give praise to him. I decided that from that point forward I wanted to miss fewer and fewer of those occasions in my life.

It's possible you've missed a few opportunities too—times when you could have done "good to all people," to fellow believers and to those who weren't yet members of God's family. It's not that the Lord *needs* you to be helpful and to be a blessing to others. He's *allowing* you to be a part of his work here on earth.

His words in Galatians 6 are an encouragement for you to take advantage of those God-ordained openings. They are not coincidences; they are God-incidences.

LET'S PRAY

Father, I don't want to miss the opportunities you provide for me to be a part of your heavenly plan. Give me eagerness not only to be helpful but also willing to invest in someone's spiritual growth.

OCTOBER 19

Priorities

"You shall have no other gods before me."
—EXODUS 20:3

I sat in the conference hall and heard a speaker encouraging each of us to establish a list of priorities. He made several valid points that convinced me of the importance of written priorities, so I did what he'd suggested. I made a list, numbered it 1–5, and put that list on the corner of my desk. Sadly, it made absolutely no difference in my life.

Years later I had an idea that I believe was from God. It lined up with his Word and was much smarter than I am.

Rather than make a list with pen and paper, I was challenged to paint my list with watercolors and a tablet set on an easel. If you know anything about watercolors, you're already shaking your head. The paper needs to be flat so the colors won't run.

That's true for a work of art, but the fact that the paint was destined to drip down the page provided the perfect illustration. The Lord, number one on my list, ran down to the bottom of the paper and colored every priority below. Any decisions made about the lesser priorities were colored by number one. Priority number two colored number three and so on down the list.

FIRST THINGS FIRST

Painting your list of priorities in this manner will help you make decisions wisely.

OCTOBER 20

Pass It On

For what I received I passed on to you as
of first importance: that Christ died for our sins
according to the Scriptures.

—1 CORINTHIANS 15:3

One of the blessings God has given you is the ability to share the gospel message with others. There are many ways that can be accomplished. When you think about your pastor, you probably imagine a multitude of opportunities he has simply because of the nature of his job. But it doesn't matter what you identify as your profession—stay-at-home mom, teacher, engineer, or truck driver; you have the ability and the opportunity to share the good news, to pass on the truth found in the Word.

Sharing your faith with someone doesn't demand formal training or great wisdom. All you need is the willingness to obey and pass on what you have received from God. It looks a little like a relay race.

In a relay, you receive the baton and run your segment of the race. Then you hand that baton to the next runner, who hands it to the next. You pass it on.

AN IDEA

Have you ever taken the time to thank the individual who passed faith on to you? A note like that is bound to make someone's day.

OCTOBER 21

The God Card

"Do not take advantage of each other,
but fear your God. I am the LORD your God."
—LEVITICUS 25:17

I've played quite a few card games with my kids—games like Go Fish and euchre, and once, only once, we gave bridge a try; it took too much thinking.

In order to play and win those games, I had to know what card outranked the others. It was always beneficial to hold a trump card in my hand. After all, playing it at the right time could mean victory.

God's Word is, in essence, the ultimate trump card. It surpasses all other plans and promises. And playing that card at the right time is also important.

For example: Your son makes a poor choice, and amid your reaction to the news you tell him how disappointed God is. You play the trump card, but it doesn't help him face his poor choice or its consequences.

Your daughter finds herself depressed over a failed relationship and you slap down the God Card by telling her to praise God in every situation. Does that help her overcome her depression?

The Word is truth, but listening to God's Spirit before playing the trump card is important.

SO

Remember your goal as you interact with your kids amid difficult situations. These are not games to win or lose; they are opportunities to transfer your faith. Play the trump card wisely.

OCTOBER 22

The Real Deal

Trust in him at all times, you people;
pour out your hearts to him, for God is our refuge.
—PSALM 62:8

How was your day yesterday? Was everything wonderful? If I were to answer the second question, I would have to say no. It was not a perfectly wonderful day.

Nothing big happened—just an accumulation of little disappointments. In retrospect I realize they were silly and unimportant, but there's something about adding one little annoyance to the next that can turn your day into something less than wonderful.

Everything isn't always perfect. Circumstances you've created and those beyond your control will do their best to rob you of joy and peace. It can be easy to become buried in your problems.

The good news is this: You can trust God at all times and in every situation. He is ready day and night, waiting for you to pour out your heart.

Your children may have an idea of the concerns you have, and they may even share them. When they see you trusting your heavenly Father regardless of the circumstances, they see you living what you say you believe. You're the real deal, and so is the Lord.

LET'S PRAY

Lord, my desire is to trust you . . . all the time, with every circumstance. Thank you for promising to be my safe haven.

OCTOBER 23

Live Your Faith

What good is it, my brothers and sisters,
if someone claims to have faith but has no deeds?
Can such faith save them?

—JAMES 2:14

Too many times moms decide that all they have to do is give their kids instructions—just tell them what to do. One classic (and disappointing) example is saying, "Do as I say and not as I do." I'm not sure who came up with that, but it should be banned from the vocabulary of every mom unless she is teaching her child some intricate skill she hasn't been able to personally accomplish—like a back handspring, for example.

When a mom declares her child should heed her words but not her actions, it merely draws attention to her actions. Mom, your kids are listening and watching. If you insist on modeling unforgiveness toward a neighbor or a family member, telling your child to forgive will bring questionable results.

Rather than teaching important biblical lessons with words only, teach them with your deeds too.

LIVE YOUR FAITH

Forgiveness, the example above, can be difficult. Only the Lord is capable of forgiving and forgetting. It isn't necessary for you to model forgetting. Your job is to model a forgiving attitude for the benefit of both you and your child.

OCTOBER 24

Lost and Found

"What good will it be for someone to gain
the whole world, yet forfeit their soul?
Or what can anyone give in exchange for their soul?"
—Matthew 16:26

I hate it when I lose things, and it happens too frequently. In fact, right now I have a pair of earrings that I cannot find. My eldest used to say, "Mom, things aren't lost. You just don't know where they are right now." That's an optimistic way to look at it, and I certainly hope that's true with my earrings. I really like them! They were one of my favorite pairs, and now they are lost.

Losing something you like can be very frustrating, but there's something more important that you never want to lose. The questions in Matthew 16:26 provide Food for Thought: "What good will it be for someone to gain the whole world, yet forfeit their soul? Or what can anyone give in exchange for their soul?"

The answers are simple: It will be of no good, and there is nothing worth exchanging for your soul. Those answers underline the importance of transferring your faith.

SO

Be intentional. Realize the magnitude of transferring your faith to your children.

OCTOBER 25

The Power of Love

If I have the gift of prophecy and can fathom all mysteries
and all knowledge, and if I have a faith that can move
mountains, but do not have love, I am nothing.
If I give all I possess to the poor and give over my
body to hardship that I may boast,
but do not have love, I gain nothing.

—1 CORINTHIANS 13:2–3

"Knowledge is power." That well-known phrase dates back to the 1500s. Knowledge is a wonderful thing, and it is capable of accomplishing a great deal.

God has given men and women knowledge that has led to cures for many life-threatening diseases. He has given knowledge that has led to great discoveries and solutions for difficult problems.

But love is more important than having "all knowledge," the "gift of prophecy," and "a faith that can move mountains." It is even more than giving "all to the poor" and giving your "body to hardship."

Love is from God, and love is power! "'What no eye has seen, what no ear has heard, and what no human mind has conceived'—the things God has prepared for those who love him" (1 Corinthians 2:9).

LET'S PRAY

Lord, thank you for loving me. Help me exhibit your power by loving others well.

OCTOBER 26

Measure Up

We, however, will not boast beyond proper limits,
but will confine our boasting to the sphere of
service God himself has assigned to us,
a sphere that also includes you.

—2 Corinthians 10:13

On the wall of our laundry room there are many, many pencil marks. Each mark is labeled with a name and a date. That's the wall where I've recorded my sons' growth through the years. Each July and January we ritually measured their heights and recorded the progress. There are even marks for several of my kids' good friends. This record of growing is a fun piece of family history.

For many years each measurement showed a few inches of growth; each boy was getting taller and taller. The mark would be made, and each one would turn around to compare their new height to their last mark on the wall. In a sense, each boy was interested in how he measured up.

Likewise, it is important to make sure that you are continually growing in the sphere of service God has assigned to you. Measure up by serving well.

LET'S PRAY

Father, I want to continually grow. You have given me an assignment, and I want to serve you well.

OCTOBER 27

Sympathy and Empathy

Because he himself suffered when he was tempted,
he is able to help those who are being tempted.

—HEBREWS 2:18

There are times I completely understand the plight of others. I have empathy because I have experienced the same distress or the same temptation.

When a dear friend lost her sister-in-law to cancer, I was able to relate to her feelings having lost my brother-in-law years before. I could remember the pain and also the comfort offered by loving friends.

Other times I am in the dark and have no idea how a friend is suffering. I had a cup of tea with a friend whose son had recently died. I could only imagine how she felt. Although I could l express my sympathy, I had never experienced the pain she was enduring. I was unable to empathize with her.

It's been my experience that when someone was able to empathize with me—when a friend could relate my experience to a similar one in her own life—she was able to offer great comfort and understanding.

Jesus can empathize with you. He has been through what you've experienced. He understands and offers compassion, kindness, and empathy. He is able to help you and share your burdens.

IT'S TRUE

God understands, and he is able to help.

OCTOBER 28

Back on Track

We have come to share in Christ,
if indeed we hold our original conviction
firmly to the very end.

—HEBREWS 3:14

It can be easy to get off track. I like to blame my smartphone. I pick it up to check the weather and notice I have three unread e-mails. I open the first one, and it's a request for information. I shift gears, go into my office, and begin sifting through the papers on my desk. After I find what I'm looking for, I look at my phone once again—remembering I haven't seen the weather forecast. Oh, look! I've got a text.

You may be wondering if I ever get back to the weather. Not always! The truth is, if I don't try to stay on track, I can start (and never finish) multiple things. I realize it's important to be faithful to the end of a project, but knowing that and doing it are two separate things.

Staying on track with God, holding on to your original conviction, is important to do! As you share your faith with others, especially your children, hold firmly to your beliefs.

SO

The idea is to stay on track. Don't let distractions sidetrack you. Trust God as firmly as you did when you first became a believer.

OCTOBER 29

How Much Time?

He asked you for life, and you gave it to him—
length of days, for ever and ever.
—PSALM 21:4

I'll always remember the sobering conversation I had with a dear friend. She had undergone a radical mastectomy seven years before, and the cancer had returned. As we ate lunch together, I finally found the courage to ask her what the doctors said about her prognosis.

She told me of the grim report she'd received, then smiled and added, "But seriously, how do they know? Only God knows for sure. Think about it: You may beat me to heaven." As she smiled wryly, I realized the truth in her words. Only God knows how long anyone will be alive on this earth.

Within a few months my friend died. Her illness taught me many things, including the importance of enjoying and actually treasuring each day. More importantly, she reminded me to honor the One who can give his children "length of days, for ever and ever."

SO

Do not waste a day. Fill each one with praise and thanksgiving for the One who will give you life eternal.

OCTOBER 30

Authentic and Forgiven

So the other disciples told him, "We have seen the Lord!" But he said to them, "Unless I see the nail marks in his hands and put my finger where the nails were, and put my hand into his side, I will not believe."

—JOHN 20:25

Thomas, one of Jesus' disciples, demanded proof of the resurrection. Christ himself gave that proof when a week later he came and stood with Thomas and the other disciples. After greeting the men, Jesus encouraged Thomas to touch the wounds on his hands and the gash on his side.

Jesus had risen from the dead, yet he still bore the scars of the crucifixion. Have you ever wondered why he did not have a perfect body? Perhaps it was because he could minister through his scars.

Everyone has scars and imperfections from the journey of life. You can choose to hide those blemishes from others, such as your own children, or you can share the stories behind those scars and watch God use them for his glory.

IT'S TRUE

God's grace and forgiveness enable you to be authentic. Your scars may lead others to the truth, to Jesus.

OCTOBER 31

Fearless Words

Pray also for me, that whenever I speak, words may be given me so that I will fearlessly make known the mystery of the gospel, for which I am an ambassador in chains. Pray that I may declare it fearlessly, as I should.

—Ephesians 6:19–20

Every Tuesday in the summer was our library day. The Children's Room was spacious and decorated with banners and pictures proclaiming the joy of reading.

Each of my young sons would hunt for a new book or two to enjoy during the week, and before we left we'd sit on the beanbag chairs to read a short story together.

One day the librarian surprised me with a question: "You are always so joyful. What's your secret?"

I was taken aback by the compliment and the question. Fumbling for an answer, I simply said, "Guess I got a good night's sleep."

Immediately after leaving the library, I realized I'd missed a golden opportunity to share my faith, and I prayed God would give me another chance.

My prayer was answered the very next week when she asked a similar question. That was when I told her of my love for Jesus and his love for her. The boys were present as God gave me the words to "make known the mystery of the gospel."

LET'S PRAY

Lord, let me fearlessly present the truth of the gospel and model that courage for my kids.

TEACH US, LITTLE CHILDREN

At that time Jesus said, “I praise you, Father, Lord of heaven and earth, because you have hidden these things from the wise and learned, and revealed them to little children.”

—Matthew 11:25

NOVEMBER 1

Follow the Rules

"As for God, his way is perfect:
The LORD's word is flawless;
he shields all who take refuge in him."
—2 SAMUEL 22:31

The young girl handed the box to her pastor. She had taken it home last Sunday and brought it back to church the next week with something inside—something, anything that would spark an idea for his children's sermon.

The box was covered with wrapping paper, and the rules were posted on the side: "No peeking, no shaking, nothing alive inside."

Pastor took the box and commented on how light it felt. "Are you sure there's something inside?"

She nodded her head. Then he asked another question. "May I shake it?"

Her answer was immediate and firm. "No shaking! That's a rule!"

"But," Pastor countered, "do we have to follow the rules if they don't make sense?" And with that question as his inspiration, he launched into the children's message for the morning.

God's rules may not make sense to you or to your kids, but the ability to completely understand them is not important. The Lord's Word is flawless.

SO

No debate, no discussion, no dispute, no deliberation. Those are all a waste of time. Instead just follow the rules.

NOVEMBER 2

Don't Be Afraid

The angel said to them, "Do not be afraid. I bring you good news that will cause great joy for all the people. Today in the town of David a Savior has been born to you; he is the Messiah, the Lord."

—LUKE 2:10–11

The little boy was playing with his Matchbox cars as his mom watched the evening news. An elderly gentleman was being interviewed, and he was extremely emotional. Over and over again he said, "I didn't mean to hurt the boys. I was just so afraid. I just wanted to scare them away. I was afraid and I lost control. I was so afraid."

When Mom realized that her son was watching the disturbing scene, she reached for the remote to change the channel. Before she could get the job done, her son spoke up. "Doesn't he know what the angels said?"

When she looked confused, he repeated his question and continued the thought. "Doesn't he know what the angels said? 'Don't be afraid. Baby Jesus is born!'"

This simple and profound paraphrase of the Scripture in Luke came from the lips of a child. The Word of God had made an impact on his life.

FOR YOU

Let God's Word influence your thinking and your life. Don't be afraid; baby Jesus is born!

NOVEMBER 3

It's Daddy's

You are no longer a slave, but God's child;
and since you are his child, God has made you also an heir.
—GALATIANS 4:7

The young boy and his father traveled to spend the weekend together at an Experimental Aircraft Association Fly-In. It's a gathering of people interested in aviation, especially recreational flying. The father and son didn't fly to the event, but drove a car and pulled a trailer carrying an ultralight airplane the father had built.

After Dad moved the plane to the display area and put the wings on, he and his son stayed close so he could answer questions about the plane's structure and performance. His son played in, on, and around the plane all day.

At one point the four-year-old climbed into the seat and pretended he was flying. A passerby took it upon himself to scold the boy for playing with the controls. The little boy looked at the man and timidly responded, "It's my daddy's plane."

His father didn't mind him enjoying the plane he had created. He encouraged him. It was his plane, and this was his child. God encourages you to enjoy what he has created. It is his world and you are his child: "For the world is mine, and all that is in it" (Psalm 50:12).

SO

Just like this little boy, remember whose it is and remember whose you are!

NOVEMBER 4

Pint-Sized Teacher

Jesus said, "Let the little children come to me,
and do not hinder them, for the kingdom
of heaven belongs to such as these."
—MATTHEW 19:14

Stop and think: What have you taught your children recently? Maybe it was a physical skill or an all-important manner that had been lacking. Maybe you taught them something that would be beneficial in the classroom. There could be many things on this list.

Now I want you to think about the things your children have taught you. "Kendra, you don't understand," you may say. "My kids are all little. They're too young to teach me anything."

The verse in Matthew 19 says that the kingdom of heaven belongs to the little children. With that in mind, I'm guessing there might be a thing or two these little ones can teach their moms.

Maybe you've missed the lesson because you haven't been paying attention, or maybe you haven't had a teachable attitude when it came to learning from a little one. Either of those things could keep you from learning what your child might be teaching.

Little children can teach compassion, care, and courage to name just a few of the lessons; and they do it best when they have assumed the role of teacher without realizing it.

LISTEN AND LEARN

Don't miss an opportunity to learn from your children. They can be remarkable teachers.

NOVEMBER 5

Heaven

"You alone are the LORD. You made the heavens,
even the highest heavens, and all their starry host,
the earth and all that is on it, the seas and all that is in them.
You give life to everything, and the multitudes
of heaven worship you."

—NEHEMIAH 9:6

"Does Grandpa have a mustache in heaven?"

That was the question posed by my five-year-old son. He was asking about my father, who died years before my son was born.

How in the world was I supposed to answer that question, and where in the world did it come from? "I'm not sure whether or not Grandpa has a mustache," I replied. "Why do you ask?"

"Well," he began, "do you see that picture of him up on the shelf? He's got a mustache in that picture, and if he doesn't have one in heaven, how am I going to recognize him?"

How indeed! When it comes to heaven, I have many more questions than answers; but I did my best that morning to share the things I knew from God's Word.

"The multitudes of heaven will worship" God Almighty. I'm certain that recognizing one another will be insignificant compared to worshiping the Lord.

LET'S PRAY

Father, help me teach my children about your glory and majesty. Direct me as I show them the path to eternal life with you.

NOVEMBER 6

Peter Sank

"Lord, if it's you," Peter replied, "tell me to come to you on the water." "Come," he said. Then Peter got down out of the boat, walked on the water and came toward Jesus. But when he saw the wind, he was afraid and, beginning to sink, cried out, "Lord, save me!"

—MATTHEW 14:28–30

The family sat gathered around the kitchen table as Mom read the devotional message for the day. It was the story of Peter walking on the water.

After Mom finished reading and after they prayed together, one of the kids surprised his mom with these words. "Hey guys," he said, addressing everyone in the family, "I know why Peter sank."

His mother had a doubtful look in her eye but gestured for him to continue. "It's simple," he said. "Peter quit lookin' at Jesus."

Yes, that is what happened. Peter took his eyes off of the Lord and instead focused on the wind and the waves. That's when he started going under.

On that day, Mom did not teach the lesson. One of her kids was the teacher.

AND

That simple explanation is true, not only for Peter but also for you. When you take your eyes off of Jesus and look at your situation, you may find yourself sinking. Keep your focus where it belongs—on the Lord.

NOVEMBER 7

Don't Keep Score

[Love] keeps no record of wrongs.

—1 CORINTHIANS 13:5

A teacher is typically an adult and a student is typically a child; but occasionally the roles are reversed. Children are very capable of teaching adults—including moms who are willing to learn.

One lesson I have seen children teach and model for their moms is found in 1 Corinthians 13, the love chapter. In that chapter the apostle Paul describes what love is and what love is not. He also includes what love does and does not do.

For example, love "keeps no record of wrongs." Love doesn't keep score. Kids are wonderfully talented at not keeping score. Sure, the neighborhood kid was irritating yesterday, but today is a new day and most kids are willing to give him another chance. They're willing to extend a little grace and forgiveness. That's a great lesson for any adult.

Pay attention to the children in your home, in your neighborhood, and in your church. Their actions and decisions might look a lot like the ones your heavenly Father recommends.

SO

Let the children teach you and be willing to learn.

NOVEMBER 8

Consulting

Plans fail for lack of counsel,
but with many advisers they succeed.
—PROVERBS 15:22

"Do you ask your mother *everything*?" said a young woman to her friend after she overheard her discussing an upcoming decision.

The response was immediate and interesting. "I wasn't asking permission," the friend said. "I was 'consulting' with her."

Great answer! This young lady wanted to make a wise decision, so she sought the counsel of her mom. My guess is that this mother had been available with godly advice from the beginning. Her accessibility contributed to making her the logical choice when a "consultant" was required.

In today's world, a consultant can earn a healthy paycheck. As a consultant to your children you'll reap a reward, but it won't be something you can deposit in the bank. It is an honor when your children ask for your advice and counsel. It means they are certain you have their best interest at heart and you have wisdom to share.

THE NEXT STEP

Becoming a consultant is a natural progression as your children move toward adulthood. Be certain you have given them good reason to ask for your advice.

NOVEMBER 9

Asking Permission

Daniel resolved not to defile himself with the royal food and wine, and he asked the chief official for permission not to defile himself this way.

—DANIEL 1:8

The king had ordered Daniel and several other young men to eat a daily amount of food and wine from his royal table. Daniel had no desire to do what was ordered, so he asked the chief official for permission to abstain from the ordered diet. He didn't ask the king. Instead he went to the one who could and would grant his request.

Kids have the same ingenuity. They ask the right person for permission to do something that someone else might consider too dangerous. They know which parent to ask when they want to participate in a social event, an event that the other might consider frivolous. Children are quick to learn exactly who they should ask to get the answer they desire.

More important than getting what you want, is doing what the Lord knows is best. When your children learn that important truth, they will know where to take their every request.

LET'S PRAY

Thank you, Father, for always being available and for being willing to lead and guide my life and the lives of my children.

NOVEMBER 10

Birth Order

"Take two onyx stones and engrave on them
the names of the sons of Israel in
the order of their birth—six names on one stone
and the remaining six on the other."

—EXODUS 28:9–10

In the Scripture above, the sons of Israel were to be listed by their birth order. Many studies have been done on the influence of birth order. There was actually a research project attempting to prove or disprove the thesis that firstborn children were inherently brighter. Ultimately the study concluded that there was no difference in intelligence based on birth order.

There are other stereotypes. The baby of the family is generally considered to be everyone's favorite, and the middle child is usually seen as overlooked.

I have one of each—a firstborn, a middle child, and a baby. In order to combat the negative middle child tag, my middle son used to refer to himself as "the glue that holds this family together."

In the family of God, Jesus is the firstborn. "The Son is the image of the invisible God, the firstborn over all creation" (Colossians 1:15).

He is also the glue and maybe even everyone's favorite.

SO

Don't believe stereotypes or attach labels to your children. The only label they need is "child of God."

NOVEMBER 11

Filthy Rags

All of us have become like one who is unclean, and all our righteous acts are like filthy rags; we all shrivel up like a leaf, and like the wind our sins sweep us away.

—ISAIAH 64:6

I was always a little surprised when my kids taught me a lesson from the Word without even trying. That's what happened one summer day.

My youngest son had been playing football outside, and when he finally came in the house, I wasn't prepared for how dirty his T-shirt was. It had been white, but now it was . . . indescribable.

So I set out to clean it. Step one was to send it through the wash cycle. It was cleaner, but could not be honestly classified as clean. Step two: send it through the cycle again, this time with bleach and even hotter water. Still not clean.

Now it was time for drastic measures. I filled the sink with hot water and more than the recommended amount of bleach and submerged the shirt. Then I walked away from the sink to let the bleach do its job.

The outcome? Let's just say all my efforts failed, producing only a useful though filthy rag.

FILTHY RAG

Those words describe my righteous acts. "As it is written: 'There is no one righteous, not even one'" (Romans 3:10). Yet: "This righteousness is given through faith in Jesus Christ to all who believe" (v. 22).

NOVEMBER 12

How Big?

His wisdom is profound, his power is vast.
Who has resisted him and come out unscathed?

—JOB 9:4

I was introduced to the sweetest little boy. He was only three years old and as cute as could be. His mom looked at him and said, "Show Mrs. Smiley your muscles."

At that request he lifted his short arms and did a great impression of a muscleman. After all that effort, I went on and on about how strong he was. He responded to my compliments by flashing a charming smile.

I remember asking my boys to show me how big they were. At my prompting they would reach up as high as they could. Of course, I'd also let them know I was thrilled about how big they were getting.

How big is God? How powerful? The verse in Job 9 answers those questions. "His wisdom is profound"; it is deep and insightful. "His power is vast"; it is enormous, immense. Our God is great!

HOW DO YOU RESPOND?

As one of his own, the fact that your heavenly Father's power and wisdom exceeds that of all others is reason to be thrilled—reason enough to "praise him for his mighty acts: praise him according to his excellent greatness" (Psalm 150:2).

NOVEMBER 13

Miracle

When he came near the place where the road
goes down the Mount of Olives,
the whole crowd of disciples began joyfully to praise God
in loud voices for all the miracles they had seen.

—LUKE 19:37

Some words are difficult to define. Furthermore, some words are difficult to understand. One example is the word *miracle.*

The dictionary says a miracle is an "act of God." I'm certain that's accurate, but I like the definition I heard from a grade-school girl: "A miracle is when God surprises you with something really good!"

You've got to love that insight. In my way of thinking, her definition outshines the official one.

God's Word is filled with reports of miracles, really good surprises from God, and they have been recorded for a specific purpose: "But these [miraculous signs] are written that you may believe that Jesus is the Messiah, the Son of God, and that by believing you may have life in his name" (John 20:31).

IT'S YOUR TURN

Take a minute and think of the various times when God has surprised you with something really good. Write down those miracles and share them as God leads you. They may lead someone to belief in Jesus.

NOVEMBER 14

Good for Dancing

Praise the LORD.
Sing to the LORD a new song,
his praise in the assembly of his faithful people.
Let Israel rejoice in their Maker;
let the people of Zion be glad in their King.
Let them praise his name with dancing
and make music to him with timbrel and harp.

—PSALM 149:1–3

The two-year-old accompanied her mom to the home that would soon be theirs. The paperwork had been signed, and it was just a matter of time before the moving van would arrive with the household belongings.

They walked through each room, and finally her mom showed the little girl the room that would be hers. As soon as she crossed the threshold, she began to twirl around with her arms outstretched. After three revolutions she stopped and announced to Mom, "This room is good for dancing!"

Are you able to find a place in your life that is "good for dancing"? A place where you find joy and peace? A place where you overflow with praise to God? God created you to rejoice and to praise him, and it is possible your joy could take the form of dancing.

YOUR ASSIGNMENT

If you cannot name a place that is "good for dancing," the place where you feel free to worship the Lord, begin your search for it today.

NOVEMBER 15

Sit Anywhere

"When you are invited, take the lowest place,
so that when your host comes, he will say to you,
'Friend, move up to a better place.' Then you will be
honored in the presence of all the other guests.
For all those who exalt themselves will be humbled,
and those who humble themselves will be exalted."

—LUKE 14:10–11

I boarded the plane and settled down in my seat. Moments later the aisle was filled with young men wearing baseball warm-ups. These middle school boys were on their way to a big tournament, and they were excited!

The first young man was about three rows from me when I heard someone behind him ask, "Where do we sit?"

"Anywhere is fine," answered the boy leading the brigade. The kids immediately began sitting in the nearest seats, paying no attention to their boarding passes.

That was the beginning of a mess that actually delayed takeoff and reminded me of the parable that is recorded in Luke 14. The boys chose the most convenient seats and ultimately had to move. It might not have been a humbling experience for them, but it was for their very apologetic chaperoning adults.

SO

There is a Bible lesson everywhere. Watch and learn.

NOVEMBER 16

Student as Teacher

"The student is not above the teacher,
but everyone who is fully trained will be like their teacher."
—LUKE 5:40

I remember a love struck young man telling me about the woman of his dreams. "She loves Jesus," he said, "and she's really funny!" What great credentials! He'd actually homed in on two important characteristics.

First, she loved Jesus. That is extremely important! Two becoming one is tricky business, and it's much easier if the two want to become one who resemble Jesus. Loving the Lord does not solve every problem a couple might face, but it helps assure that the problems will be faced from the proper perspective.

Second, she was really funny. That's an important attribute. Life is not always easy, but a sense of humor, a cheerful heart, is good medicine (Proverbs 17:22).

I expressed my interest in meeting this young lady. As he went on his way, I silently congratulated his mom for helping him know what to look for in a friend and possible bride. She had taught him well, and perhaps now he is teaching others.

IT'S TRUE

What you teach your children will provide them with important lessons to teach others. The student becomes the teacher.

NOVEMBER 17

Keep It Simple

Follow God's example, therefore, as dearly loved children and walk in the way of love, just as Christ loved us and gave himself up for us as a fragrant offering and sacrifice to God.

—EPHESIANS 5:1–2

The young man had been in church for several Sundays, and on this particular day he was waiting at the back of the church for the youth leader. As they talked he explained that he had gotten a Bible as a gift and was doing his best to understand what he'd been reading.

He went on to tell her that the whole thing was confusing: so many laws, so many words he'd never heard before. This young man had already decided that Christianity—or more importantly, Jesus Christ—was not for him. "Can't they make this a little simpler?"

After a whispered prayer, the youth leader tried to do just that. "It boils down to two basic things," she began. "The first is that God wants you to know he loves you. And the second is that he wants you to choose to love him back. That's it. Making that choice means accepting the sacrifice that Jesus made for the world."

KEEP IT SIMPLE

First: Know that God loves you. Jesus died for your sins. Second: Choose to love him back and become a member of the family of God.

NOVEMBER 18

Go to the Refrigerator

A voice came from the cloud, saying,
"This is my Son, whom I have chosen; listen to him."
—LUKE 9:35

Listening to the Lord isn't always easy, and the message you initially hear or read in his Word may simply be that: the *initial* message. That was the lesson that the Bible study teacher was trying to communicate to the teenagers.

"Here's a far-fetched example," she said. "Let's say you know that God told you to go to the refrigerator, so you immediately head in that direction. The fact is, you're moving so fast that you fail to pay attention and listen for him to speak again. You arrive at what you've determined was the destination, the refrigerator, and wonder why God sent you there.

"The problem is you're confused because you kept going when God was trying to get your attention. He wanted you to go to the refrigerator and then turn to the left."

The teacher knew that it wasn't a perfect example, but the simplicity of it was great for the teenagers. It's good for adults too.

SO

When God has sent you in one direction, keep listening. He might want you to take a left.

NOVEMBER 19

Community

"This, then, is how you should pray: 'Our Father in heaven, hallowed be your name, your kingdom come, your will be done, on earth as it is in heaven. Give us today our daily bread. And forgive us our debts, as we also have forgiven our debtors. And lead us not into temptation, but deliver us from the evil one.'"

—MATTHEW 6:9–13

I've had the Lord's Prayer memorized since I was a young girl. One day I realized that the prayer was written in the plural: "*Our* Father," "Give *us* today *our* daily bread," "Forgive *us our* debts, as *we* also have forgiven *our* debtors. And lead *us* not into temptation, but deliver *us* . . ."

As Christians, we live in community. The instructions from God's Word to encourage one another and pray for one another further illustrate the fact that you're not alone in your walk with the Lord.

Your brothers and sisters in Christ can have a very positive impact on your children, and if you're paying attention, you might learn something from their kids too. Keep your eyes and ears open.

LET'S PRAY

Lord, forgive me when I don't appreciate the gift of community. Thank you for giving me the family of God. Help me be teachable and learn from other members of the family, young and old.

NOVEMBER 20

Suggestions

Humble yourselves before the Lord,
and he will lift you up.

—JAMES 4:10

In college one of my sons attended a church with a non-traditional worship style. Even though he thoroughly enjoyed the church and the music, he longed to hear hymns of a traditional nature—hymns he had learned in our home church.

The church had a suggestion box, and one Sunday he dropped in a slip of paper with these words: "Can we sing a hymn like 'Amazing Grace' or 'How Great Thou Art' sometime?"

Sure enough, the very next week, what do you think the congregation sang? "Amazing Grace." And a few weeks later, they all joined in singing "How Great Thou Art." That wonderful church was able to take a suggestion—a suggestion given by a student.

God wants you to be like that church: to humble yourself, take legitimate suggestions, and be teachable, even when the suggestion comes from someone a generation younger.

THINK ABOUT IT

Have you received any suggestions recently? Do those suggestions line up with the Word of God? If the answer is yes, it's time to humble yourself and take those suggestions. God has promised to lift you up as you humble yourself before him.

NOVEMBER 21

Training Manual

All Scripture is God-breathed and is useful for teaching, rebuking, correcting and training in righteousness.
—2 TIMOTHY 3:16

When my sons turned sixteen and were old enough to get a driver's license, I didn't have the anxiety so many mothers experience. I've known moms who got close to a panic attack at the mere thought of their son or daughter turning sixteen and becoming a licensed driver.

The explanation for my calm demeanor is simple: The boys all grew up on our farm. They had oodles of teaching, warning, correcting, and training when it came to driving a motorized vehicle—in this case, a tractor. That meant they were more than prepared for driving a car.

Each one began driving at an early age in the confines of a corn or soybean field. When they actually transitioned from driving an expensive tractor to driving a used car, it was a monetary downgrade. Each of the boys had a time of preparation before having to take a driver's test—preparation that is unique to being raised in the country.

God is willing to prepare you and your children for every challenge of life, regardless of where you were raised. His love letter, the Bible, is the training manual. It will teach, rebuke, correct, and train you in righteousness.

LET'S PRAY

Lord, help me saturate myself in your Word and be open to the things it will teach me.

November 22

Evangelism 101

He replied, "Whether he is a sinner or not, I don't know. One thing I do know. I was blind but now I see!"

—John 9:25

I heard a teenage girl who had recently come to a saving knowledge of Christ say, "I'm not very gifted when it comes to evangelism. I don't know much about the Bible."

Her words made me think: How much do you need to know before you can be effective in sharing the message of God's love? Do you have to know a certain number of Bible verses by heart? Do you need a degree in theology? Is there a minimum or maximum age?

My favorite example of powerful, life-changing evangelism is found in the words of John 9:25. Jesus had healed a young man who had been born blind, and this amazing miracle had been performed on the Sabbath.

Some of the Pharisees said, "This man is not from God, for he does not keep the Sabbath" (v. 16). Then they challenged the young man who could now see. "Give glory to God by telling the truth," they said. "We know this man is a sinner" (v. 24).

His response is priceless and powerful: "I was blind but now I see!"

Your Turn

You can be an effective evangelist simply by sharing what God has done in your life.

NOVEMBER 23

Count Backward

"Therefore keep watch,
because you do not know the day or the hour."
—MATTHEW 25:13

It can be difficult to be on time. You might encounter interruptions that slow you down, or maybe you just didn't start soon enough. When the kids were little, I introduced them to a plan to be certain they were ready to leave home and arrive at their destination on time. Here's how it worked.

"What time should we get ready to go?" they'd ask. "Let's count backward," was my reply. "We need to be at the junior high school by eleven a.m. The drive will take fifteen minutes; that's 10:45. You need to shower and get dressed; thirty minutes? Now we're at 10:15. And before you do that, please go outside, feed the dog, and put your bikes in the garage. That should take another fifteen minutes. Looks like you need to start getting ready no later than 10:00."

Five of the ten virgins described in the parable in Matthew 25 did not start getting ready on time. They had their lamps, but no oil. When they needed to light the lamps, they had to go and buy oil. They hadn't allowed time for that, and missed an important opportunity.

AND

You don't know when Christ will come again. You can't count backward. Be prepared and help your kids be prepared too.

NOVEMBER 24

Catch the 9:05

He said to them, "Go into all the world and preach the gospel to all creation."
—MARK 16:15

"Mom, I missed it! I had the perfect opening to tell our neighbor about Christ, and I didn't do it. I can't believe I didn't take advantage of the opportunity!"

No mom wants to hear the angst and agony that accompanies a confession like that. This young man's grief was a reflection of his love for this neighbor and his love for Christ.

It's possible you've faced a similar situation with your child: God provided an opening for him to share the truth of the gospel, but for whatever reason, the opportunity came and went.

Why that happened doesn't really matter. The important thing for you to do is to let your child know that all is not lost. How about sharing this analogy?

"This is what I think. You missed the 8:05, and the train has come and gone. Rather than lament that reality, start watching for the 9:05. It's possible another opportunity will come before you know it."

IT'S TRUE

Both moms and kids can "miss the 8:05." But take heart: If that happens, know that God might be preparing to send the 9:05. Don't miss the next opportunity!

NOVEMBER 25

A Pleaser

"What shall I do, then, with the one you call the king of the Jews?" Pilate asked them. "Crucify him!" they shouted. "Why? What crime has he committed?" asked Pilate. But they shouted all the louder, "Crucify him!" Wanting to satisfy the crowd, Pilate released Barabbas to them. He had Jesus flogged, and handed him over to be crucified.

—MARK 15:12–15

Pilate found himself in a difficult situation. He knew that Jesus had not committed a crime, but the crowd didn't seem to care. Pilate knew Christ was an innocent man—perhaps even the Son of God, as he claimed; but no one in the crowd thought that was of any importance. "Crucify him!" was the response to each of Pilate's questions.

Pilate knew the truth, yet he did not release Jesus from prison. Instead, he ordered the flogging and crucifixion. Why would Pilate demand the death of an innocent man?

In today's terms, the answer to that question is simple: peer pressure. Pilate wanted to "satisfy the crowd." That was his goal.

As you teach your children about the Lord and help them understand the boundaries he has set, encourage them to look for ways to please God and not "satisfy the crowd."

IT CAN BE TOUGH

God speaks to his children through the Word and occasionally in a still small voice. The crowd tends to shout! Teach your children to listen, learn, and make it their goal to please God.

NOVEMBER 26

Prayer

Jesus often withdrew to lonely places and prayed.
—LUKE 5:16

As a Christian, Jesus is your model. He is the plumb line serving as your guide. With that in mind, consider the words of Luke 5:16: "Jesus often withdrew to lonely places and prayed."

It can be difficult to find that lonely place to pray; and even if you can, it's not easy for a mom to withdraw. Withdrawal demands a large segment of time, and those segments can be hard to find.

Hard to find? Maybe. A reasonable excuse for not following the model of Christ? Probably not.

That's not to say that every time you pray you must withdraw to a lonely place. After all, you are to pray without ceasing and you cannot always be in a place of solitude.

Perhaps the question is: Are you ever in a place of solitude? Are all of your prayers done in a rush—as you're cooking breakfast, when you're waiting in line at the Starbucks drive-through, when you're walking on your treadmill?

Those may be great examples of multitasking, but if you never find time to withdraw to a lonely place, you might want to step back and reevaluate.

MAYBE IT'S TIME

Withdraw to a lonely place and pray. If you can't do it today, do it tomorrow.

NOVEMBER 27

Your Choice

"Be merciful, just as your Father is merciful. Do not judge, and you will not be judged. Do not condemn, and you will not be condemned. Forgive, and you will be forgiven."

—LUKE 6:36–37

The teenager was at her wit's end, standing in the middle of the room, simultaneously crying and shouting, "I can't forgive him."

I thought about her statement for a minute or two. It made me sad to see how upset this young woman was as she vented her anger and frustration.

She said those words with great resolve and also with some remorse. "I can't forgive him."

I knew her statement wasn't correct, yet I couldn't put it in perspective until I remembered something a friend had shared with me. Gently, I told her what I'd learned long ago.

"When you say, 'I can't forgive,' that isn't really true," I began. "Forgiveness is a choice, and God is with you to help you choose to forgive."

IT'S TRUE

It is easy to say, "I can't" when it comes to following God's instruction. But in reality, that "I can't" is actually "I won't" or "I choose not to." Choose to do as the Lord directs.

NOVEMBER 28

Slow Learner

"Take my yoke upon you and learn from me,
for I am gentle and humble in heart,
and you will find rest for your souls."
—MATTHEW 11:29

There have been times in my life I've felt like a slow learner when it comes to following the instructions of the Lord. I know that he gives me commands and directives as a result of his great love for me, but sometimes my actions don't reflect that "knowing."

Thankfully there has been forward progress through the years; but even with that progress, it can be quite frustrating and disappointing that I haven't arrived at perfection.

Years ago as I wrote in my journal, I addressed this very issue: my desire to be obedient to the loving instruction of the Lord and my inability to do so on a consistent basis. At the end of my entry, I penned these words, probably as an encouragement: *I may be a slow learner, but at least I'm not a "no learner."*

God knows each of his children well enough to refrain from expecting perfection. He is pleased when the learning and spiritual growth moves forward, regardless of our speed.

FOR YOU

Don't be concerned about the speed or the lack of perfection. Simply be a learner, learning more and more and becoming more obedient to the Lord.

NOVEMBER 29

The Tea Bag

Do not let any unwholesome talk come out of your mouths, but only what is helpful for building others up according to their needs, that it may benefit those who listen. And do not grieve the Holy Spirit of God, with whom you were sealed for the day of redemption. Get rid of all bitterness, rage and anger, brawling and slander, along with every form of malice.
—EPHESIANS 4:29–31

A teenage girl brought me a special treat one day. She had been to a gourmet coffee shop with her mom and, knowing I wasn't a coffee drinker, she'd picked up several unique and exclusive tea bags for me.

Along with this gift came some very specific instructions she had received from the barista who checked her out. "Don't let the tea brew too long. If you do, it will get bitter."

That directive is similar to the words of Ephesians 4:31. If you allow rage, anger, brawling, slander, or any form of malice to "brew too long" in your life, your days will not be as satisfying as they could be and you run the risk of becoming bitter.

Everywhere you look there are illustrations of the lessons in God's Word.

SO

Take note of things that might have been brewing in your heart, mind, or memory and get rid of them sooner rather than later.

NOVEMBER 30

Encouragement

Finally, brothers and sisters, rejoice!
Strive for full restoration, encourage one another,
be of one mind, live in peace.
And the God of love and peace will be with you.

—2 CORINTHIANS 13:11

I often display cartoons on my refrigerator. One of my favorites from years ago featured a little boy who was obviously discouraged. In the first frame, his mother is concerned about his sad countenance.

"What's wrong?" his mother asks.

Without missing a beat, the young boy replies, "No one likes me."

The next frame finds the mom reassuring her offspring.

"That's not true," she says encouragingly. "I like you!"

In the final frame, the little boy looks up at his mom and responds, "Of course you do. That's your job!"

I guess that *is* your job as a mom. You want to encourage your children and help them overcome adversity in every form. But the task of encouraging others isn't limited to your relationship with your children. Imagine the state of our world if every believer made a conscious effort to encourage others.

LET'S PRAY

Father, I want to be an encourager to the people in my family, in my church, in my neighborhood, and in the world beyond. Teach me to encourage others with my words and with my actions.

GIVE YOUR CHILDREN ROOTS AND WINGS

“‘For this reason a man will leave his father
and mother and be united to his wife,
and the two will become one flesh.’
So they are no longer two, but one flesh.”

—MARK 10:7–8

DECEMBER 1

The Powerful Gospel

Jesus looked at them and said,
"With man this is impossible,
but with God all things are possible."
—MATTHEW 19:26

With God all things are possible. Nothing is impossible—absolutely nothing. Recently I heard that truth in a context I had never considered before. The exact quote was, "The gospel is more powerful than your past. Nothing is impossible for God!"

Do you know anyone who has been trapped in the web of negative past experiences? Maybe you fall into that category. Your past may have been colored with the results of others' poor decisions or actions. You may carry destructive baggage that was packed for you; circumstances totally beyond your control have colored both your past and your present.

Maybe the circumstances you battle are the result of your own poor choices. Regardless, the incidents from your past that have carried over to your present do not have to be a part of your future! That is true for your children too.

REMEMBER THIS TRUTH

The gospel is more powerful than your past. Nothing is impossible for God!

DECEMBER 2

A Time and Season

There is a time for everything,
and a season for every activity under the heavens.
—ECCLESIASTES 3:1

I have a magnet on my refrigerator that reads, "Time flies whether or not you're having fun." There's a degree of humor in those words, and also a great deal of truth.

My eldest son had a four-year commitment to the Air Force following his college graduation. Weeks before he finished school, we were discussing the upcoming change in his life and wondering where he might be stationed.

"Four years is a long time," he momentarily lamented. Then he reflected on how rapidly the four years of college had flown by and added, "I guess it really isn't that long."

Time does fly. My magnet is correct. And it doesn't matter whether you're having fun or not. "There is a time for everything, and a season for every activity under the heavens." Because those seasons rapidly come and go, be sure to enjoy each day. This day is not a dress rehearsal; it is a gift from your heavenly Father.

LET'S PRAY

Lord, I do not want to squander a single day of the life you have given me here on earth. Help me to live each day in your love.

DECEMBER 3

No More Lectures

We have heard it with our ears, O God;
our ancestors have told us
what you did in their days,
in days long ago.

—PSALM 44:1

I remember when my children got to the stage of life when it was no longer appropriate to sit them down and teach a Bible lesson. They were gone from home and independent, for the most part. They were no longer at my breakfast table each morning ready to hear a Scripture lesson and pray. They were probably grabbing a bagel and running to their eight o'clock class. Hopefully they were taking time in the evening to be in the Word.

The old routine would no longer work; it was no longer applicable. So now what? Did my spiritual influence stop? No, it simply took on a different shape.

Our spiritual discussions became a time of sharing what God had been teaching each of us. It was talking and listening with the hope that all would grow closer to the Lord. It was a time when everyone could talk about the things God had been doing "in their days."

THE TRANSITION

As your children grow up and move toward adulthood, you will no longer be the one responsible for their learning. Give them a firm foundation and let them build upon it.

DECEMBER 4

Holding Hands

Yet I am always with you;
you hold me by my right hand.
You guide me with your counsel,
and afterward you will take me into glory.

—PSALM 73:23–24

My granddaughter and I were walking together, holding hands. She had been my constant companion throughout the day as we traveled through the children's museum.

At one point I gave her little three-year-old hand a squeeze and said how much I loved holding hands with her. She smiled, looked up at me, and said, "Grandma KK, I will hold your hand forever, even when I'm big!"

Her older sisters heard her comment, turned to me, and gave me a smile and an unsurprising eye roll. Their nonverbal communication was clear: "Don't hold your breath, Grandma. She'll probably grow out of this stage pretty soon."

I knew what they were thinking was accurate. Before long she would be all grown up and holding her own children's hands. Maybe she would remember the day we spent walking hand in hand, and maybe not.

The important thing is that she knows that even after Grandma has gone back home, her heavenly Father is with her, longing to hold her hand. He'll hold your hand and the hand of your child too.

SO

Take his hand right now and let him lead and guide you.

DECEMBER 5

Long Days

God saw all that he had made, and it was very good.
And there was evening, and there was morning—
the sixth day. Thus the heavens and the earth were
completed in all their vast array. By the seventh day
God had finished the work he had been doing;
so on the seventh day he rested from all his work.

—GENESIS 1:31; 2:1–2

The Lord created the heavens, the earth, man, and woman in six days; and on the seventh day he rested. Not only had he done all of this in record time, but also everything he created was "very good."

Mom, you're in the business of raising responsible adults. The hope is that when you work your way out of that job, you will be able to respond as the Lord did when he had completed creation.

We have no idea how long each day of creation was—no idea how many hours passed by. We do, however, know what 2 Peter 3:8 says: "With the Lord a day is like a thousand years, and a thousand years are like a day."

No doubt you've discovered that in parenting some days feel very long. Maybe you haven't reached the point when you realize that even though the days are long, the years are short.

IT'S TRUE

You can choose to enjoy each long day and create memories for the future.

DECEMBER 6

Hard Work

Epaphras, who is one of you and a servant of Christ Jesus, sends greetings. He is always wrestling in prayer for you, that you may stand firm in all the will of God, mature and fully assured. I vouch for him that he is working hard for you and for those at Laodicea and Hierapolis.

—Colossians 4:12–13

The definition of hard work can vary from mom to mom. Maybe you think that hard work means physical labor—digging ditches, doing construction, laying brick, cleaning the bathtub. Those are jobs that require a degree of physical exertion. There are other jobs that might qualify as "hard," but you're not lifting a hand or leaving your easy chair. The Scripture in Colossians provides a wonderful example.

Epaphras was "wrestling in prayer"; praying that the Colossians who were following Christ would stand firm in the center of God's will. Paul even remarked that Epaphras was working hard.

I don't know if your prayers could be classified as "wrestling," but perhaps you're struggling right now. Maybe you're working hard to stay focused, to know the mind of Christ, to remember it's not about you but all about God.

SO

Keep working hard. Keep praying for yourself and for your kids, that each of you will stand firm in the will of God.

DECEMBER 7

A Worthy Life

As a prisoner for the Lord, then,
I urge you to live a life worthy of
the calling you have received.
—Ephesians 4:1

Take just a minute and reread the words of Ephesians 4:1. Paul is urging you "to live a life worthy of the calling you have received." One day it dawned on me that following a list of rules might be a much easier task.

God has called you to be a mom so imagine this list of what you need to do. Number one: Always tell your child, "I love you" first thing in the morning. Number two: Have every permission slip signed at least five minutes before your child must leave for school. Number three: Change the sheets on your kid's bed every two weeks under normal circumstances. Number four: Provide a choice of two after-school snacks. Number five . . .

You can spend your life trying to live by your list, or you can focus on God's shorter list: to live a life worthy of your calling. Number one: Recognize your calling from God. Number two: Determine how your life can reflect that calling. And number three: Live the life he is calling you to live.

THE GOOD NEWS

The Lord will help you accomplish the task he has given you—to live a life worthy of your calling.

DECEMBER 8

At Home

"My Father's house has many rooms;
if that were not so, would I have told you
that I am going there to prepare a place for you?"
—JOHN 14:2

As a young girl, I was always a little frightened when I watched the movie *The Wizard of Oz.* There was, however, one line I especially liked. Toward the end of the movie, Dorothy clicked her heels together and said, "There's no place like home. There's no place like home. There's no place like home."

It's true, isn't it? There's no place like home, whether your home was a place of peace and encouragement as you grew up or exactly the opposite. There is no place like home.

I'm guessing one of your goals is or was to make the home where your children were raised a place of joy and contentment. As your children leave home—the place where their roots were established—be certain to give them your blessing. They will be establishing a new place of residence, a new address where you no longer reside.

Always remember, much more important than the return address on a letter is the home Christ is preparing for you and for all who love him—the home in heaven.

SO

As those kids of yours sprout wings to fly to the next adventure in their lives, rejoice with them, knowing the final adventure for all who love the Lord will be the adventure of heaven.

DECEMBER 9

Look Ahead

In all this you greatly rejoice,
though now for a little while
you may have had to suffer grief
in all kinds of trials.

—1 PETER 1:6

I remember seeing a humorous poster that read "Plan Ahead," and by the time the writer got to the last letter of the word *ahead*, he had run out of room. The *d* was sort of dangling in space, an excellent example of someone who did not plan ahead.

Planning ahead is a great idea. It never hurts to plan for the future, unless of course you are so tuned in to the future that you fail to enjoy the present.

That can happen. So can lagging behind in the past. Living in the past can rob you of the joy of the present. But what if the present seems to offer no joy? Then rather than planning ahead, the key may be to *look* ahead.

The words of 1 Peter 1:6 encourage you to rejoice. If your day has been a rough one, look ahead. If your day here on earth has been less than perfect, look ahead. If your joy has been lacking, look ahead and know there is wonderful joy yet to come. Look ahead.

LIVE IT

Now for a little while you may have to suffer grief, but look ahead to heaven, your eternal home.

DECEMBER 10

Warning Signs

Whoever scorns instruction will pay for it,
but whoever respects a command is rewarded.

—PROVERBS 13:13

Some of the signs encountered on the roadways of the Midwest can be very funny. I love the "Dip" sign. You don't have to travel very far to come across one of those. Usually the word *dip* is not sufficient to describe the drop-off you are about to encounter. Furthermore, the sign is typically on the very edge of the dip, which means that by the time your brain has logged the upcoming problem you have already experienced it!

"Rough Road" is another good one, and another understatement. The word *rough* is accurate. The word *road* is the one I question. Maybe it should read "Rough Path" or "Rough Trail." At least with this particular sign, there is usually adequate preparation time between the location of the sign and the beginning of the road.

That all-important lead time can really make a difference. I've learned that the sign "Rough Road" means slow down and try to stay in the center, away from the shoulder.

When you know a hazard is ahead you can make adjustments. If you choose to "scorn instruction" and ignore the warning signs, you will pay a price.

SO

Pay attention to the advice of a wise man. It can keep you safe and help you avoid the pitfalls ahead.

DECEMBER 11

Your Prayer List

For this reason, since the day we heard about you,
we have not stopped praying for you. We continually ask
God to fill you with the knowledge of his will through all
the wisdom and understanding that the Spirit gives.

—Colossians 1:9

I began praying for my sons as soon as I learned they'd been conceived. Because I chose not to find out the gender, I'd pray for little Matthew or Gretchen, little Aaron or Erin, and little Jonathan or Kyra.

After each one was born, the prayers continued. I prayed for them before they could talk and prayed for and with them before bed until they were old enough to pray on their own. A mother's prayers seldom stop, even when her children become adults.

As they were married, I added their wives to my prayer list, and ultimately their children too. My list grew and I was aware of the fact that I didn't really know the challenges each one faced. At one point I asked each couple how I could pray for them. I learned of the concerns on each heart and could pray more specifically for each individual.

AN IDEA

You might consider asking your children how you can pray for them. Praying for those you love is a privilege.

DECEMBER 12

Affirmation

Gracious words are a honeycomb,
sweet to the soul and healing to the bones.
—Proverbs 16:24

We all know how refreshing it is to hear words of encouragement and affirmation. They can help your performance and brighten your attitude. Encouragement can bring you renewed vigor for a task and can challenge you to improve. Those benefits also apply to your children.

Not long ago, I attended the funeral of a friend. She had three children and her youngest child, a daughter, had just graduated from high school. In so many ways it was an extremely sad occasion, but because of this woman's faith, the sorrow was laced with joy. There was no doubt where she would spend eternity.

Before her death, she and her husband took the time to write words of affirmation for each of their children. At the funeral, the pastor shared them with the kids and with everyone who had gathered to pay tribute to this remarkable woman.

This mom left her children with a legacy of faith and love and also with sweet words they can read again and again and treasure for a lifetime.

JUST A THOUGHT

It's never too early to jot down words of affirmation for someone you love. Take time today to begin the process of creating a note of encouragement for each of your children.

DECEMBER 13

More Like Jesus

"Produce fruit that is consistent with repentance [demonstrating new behavior that proves a change of heart, and a conscious decision to turn away from sin]."

—MATTHEW 3:8 AMP

I can still hear the words of the noted author and speaker Ray Stedman as he addressed those of us who had gathered for morning devotions. Ever quick-witted, he began with these words: "So often I wake up, look in the mirror, and wonder: What's a young man like me doing in such an old body?"

The listeners responded exactly as he'd anticipated, with smiles and laughter. Maybe you can relate to his words and maybe not. He was obviously referring to the physical changes he had undergone—changes that were reflected in the mirror.

Everyone experiences those changes. You don't look the way you did ten years ago. Depending on the ages of your children, they may not look like they did *two* years ago.

You are always able to look in a mirror and see the reflection of the changes in your appearance. The hope is that the changes in your heart, the reflection of your heavenly Father, are demonstrated by your behavior.

LET'S PRAY

Lord, I want to reflect your nature. Help me be more like you today than I was yesterday, and more like you tomorrow than I am today.

DECEMBER 14

A Safe Place to Grow

Like newborn babies, crave pure spiritual milk,
so that by it you may grow up in your salvation.
—1 PETER 2:2

I tried in vain to grow rosebushes in my yard. They looked very good on the day they were planted, but their good looks quickly faded. I soon discovered that the problem was rabbits. The cute little bunnies were destroying my rosebushes!

The small fences circling each bush did no good; the clever critters managed to nuzzle under the wire or reach over the top in order to get a bite of the evidently delicious rosebuds. As a last resort, I searched and searched until I found some fencing that proved to be rabbit-proof. Finally my bushes had a safe place to grow.

Your children need the same thing. No, not a rabbit-proof fence, but a safe place to grow up in Christ. Your home can provide just that: a place where they can grow and mature and bloom in his love. Do your best to see that there is nothing prohibiting their spiritual growth.

IT'S TRUE

Your children aren't the only ones who need that safe place to grow. It's important for you too. Your home and your church can both meet that need.

DECEMBER 15

Preparation

The angel answered, "The Holy Spirit will come on you,
and the power of the Most High will overshadow you.
So the holy one to be born will be called the Son of God . . .
For no word from God will ever fail."
"I am the Lord's servant," Mary answered.
"May your word to me be fulfilled."
Then the angel left her.
—LUKE 1:35–36, 37–38

Christmas is almost here, and you've probably been preparing for it for several weeks. There are many things most moms have on their to-do list as Christmas approaches.

There's cooking and cleaning and sending cards and shopping and wrapping and baking and parties and caroling and programs and . . . I'm beginning to think that simply making your list could be tiring.

Mary the mother of Jesus had only one thing to do in order to prepare for the birth of the Christ child. Mary's only responsibility was to prepare her heart for what the Lord had promised. She had confidence that God's message, delivered by the angel, would come to pass. She was destined to celebrate the first Christmas by holding the Son of God in her arms.

IT'S TRUE

The Lord made a promise to Mary, and he has made promises to you. They're found in his Word. May his word to you be fulfilled.

DECEMBER 16

Listen and Learn

Let the wise listen and add to their learning,
and let the discerning get guidance.
—Proverbs 1:5

Mom, it's important for you to be available for your older child but to refrain from being an interruption in his life. That may sound a little confusing. What does it mean to be available without interrupting? Let me give you a practical example.

I would encourage you to volunteer to drive a carload of kids to an event, either school or church related. If you are quiet and don't interrupt as you drive, you'll discover a vast amount of information. What are these kids interested in? Are they boy crazy, girl crazy, or sports crazy? Do they have an interest in spiritual things? Are they respectful or teasing as they talk to one another?

If you chauffer the kids and don't interrupt, before long you'll become invisible—and from that invisible state you can be a student of your own child and his peers. You're offering a service to the kids, not companionship; and by listening you'll learn a great deal that can be of help to you as a mom.

IT'S TRUE

Too often moms miss an opportunity to learn more about their child because of: (1) not wanting to take the time or (2) interrupting rather than listening.

DECEMBER 17

Christmas List

He has saved us and called us to a holy life—
not because of anything we have done
but because of his own purpose and grace.
This grace was given us in Christ Jesus
before the beginning of time.

—2 TIMOTHY 1:9

Who's on your Christmas list? I'm guessing the "regulars" made the list—your kids, your parents, your grandkids (if you have any), and maybe your siblings. There may be others too. Even though I don't know the actual names of the folks on your list, I'm guessing every person is there because of who they are.

That's how it is with my Christmas list. There are six people on my list because they are my three sons and their wives. There are ten—count 'em, *ten* so far!—grandkids on the list because . . . well, you get the idea. These folks will receive gifts from me because of who they are, and there's nothing wrong with that. It is, however, in sharp contrast to the gift given by God.

God has chosen to give the most precious gift, the gift of grace and salvation, to you and to your children not because of anything you have done but because of who *he* is.

YOUR CHOICE

God chose to love you and your children with an everlasting love. The best choice anyone can make is to love him back.

DECEMBER 18

'Tis the Season

"The virgin will conceive and give birth to a son,
and they will call him Immanuel"
(which means "God with us").

—MATTHEW 1:23

Christmas is a time of year that elicits many different feelings. If we believed the secular Christmas songs, we'd be convinced that it was our duty to be jolly.

There are moments in every Christmas season when I definitely feel cheerful. There are other times when the miracle of the season, the miracle of God's love, absolutely overwhelms me and I am filled with awe. Those are the times I am aware of who God is and how incredible it is that he chose to love me.

Other times, when I reflect on some of the Christmas mornings from my childhood, I feel a sense of sorrow. Those days were not filled with peace or joy.

It is interesting that those particular thoughts almost always lead me to thankfulness for my Christmas celebrations as an adult.

Regardless of how you are feeling today, my hope is that you will know the very real presence of God and choose to rest in his love.

LET'S PRAY

Lord, help me focus on the gift of your Son, Jesus. Thank you for loving me and for loving my children. Thank you for being with me every moment of every day.

DECEMBER 19

To: God From: You

He has told you, O man, what is good; And what does the LORD require of you except to be just, and to love [and to diligently practice] kindness (compassion), And to walk humbly with your God [setting aside any overblown sense of importance or self-righteousness]?

—MICAH 6:8 AMP

Imagine this: After church you receive a surprise from a new friend in your Bible study. She has a Christmas gift for you. How very nice of her—but wait! You are now required to reciprocate and buy a gift for her.

This is going to be tough because you really don't know her very well. It looks like you'll have to settle for a one-size-fits-all gift. It would be so much easier if you knew what she wanted.

Chances are you've experienced a scenario similar to the one above: receiving a gift and then not knowing how to respond appropriately. The Lord has given you countless gifts, amazing gifts, including the priceless gift of his Son. What can you give to him in return?

His Word is clear. His desire is for you to act justly, love mercy, and walk humbly. That's what is required; that's the gift you can give to him.

IT'S TRUE

God not only requires this of you, but he will also help you do what he has asked.

DECEMBER 20

Do You See What I See?

"Do you have eyes but fail to see, and ears but fail to hear? And don't you remember?"
—MARK 8:18

There is a beautiful Christmas song with the repetitive phrase: "Do you see what I see?"* That is a very interesting question. How many times do two or more people see or hear the same thing differently?

It's the old problem of eyewitnesses at the scene of a crime. One eyewitness saw an older man of small stature pulling away from the scene in a light blue Ford. The other eyewitness saw a woman, rather tall, driving south in a green Chevrolet. Who was right and who was wrong?

Even though an eyewitness might be able to provide important information, that's not always the case. I have to admit that my eyes don't see with 100 percent accuracy. Sometimes they reflect my bias.

If you share that same problem, occasionally experiencing faulty eyes, I have a suggestion for you. It's something that's been working for me.

How can you improve your vision? By trying to see others through the eyes of Jesus.

LET'S PRAY

Lord, I don't always view people or situations with love and compassion. Please help me. I want to be more like you.

---

* "Do You Hear What I Hear?," lyrics by Noël Regney (1962).

DECEMBER 21

Wrapped in Love

To bestow on them a crown of beauty instead of ashes,
the oil of joy instead of mourning,
and a garment of praise instead of a spirit of despair.
They will be called oaks of righteousness,
a planting of the LORD for the display of his splendor.
—ISAIAH 61:3

I enjoy wrapping Christmas gifts. Years ago I made an exchange with a friend. I wrapped her family's gifts, and she baked goodies for me. I considered myself the big winner in that trade.

The packaging and wrapping of a gift can be functional, beautiful, or even creative. Have you noticed that occasionally you receive a gift from God that didn't come in the packaging you had anticipated?

Sometimes his gifts are wrapped in something that you consider unpleasant or painful. You might even be certain the circumstance is bad and that you absolutely, positively don't want it. Then days, weeks, maybe even years later you realize it was a blessing—a blessing in disguise.

Don't be distracted by the wrapping. Just as God sent Isaiah to give the people beauty for ashes, the Lord will give you the oil of joy. Accept his gifts with thankfulness.

SO

God can use any circumstance in your life for good. Don't be quick to label something as bad news. Give the Lord time to work. His timetable is not the same as yours.

DECEMBER 22

Home Sweet Home

Therefore we are always confident and know
that as long as we are at home in the body we are
away from the Lord. For we live by faith, not by sight.
We are confident, I say, and would prefer to be away
from the body and at home with the Lord.

—2 CORINTHIANS 5:6–8

"I'll Be Home for Christmas" is a very old Christmas song. As the mom of three grown sons, I am well aware that they all have homes of their own where each one lives with his wife and children. No longer is their physical address the same as mine, but when it comes to the holidays, they talk about coming "home" to spend time together.

The house where they were raised is not truly their home, nor is it their current address. As believers, their home is in heaven where they will live eternally with the Lord.

They are my children, but they are also children of the King of Kings; and he has promised them a home in heaven. He's promised that home to everyone who has come to a saving knowledge of Christ.

IT'S TRUE

As a believer, your permanent home will be with the Lord; and when you arrive there, you can say without reserve, "There's no place like home!"

DECEMBER 23

The Goal

My goal is that they may be encouraged in heart
and united in love, so that they may have the full riches
of complete understanding, in order that they may
know the mystery of God, namely, Christ.
—COLOSSIANS 2:2

Things have changed and I now start preparing for Christmas much earlier than I did when the children were young. It's not that I'm incredibly organized (but thank you for considering that as an explanation!) or that I now am more extravagant in my decorating or shopping.

No, I plan ahead because in the last few years our family has celebrated the birth of Christ weeks before the rest of the world.

With three sons and their families in three different states, flexibility is the key to getting together for the holidays. If rearranging our former traditions or completely ignoring them means that I have the joy of being in the same room with all my kids, kids-in-law, and grandkids, I support that change 100 percent!

Being willing to change and let go of many of the traditions of the past can be difficult, but it's easier when you focus on your goal. My goal is to join with many of the folks I love and celebrate the birthday of the One who loves each one of us best.

SO

Don't be afraid to let some traditions go.

DECEMBER 24

No Room

He went there to register with Mary, who was
pledged to be married to him and was expecting a child.
While they were there, the time came for the baby to be born,
and she gave birth to her firstborn, a son.
She wrapped him in cloths and placed him in a manger,
because there was no guest room available for them.

—Luke 2:5–7

The innkeeper had no room for Mary and Joseph in his establishment even though she was ready to give birth at any moment. More than once I've wondered if, after the fact, he realized that Christ the Lord had been born in his lowly stable.

Couldn't he have found a space and a bed somewhere? Maybe he would have sacrificed his own comfort if he had known who was ready to be born. "No room . . . no room at the inn."

Is there someone you love who hasn't yet made room in her life for Jesus? Is that loved one like the innkeeper, believing she has no room for the Lord?

When the innkeeper sent this young couple to the stable, he had no idea who would be born. Maybe he realized after the fact, maybe not.

The person on your heart today, the loved one who is not a believer yet, may soon be ready to make room for Christ.

BE PREPARED

Be ready to share about the hope you have in Christ.

DECEMBER 25

All You Need

My God will meet all your needs according to
the riches of his glory in Christ Jesus.
—PHILIPPIANS 4:19

"Just what I needed!" exclaimed my second son as he excitedly tore open the package holding his Christmas present. Inside the box was a pair of cowboy boots that were, evidently, absolutely perfect!

Did this four-year-old really *need* cowboy boots? The answer is no. Did he *want* those boots? He did, and his enthusiasm was obvious to all.

Sometimes that happens. Sometimes you give or receive a gift that is perfect. Occasionally the gift is also what was needed.

The Lord is a giver, and his gifts to you and your children are always good, meeting your every need. He promises that in his Word. He doesn't, however, promise that he'll meet all your wants.

Mom, you may not get that big raise allowing you to redecorate, and your children may not proclaim "Just what I wanted!" as they open their Christmas gifts. But you can be certain that any gift received from God will be just what is needed.

SO

Teach your children to distinguish the difference between a need and a want and to thank God for meeting their needs.

DECEMBER 26

Up and Down

"Therefore the Lord himself will give you a sign:
The virgin will conceive and give birth to a son,
and will call him Immanuel."

—Isaiah 7:14

Isaac Newton once aptly said, "What goes up must come down." This is true in regard to gravity, but it also applies to Christmas decorations. What goes up must come down. That specific fact usually keeps my decorating urges under control, at least to some extent.

It's likely you are now dealing with the thought of undecorating and undoing all the festive beauty you recently created. What goes up must come down. Even if you got a little help with step one (putting the decorations up), there's probably no one around to help with step two (taking them down).

Add to that tiring assignment the predictable melancholy surrounding the job of packing up all the holiday goodies and putting them away for another year, and you might be feeling a little down in the dumps.

If that's the case, it's time for some good news. You already know this, but a little refresher might be welcome. The celebration of Christ's birth, his arrival on this earth, can continue long after the decorations have been put away, for he is Immanuel, God with us.

IT'S TRUE

God is always with you, every day in every month of the year.

DECEMBER 27

Rise and Go

"Rise! Let us go! Here comes my betrayer!"
—MATTHEW 26:46

I may never have had the privilege of meeting you personally. Even so, I do know something about you. I know you've experienced a failure of some sort in your life, and so have your children.

How can I be so certain? Because no one can escape the reality that failure is a part of being human. It is inevitable, and when the failure involves not following God's instructions, it can be accompanied by a feeling of despair.

Maybe the disciples felt that way when they fell asleep in the garden after the Lord's command to watch and pray. I find the response Jesus gave so long ago to those resting men very encouraging for moms today.

Jesus didn't scold the men, he didn't ask them for an explanation, and he didn't listen to any excuses; he simply told them to rise and get going.

You and your children will experience failure when it comes to following the Lord's instructions. When that happens it's reassuring to know that God will lovingly encourage you to rise above your failure and press on with him.

LET'S PRAY

Father, you know my heart and my desire to make choices in line with your Word. You also know I fall short. Thank you for helping me in every situation—helping me to rise up and go forward.

DECEMBER 28

He's There

"Therefore go and make disciples of all nations,
baptizing them in the name of the Father and of the
Son and of the Holy Spirit, and teaching them to obey
everything I have commanded you. And surely I am
with you always, to the very end of the age."

—MATTHEW 28:19–20

The Scripture above is a directive Jesus gave to the disciples after his resurrection. It is also a promise, an assurance. Every word is significant, but recently the absolute truth of his final statement became even more significant to me: "And surely I am with you always, to the very end of the age."

God's Holy Spirit is with you right now. He was with you when you woke up this morning. He was with you before you opened your eyes.

The Holy Spirit is not limited the way you are as a human being. He is with you, with me, and with every believer. We don't have to go to church, to our quiet place, or to a mountaintop to connect with the Lord.

HIS PROMISE

God's Holy Spirit is with every believer. When you cannot comfort your children, God's Holy Spirit is with them. When you cannot see your children, God's Holy Spirit is with them. When your children need the assurance of God's love, his Holy Spirit is with them.

DECEMBER 29

Thank You

Thanks be to God for his indescribable gift!

—2 CORINTHIANS 9:15

Moms typically appreciate good manners, such as saying please and thank you. When I was young my mother would prompt me by asking, "What's the magic word?" That was my cue to say please or thank you, whichever applied at the time.

I'm not sure when I was able to correctly respond without Mom's help, but I'm guessing it didn't take too long to learn. The approach I used with my boys was to simply ask, "What do you say?" Then they would respond appropriately.

With my grandkids I had fun with a different approach. Rather than ask a question to elicit the correct response, I chose to reward them with points when they said those words without any prompting.

I'd hear the phrase, "Please pass the bread," then I'd award that particular child a thousand points! You might be wondering what they could do with those points.

The honest answer is, absolutely nothing—except feel rewarded. I used to say the points were "useless but fun." And yes, they did the trick.

Expressing gratitude to someone with a "thank you" is a good idea. Giving thanks to God for his indescribable gift is a privilege.

THANK YOU

Thank you, God, for sending Jesus. Thank you, Jesus, that you came and gave believers the gift of your Holy Spirit.

DECEMBER 30

Straight to the Top

Zacchaeus stood up and said to the Lord, "Look, Lord!
Here and now I give half of my possessions to the poor,
and if I have cheated anybody out of anything,
I will pay back four times the amount."

—LUKE 19:8

As your children grow up and go out into the world, they're bound to encounter criticism. Some of it will be honest and constructive, but some will not. One of your responsibilities is to teach them how to respond to the critics.

God's Word provides a beautiful illustration of the correct response. Jesus encountered Zacchaeus and declared he would stay in the home of this notorious tax collector. The people were appalled and began to mutter. They didn't like the idea of Jesus honoring this man with his presence.

Rather than try to explain his position to the townspeople, Zacchaeus took his concern straight to the top and addressed the Lord: "Look, Lord!"

Mom, teach your children to take any accusation to God. Then, just like the tax collector, they will need to listen to the Lord's response.

Zacchaeus was willing to do whatever God commanded, including paying back four times the amount.

IT'S TRUE

Not all criticism is valid; not all is worthless. As your kids fly from the nest, be certain they know what to do when criticism comes their way: Take it straight to the top!

DECEMBER 31

Wings

Those who hope in the LORD will renew their strength. They will soar on wings like eagles; they will run and not grow weary, they will walk and not be faint.

—ISAIAH 40:31

Mom, you've done your best to help your children build a firm foundation on the Lord. You haven't done it perfectly, but you've tried to teach them the importance of living as the Word instructs.

Mom, you've done your best to model belief and trust in Jesus. You haven't done it perfectly, but you've made every effort to live in God's love.

Mom, you've done your best to correct your child in love, just as the Lord corrects you. You haven't done it perfectly, but you've tried to give them an example of justice and mercy.

Mom, you've done your best to teach your children to think long-term. You haven't done it perfectly, but you've seen evidence that your teaching has made a difference.

Mom, you've done your best to celebrate your position in the family of God. You haven't done it perfectly, but you've found joy, resting in his love.

Mom, you've learned from your children. You haven't done it perfectly, but you've allowed them to teach you things about your heavenly Father.

Mom, you've given your children roots. You haven't done it perfectly, but when the time comes, you can give them wings too.

AMEN!

CONCLUSION

Choose to Obey

His mother said to the servants,
"Do whatever he tells you."
—JOHN 2:5

Those words from John 2:5, words spoken by Mary the mother of Jesus, don't only apply to those serving at the wedding feast (John 2:1–11). Those words are for you, for me, and for our children. "Do whatever he tells you."

In order to follow that very wise instruction, it's necessary to know what the Lord is telling you to do. It is necessary to read the Word and to let the truth of his Word permeate your very being.

The chances are great we have walked together in his Word for the last few days or weeks or months. We have shared thoughts about the adventure of motherhood, the ups and downs, the joys and sorrows; and I'm willing to begin again tomorrow on January 1.

Please join me again or again and again. The daily walk through motherhood is always better when you walk hand in hand with a friend.

About the Author

Kendra Smiley is a popular author and speaker, ministering to women nationally and internationally. She brings wit and wisdom to her writing, speaking, and national radio program, "Live Life Intentionally," heard on over 350 stations. Named Illinois Mother of the Year in 2001, Kendra and her husband, John, a former military pilot, live on a farm in central Illinois where they raised their three sons, all of whom are married and are parents themselves. Kendra is the author of nine books and has contributed to many others.

KENDRASMILEY.COM

KENDRASMILEY.COM